LIFE IN A LIBERTY BODICE

Betsy and her cronies

Life in a Liberty Bodice

random recollections of a Yorkshire childhood

Christabel Burniston

Colour illustrations
by
Margaret Clarkson

WESTBURY
2004

First published in 1991
by Highgate Publications

Republished in hardback in 1995
by Smith Settle and reprinted in 2000

This new edition published on behalf of
a publishing consortium by
Westbury Publishing
Ilkley Road, Otley
West Yorkshire LS21 3JP

Westbury Publishing is an imprint of
Smith Settle Printing & Bookbinding Ltd

ISBN 1 84103 029 5

Set in Bembo

Designed, printed and bound by
Smith Settle Printing & Bookbinding Ltd
Ilkley Road, Otley, West Yorkshire LS21 3JP

Dedicated to my loving and delightful family
my daughter Liz and my grandchildren Magnus, Tamara,
Gus and Daisy, and my great granddaughter Lily,
all of whom were born long after 1925
when this book ends.

CONTENTS

ACKNOWLEDGEMENTS
For the special edition 2004

I would like to thank the principal of the Swan School of English in Oxford, H. A. Swan, former principal of London Schools of Langauge, Peter Fabian and vice-president of the English Speaking Board (International) Ltd., Jocelyn Bell as the major influences in this re-launch of *Life in a Liberty Bodice.*

This has re-kindled the enthusiastic support of many readers. It is good to be in touch with you all again.

For the hardback edition 1995

Rhoda and Babs Danby, my nonagenarian cousins with longer memories than mine, have both made Sunday telephoning productive, informative and delightful.

John Hyde, who again has added still more pieces to the family jigsaw.

Frank and Valerie Gray for the loan of Danby family photographs.

Barbie Errington for the Mackintosh letter and photograph of her husband: Sydney Errington.

My nieces Jill and Mary Sheppard for adding to the William Smith records and photographs.

The Megginsons, Jack and Irene, have once more soaked me in the glorious Wolds air, language and lore.

Roger Smith, for his help in finding and photographing Little and Great Woolstone, trapped as both these villages are in monstrous Milton Keynes.

The photographer Michael Carter for providing the photograph of my youngest grand-daughter Daisy and her friend Beatrice Beazley performing in the James Allen Prep. School performance of *Bugsy Malone.*

The residents of Morritt Avenue, especially Bernard and Mary Todd (who live in my old home—Number 17) for recent photographs, and Nigel and Ros at Number 13 for supplying the 1903 photograph.

Jack Danby for pen and ink drawing of Morritt Avenue, 1903.

For Woodhouse Grove School retired and serving staff, in particular Keith Rawlings, forester to the school, who, after cutting down 200 years of history in the ancient chestnut tree, converted one slice of it into a ringed record of historical fact.

For Judy Thompson in arranging for the photograph to be included in *Life in a Liberty Bodice 2* and for John Hyde's delving into the archives for records of Austin Hyde.

Rev. Trevor Davidson for gravestone records of Carnaby Churchyard.

David and Christine Jackson of Carnaby House for their detailed record of the Jacksons in the Bridlington area.

Don Bramley of South Milford for still more information on the Wainwright and other farms in the Sherburn-in-Elmet area.

Special thanks are due to the many people in both the West and East Ridings who made festive signing sessions in the year following the initial publication, in particular Sheila Lennon for arranging the Grand Hall of the Grand Theatre in Leeds.

Jill and Pat Nutt of Foulbridge Farm who opened new vistas for this new edition by generously hosting two sessions in the recently discovered and restored Knights Templar Hall. They also have given permission to reproduce drawings from their booklet to which Jean Mansfield, the artist, willingly agreed.

I am grateful to Thelma Falls-Hand who rounded up all her 'singing' friends to produce 1920s songsheets. From these I selected those sent by Margaret Hill and Dr Phil Margham and Mandy.

New light has been shed on the history of Auburn by my meeting Mary and Robin Jackson who also set me tracking down the old church bell and the font.

Mr. Marriott of Boynton Hall, where the bell now hangs, gave further information.

Norman Hirst for the Auburn Farm photograph.

Professional thanks are due for permission to reproduce photographs where copyright is held:

The Harrogate International Centre (photographs of Ripon).

Miss Willmott, Librarian for Local Studies, Bradford Central Library, for information on the 'steaming pie' end Swan Arcade.

The Curator of the Museum of Market Harborough for designs and advertisements of the Liberty Bodice.

David Mitchell, author of *Queen Christabel,* and the London Museum for the photographs of Christabel Pankhurst.

The Historian of the Local History Dept. of the Hull City Library.

The National Railway Museum for the LNER train.

Michael and Christine Waddington of Farrah's Toffee.

Rob Stanley of Humberside County Council Central Library for the list of the 'in-house' domestic staff at Tranby Croft [John Jackson was of course privately engaged to accompany HRH the Prince of Wales (later Edward VII)].

Skyview and General for permission to reproduce the aerial photograph of Auburn.

National Motor Museum, Beaulieu, for photographs and diagrams of 1920s cars.

Victor Jowett, former director of the Jowett Motor Company.

My personal appreciation of the encouragement and advice I have received over the last year from Martyn and Irene Kirby, formerly of Highgate, now working freelance, much in demand, as writers and lecturers.

Finally may I express my good fortune in working with, and being hosted by, Margaret and Mac Clarkson and being published and printed by Smith Settle whose work is all of the highest quality.

Christabel Burniston

ACKNOWLEDGEMENTS
For *Life in a Liberty Bodice* original edition

For the many official organisations which have contributed to my research I should like especially to thank: Buckinghamshire County Council; Cadbury Ltd; Doncaster Museum and Art Gallery; Elkin Music Services (The Marching Song); Forestry Commission North York Moors; Humberside Libraries; Jaegar Ltd; Local History Librarian, Mrs A Heap; International Music Publication; Milton Keynes Development Corporation; Linsay Sutton (3 railway pictures); Model Engineer (Editor Ted Jolliffe); National Railway Museum, York; Old People's Centre, Swadlincote; Rowntree Mackintosh; Terry's Group; Robert Thompson's Craftsmen Ltd; West Yorkshire Archive Service.

To the many relations and friends (and strangers who became friends) my grateful thanks for: photographs; press-cuttings; correspondence; conversations and hospitality.

Edie Baker (neé Wilson) and Winifred Price, old girls at Chapel Allerton; Paul Bookbinder former archivist to Marks & Spencer; Don Bramley, the Rev David Post and Madge Copley of Sherburn-in-Elmet, Stan Burniston, Bettine Cross, John Hyde and Peter Mallett of West Yorkshire; Babs and Rhoda Danby and Jack Danby (writer and artist) of the East Riding; Stanley Ellis and Brian Spencer of the Yorkshire and East Riding Dialect Societies; Daisy Fairbrother, Graham Nutt, Ruth Lovett and the Rev Roy Upton of Swadlingcote and district; Jack and Irene Megginson of the Yorkshire Wolds; the late Henry Hyde and Mr and Mrs Barry Read, former and present occupants of The Lodge, Fraisthorpe; W Jackson and D Nesfield of North Yorkshire Dales.

To those who have helped in the compilation of this book (including generous and helpful publishers and printers) I am deeply grateful: Valerie James for typing and re-typing; Jocelyn Bell for patient and perceptive proofing. Stella Lewis for wise and shrewd comments on the final manuscript. Special thanks to Mollie Hargreaves and Donald Sadler — both Yorkshire born — who have received the manuscript chapter by chapter and added expert pencillings of cool judgement and warm encouragement.

INTRODUCTION TO THE NEW EXTENDED EDITION

The joy of writing *Life in a Liberty Bodice* has been the overwhelming response from readers. Through their letters I have made new friends and miraculously linked up with old friends, relations and colleagues with whom I had lost touch.

How could an author resist a letter which began: 'This is the book I have been waiting for all my life ...' for that is how Moyra Platts' home in Menston has become a second home where I have shared much fun and wisdom and made contact with my splendid publishers.

Almost every letter added some gem of information or extended an invitation to meet or to lecture giving me an excuse for a whole host of 'Yorkshire revisited' delights.

Surprises came every day. One wrote that in reading a biography on Dulcie Yelland (an energetic Leeds socialist) by her husband, he and Dulcie frequently visited the Hyde family in Halton and how, following one of my mother's lectures in Leeds Theosophical Hall: 'The Pursuit of the Laughing God', Charles and Dulcie became engaged. They had a great admiration for my mother so possibly, as the lecture was on laughter, love and life, she influenced them. Charles Yelland compares our family with the Orgreaves of the Clayhanger trilogy by Arnold Bennett. Certainly the open house and liberal talk of the Orgreaves — unusual in that period and tough industrial area — compared significantly with our own.

This edition, therefore, includes extensive new material for I have seen and heard much of the West Riding's former industrial eminence in the textile world and appreciated the sweat and soot which created Bradford and the clutch of small towns encircling it. Leeds, old and new, resonates with success; buildings I took for granted as a child I look at now with a sharpened focus. Areas which were hidden in the smudge of the old city have now been rescued; I could not believe that in a square half-mile of one-time residences in the city centre one could be shown 36 blue plaques!

Some characters in our extended family, only mentioned obliquely in the first edition, have come centre-stage speaking to me through rescued letters and faded sepia photographs. Of these Austin Hyde — still lovingly remembered by older readers — had preserved the letters and verses of Grandma Hyde.

One of the highlights of my early research was to discover Irene and Jack Megginson — formerly closely connected with the Hydes of Fraisthorpe as farming neighbours. Their house in Bishop Wilton vibrated with the language, lore and laughter of the Wolds. It was in this house — on their wall — that I spotted a Margaret Clarkson colour print full of human life, and knew at once that Margaret would be the artist to catch the earthy antics of my cavalcade of characters.

We were *en rapport* from the moment we met, revelling in all the minutiae of ordinary folk in everyday actions. An extra bonus was finding that her husband, Mac, focused his camera with an artist's eye and was willing to travel.

So Margaret, Mac and I went on a memory lane photographing expedition to Morritt Avenue and posted ourselves at different points of the road. Margaret sketching, Mac, with his camera taking up weird angles, and I peering at people's houses. We should not have been surprised that two men appeared, and another pretended he was cleaning his window, for this was Neighbourhood Watch at work. They soon co-operated in every possible way and brought their copies of *Life in a Liberty Bodice* out to be autographed.

Nigel Pattison, of Number 13, to my great delight owned a copy of the photograph showing the former gated entrance to Morritt Avenue in 1903, and there and then made a photocopy, which Jack Danby has brought to sharper life in a pen-and-ink drawing.

Bernard Todd, of Number 17, the house where I was born, took us round and showed us every nook and cranny. It had all been lovingly changed but preserved. Perhaps the large top floor room gave most delight for it *was* larger than I remembered. This was where we put on our plays and where, at party times or in school holidays, it became a dormitory with three little iron beds for friends or siblings. A kaleidoscope of memories flitted into view. Could it really have been over 60 years since I had been in that room?

Writer-friends had warned me that signing sessions, especially in bookshops, could be tedious. Not so for me. I found that complete strangers chatted. From a host of memories I recall an exhausted elderly married couple rushing into the Malton bookshop saying that they had tried bookshops for miles around to get a copy of *Life in a Liberty Bodice* without success and now they'd seen it in the window. 'In York there was so much ground to cover that we went off in separate directions', said the wife, 'but not without a grumble on his part. He said he'd be embarrassed asking for a book with *that* title so I wrote it out for him on a piece of paper so he could just hand it over the counter and spare his blushes!'.

The privately arranged signing sessions in houses and halls were joyous occasions; among the variety of friends and colleagues distant relatives made valiant efforts to come and immediately became not 'distant' but 'instant' and closed gaps of many years. This was especially so at Foulbridge Hall.

In the Grand Hall of the Grand Theatre in Leeds (where over a hundred guests were present) several residents from Morritt Avenue — tuned into the grape-vine — turned up, one with the 1903 photograph showing The Avenue's former glory. One unexpected visitor was my very close school-friend Rosalie Hartley whose lovely face I recognised even though sorrows had left their signature. We had not met since early in her marriage, about 60 years before, but, as with all true friendships, gaps of time dissolve and shared memories of past days quicken and illuminate the present.

I hope you enjoy *Liberty Bodice* whether it is a first reading or *Liberty Bodice* revisited. Keep in touch.

3 Clent Lodge
Cranham Road
CHELTENHAM GL52 6BQ
Tel. 01242 245584

PREFACE

Time remembered is seldom sequential, for memory is as mercurial as Ariel, conjuring up sights, sounds, songs and smells as vivid as they are irrational.

These random recollections, inconsequential in time and light-hearted in content, have been tidied up with hindsight so that the family characters, comic or serious, are framed in the period and setting which was not apparent to the child. Past and future are outside a child's concepts for the present is all enveloping and even tomorrow is an eternity away.

Subjects for autobiographies or biographies are usually either aristocrats or celebrities. There are none in my family nor is there a case of 'rags to riches' nor even a face made familiar by TV. Not one was born with a silver spoon in his mouth with the retinue of butlers, nannies, cooks, housemaids and parlour maids to select, manipulate, fill, clean and clear the silver spoon. No, we were a middle-of-the-middle-class family —'middling' in Yorkshire terms — with modest incomes but a wealth of characters.

Every family goes back to the beginning of time and has created its own tradition. Both my paternal and maternal ancestors farmed for generations in the broad acres of Yorkshire and they, like all farmers, created their own sense of inheritance and earthy aristocracy.

Hindsight tempers, modifies and amplifies the limited memories of childhood and one can never be quite sure whether one remembers the actual event or the chat about it. Some of the pictures come straight from the magic lantern memory of the child-I-was, and these are in the child's primary colours .

Other events, through constant recall and retelling, have acquired a polish and patina, blending the child's black, white and primary colours with more subtle shades.

And why, you might ask, the 'Liberty bodice?' In the early 1900s women were tightened and trussed into whaleboned corsets and even little girls were pressed into boned stays. In 1908 the corset firm of Symingtons, sensing that fashions were becoming more relaxed, especially for children, bravely launched the Liberty bodice, the most sensational flag of freedom ever to be flown in the fashion world.

My mother, well ahead of her time, soon had her three daughters wearing the heavy cotton bodices with their upright bands of braid. Designed as they were to flatten the bust and release the waist, they were not intended to charm but rather to disguise. Rubber buttons dangling above a button-holed tape hoisted woollen or

Liberty Bodices

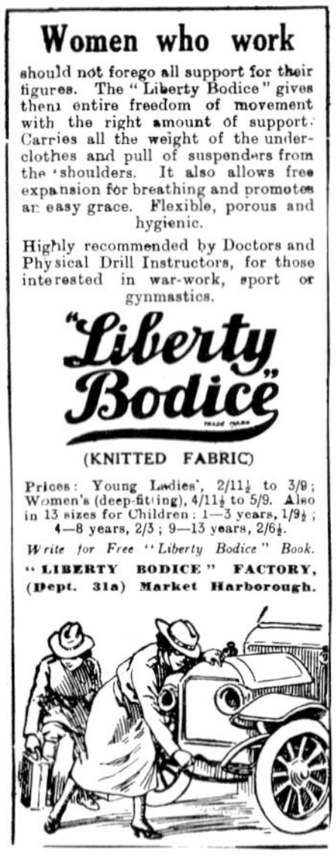

Made by Symingtons of Market Harborough 1908 to 2nd World War.

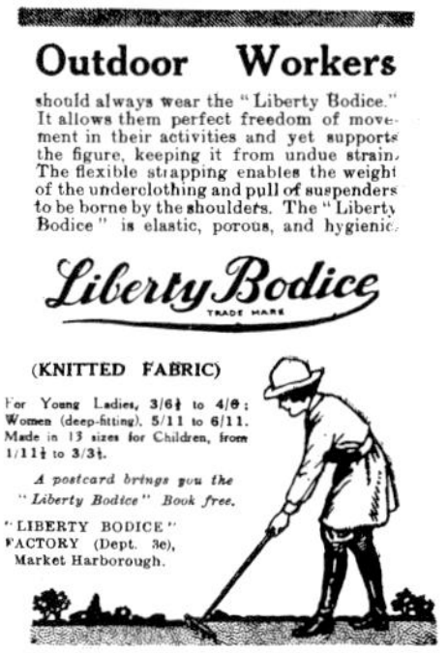

lisle stockings into position. Such was the basic garment of the avant garde. After three years in a woollen baby binder, I too graduated into the Liberty bodice brigade which I wore, on and off, until 1925.

By the time the First World War broke out, millions of young girls were wearing this uniform and I believe Liberty bodices were still being manufactured during the Second World War but for the Hyde family — and other enlightened families of my generation — the word 'liberty' had a wider and deeper connotation.

Contrary to the accepted idea that children of that era were repressed, we children enjoyed more freedom of movement and mind, albeit localised, than is possible in today's world of terrorism and trendiness titivated by television.

With our chosen friends, we young girls camped out unchaperoned sixty miles away from home for weeks on end. We could wander miles on our own without fear of rape or mugging; we could invite friends to tea without formal invitation, parent chauffeuring or television viewing. We could present plays and concerts with candles in bottles for footlights without anyone bothering about fire regulations. We could leave doors of houses and cars unlocked without fear of thieves or vandals. We picked wild flowers—which grew in wanton profusion— without censure from the conservationists. Even around our suburban home there were meadows of long lush grass through which we could wander and when the hay was cut we could picnic in the fields leaning against the igloo-shaped haycocks. At harvest time we took our food into the cornfields and sat leaning against the wig-wam stooks. On the farms in the holidays we drank milk which had only travelled a few yards from the cow to the kitchen. We ate butter, dewy wet with buttermilk, straight from the churn, drank water from the pump in complete innocence and ignorance of health and health warnings. I suppose we were both careless and carefree, but a large family, bonded by affectionate trust, creates its own survival kit.

However there was an invisible and intangible framework of discipline inside which liberty was not violated and freedom could flourish. We were protected from our own ignorance, stupidity, lust, prurient curiosity and aggression by knowing the frontiers: a silent signal said 'stop here.' If we overstepped the mark we were accused of 'taking liberties' which I, as a very young child, thought had something to do with missing Liberty bodices.

Reading was also liberated and liberal for it was not confined to examination syllabuses nor retarded by 'reading-readiness'. We read and read, anything we could lay our hands on, without teachers or censors.

We were also liberated care-free amateurs proving G K Chesterton's paradox: 'If a thing's worth doing, it's worth doing badly'. Only on rare and prized occasions were we spectators.

No attempt was made to keep up with the Joneses or buy every new gadget which came on the market. Our needs were paid for 'on the nail'. Our wants were not discussed. Life was simplified by limited choice.

Young folk today have opportunities far beyond our wildest dreams. The best of them have never been so healthy, attractive, idealistic, hard-working, courageous, honest and enterprising but the sad truth is that far too many of our young are lost in a world where the protective frontiers have been removed and the signposts and guide-lines have been obliterated. I could wish for them the limitations, security and liberality of my childhood.

To the countless men and women who, in some way, either by their presence or through their poetry, prose or music, have contributed to my life I offer my deepest thanks. It was they who gave me a foothold on this rickety ladder of life.

AUTHOR'S NOTE

The names of my family, relatives and friends have not been altered but a few teachers and neighbours have been given pseudonyms to avoid hurting or embarrassing any living descendants.

CHAPTER ONE
ANOTHER GIRL

The author in the family christening gown, in the arms of Aunt Selina 1909.

The year 1909 was not the brightest spot in my parents' married life, for in that year, on 12 September, I was born: the fourth girl. Letters of condolence arrived: 'Sorry it's not a boy'; 'Better luck next time'; 'Never mind, I'm sure you'll learn to love her'. The word 'learn' seemed ominous. Can we learn to love? I think they did.

Anyhow, they cared enough to engage the ubiquitous monthly nurse (we were all five born at home and, of course, breast-fed; no thoughts of maternity hospitals or nursing homes in those days). I can see Nurse Malthouse now, though it can only be through photographs and her regular return visits, an imposing rigid figure wearing a long starched apron, stiff white cap clamped down to keep every hair out of sight, floor length navy and white striped cotton dress, eight inch long stiffly starched white cuffs with gold cuff links, and a huge wrist-watch completely encased in leather. It was a totally inappropriate garb for dealing with the sucking, spitting and exploding which punctuates a baby's life. The 'morning-daily' was faced not only with an extra baby's washing, including Turkish towelling nappies, but with Nurse Malthouse's daunting uniform.

Even though I was the fourth girl and money was short, my parents had not run out of names, and endowed me with the rather grand name of: Sarah Elizabeth Christabel Hyde, a splendid 4/4 rhythm which lent itself to doggerel verse and song.

My mother was an ardent Suffragette, albeit a gentle one, who, I feel sure, in 1909 would rather have been carrying a banner than a baby. It was a critical year for the Suffragettes for, by this time, frustrated by the failure of persuasive protest to the Government, they mounted their military campaign. The eloquence of Mrs Emmeline Pankhurst and her daughter Christabel reached a peak. My mother sublimated her fervour, frustration and faith into christening her fourth daughter 'Christabel'.

I often wonder if my chronic insomnia may hark back to the 'Christabel' song, hardly a soporific lullaby:

> Work! Work! Work! The vote is coming!
> Cheer up girls! The day's at hand
> When for all their chaff and knocks
> We shall get the ballot-box
> And a vote for the leaders of the land

1909 was also the year when Lloyd George (my father's hero but not my mother's as he had done nothing for the women's cause) presented the famous 'People's Budget' and Finance Bill. It was the year that Blériot flew the first aircraft across the Channel; Selfridges opened, and the Ford T model was launched — the first car within the economic range of the hoi polloi.

1909 was also a critical year for King Edward VII who fought gallantly against terminal illness until he died in May 1910.

I liked to describe myself as an Edwardian, since it seemed to be more colourful than Victorian or Georgian but in fact I can only claim this doubtful distinction for the first eight months of my life!

It was the same period of the same year — April and May 1910 — when both my Hyde grandparents died, their lives spanning the reign of Victoria and Edward. It was a sensible time to die for they never saw the barbed wire and the concrete pillboxes foul their Fraisthorpe and Auburn sand-bordered fields nor mourn their wagoners who died on Flanders Fields in the First World War.

There must have been a lull in my mother's unconventional religious ventures — which I shall report later — because I was conventionally christened in the Anglican Church in Whitkirk near Leeds, a mile walk from my home.

Walking was the operative word for most of the family outings, and, as the baby period stretched through 18 years of my mother's married life, walking meant pram pushing. And what a pram! I suppose that, by the time my turn came for this heirloom, it had already covered the sort of mileage we expect of a mini-car. Those prams

Betsy, Coidy and Kathleen at the gate in Morritt Avenue.

were built to last and to serve several generations, and they did — even in Royal households.

Ours was a very large, very high, huge-wheeled affair, a deep cavernous navy blue boat. Inside, at deck level, three flat leather buttoned cushions fitted on to

Artist's impression of the entrance to Morritt Avenue as it looked before the First World War. The gates ensured absolute privacy but they were removed at the outbreak of the First World War. The house on the left was where my adopted aunts Carrie and Annie lived and later Carrie's husband.

Kathleen, Nancy, Betsy and Coidy (in age order)

ledges to cover the hull, and in the three cavities of the hull could be stowed luggage for a family holiday and the baby's needs. Over this, a firm mattress was covered with a solid rubber sheet, white linen sheets, and a lace-edged pillow. A leather apron and leather hood made it a pram for all seasons. It was to re-emerge seven years later, in the middle of the Great War, for the fifth child, mercifully, a *son*.

I cannot think that babies nowadays in their jolty little canvas contraptions with Lego size erratic wheels have the same comfort and security, but how peripatetic they, and their mothers, are. And where could you put a Silver Cross pram in a modern semi or high rise flat? In any case, children's bottoms, like the rest of their bodies, adapt to modern mobility: car and aircraft seats; safety belts; supermarket trolleys; and mother-hugging baby harnesses. I suppose in those first two years I never travelled more than four or five miles from home; my grand-children very quickly notch up four or five thousand miles!

My sisters told me that instead of the usual 'pink for a girl' I was decked out in the purple, white and green of the Suffragette movement, and that the white pillow of my pram was heavily appliqued with purple clematis and green leaves. I still possess a piece of purple, white and green striped ribbon which, we were told, came direct from Christabel Pankhurst. Incongruously, my mother's dedication to the cause was interpreted in some rather twee feminine *objects d'art:* a large white satin tea cosy lavishly embroidered with purple irises and green leaves; white linen cone-shaped hair tidies with purple violets and green ribbons; needle-cases of white flannel with lavender covers and of course delicate white china cups with purple pansies, all presents, I should think, from some of the genteel passion-spent aunts.

These art nouveau embellishments were a far cry from the women chained to the Downing Street railings and the forced feeding of those courageous women in Holloway Gaol. I was only to know years later that, on the day of my christening, Christabel Pankhurst and Lady Constance Lytton were leading a stone-throwing group of twelve Suffragettes in Newcastle-on-Tyne, aiming at what they thought was Lloyd George's car. When I was a year or so old, Dame Ethel Smyth wrote the stirring *March of the Women* for the Suffragettes, and this became part of my mother's singing repertoire in which we children joined round the piano. Later I learnt that when Dame Ethel Smyth was jailed in Holloway prison and her Suffragette supporters came to cheer her from the prison yard, Dame Ethel conducted their singing of her marching song from her cell window, brandishing her tooth-brush as a baton!

Here is an extract from a speech given by Christabel Pankhurst in 1910 and reported in the paper 'Votes for Women' in 1911:

"The present year is one of national rejoicing, and the Coronation ceremonies [for George V] will be symbolic of the unity and of the freedom of our Empire, but that unity and that freedom cannot be complete so long as the stigma of disfranchisement and political outlawry rests upon half the people. Women have a right to demand that in this year, of all years, their political liberty shall be accorded to them.

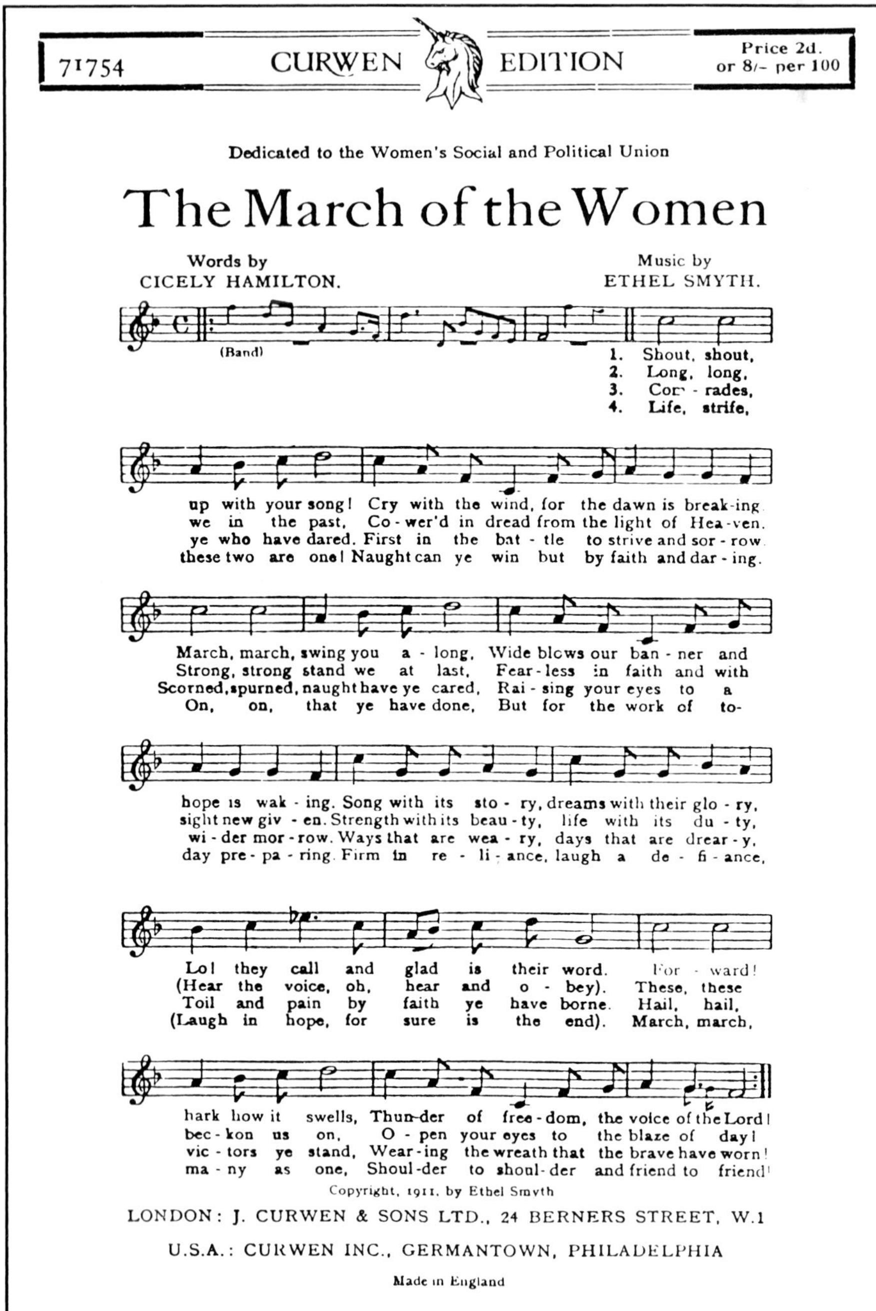
71754
CURWEN EDITION
Price 2d.
or 8/- per 100
Dedicated to the Women's Social and Political Union
The March of the Women
Words by
CICELY HAMILTON.
Music by
ETHEL SMYTH.
(Band)
1. Shout, shout,
2. Long, long,
3. Com - rades,
4. Life, strife,
up with your song! Cry with the wind, for the dawn is break-ing
we in the past, Co - wer'd in dread from the light of Hea-ven.
ye who have dared. First in the bat - tle to strive and sor - row.
these two are one! Naught can ye win but by faith and dar - ing.
March, march, swing you a - long, Wide blows our ban - ner and
Strong, strong stand we at last, Fear - less in faith and with
Scorned, spurned, naught have ye cared, Rai - sing your eyes to a
On, on, that ye have done, But for the work of to-
hope is wak - ing. Song with its sto - ry, dreams with their glo - ry,
sight new giv - en. Strength with its beau - ty, life with its du - ty,
wi - der mor - row. Ways that are wea - ry, days that are drear - y,
day pre - pa - ring. Firm in re - li - ance, laugh a de - fi - ance,
Lo! they call and glad is their word. For - ward!
(Hear the voice, oh, hear and o - bey). These, these
Toil and pain by faith ye have borne. Hail, hail,
(Laugh in hope, for sure is the end). March, march,
hark how it swells, Thun-der of free - dom, the voice of the Lord!
bec - kon us on, O - pen your eyes to the blaze of day!
vic - tors ye stand, Wear - ing the wreath that the brave have worn!
ma - ny as one, Shoul - der to shoul - der and friend to friend!
Copyright, 1911, by Ethel Smyth
LONDON: J. CURWEN & SONS LTD., 24 BERNERS STREET, W.1
U.S.A.: CURWEN INC., GERMANTOWN, PHILADELPHIA
Made in England

The feeling is universal that we have come to a turning point in the history of our Empire, to a time of new growth and new development. Mr Winston Churchill, in winding up the third reading debate on the Parliament Bill, declared that we have reached the end of an era in our politics — the end of strife, and the beginning of settlement. 'The time', he said, 'has surely come when this country can clear off its arrears of reform. The time has come when the worn-out controversies of the Victorian period should be finally settled and cleared out of the way', and he declared that we ought now to turn with all our strength to the 'social, national, and Imperial organisation on which the wealth and future of our nation depend'. If these words mean anything, they mean that the Woman Suffrage question should now be settled. It certainly forms part of the arrears of reform long overdue. It is one of the controversies of the Victorian period which ought to have been over and done with before that period expired. The help of women in social, national and Imperial organisation is needed to-day as it was never needed before. Women have taken their full share of the hardships and perils suffered by those who laid the foundations of Empire; they deserve, and they are supremely fitted for, a share in the great constructive work which it is now necessary for the men and women of this Empire to undertake."

— Christabel Pankhurst

My memories of childhood are very sketchy and irrational, and bear little relation to their significance. What quirk of memory makes me remember oddments of no consequence and forget the decisive moments of life? One little scene, for example, is firmly embedded in my brain cells and yet will flash up incongruously without any recognisable association of ideas. I could not have been more than a year old when I wormed my way between the bars and legs of a bentwood cane-seated chair and sat in that circular Lilliputian world. My toy was a long silver button hook which I was trying to manipulate so that it would hang down suspended from one of the holes. As I pushed the hook up and went through the operation of fixing it to the cane, I synchronised the movement with my first independent word: 'Coidy.' Through repetition by the family, the word became my name and has remained so for over 80 years. The triumph of fixing the hook and calling the word were signals for my mother to leave the huge earthenware bread bowl and peer down through the cane-seat holes and call back: 'Coidy, Coidy.' It was, I should also think, a clever guise to keep me stable and occupied in my tiny self-made play-pen.

Nothing is as clear as that until I was five. My fifth birthday came just after the outbreak of the First World War, September 1914, but that meant nothing to me. A far greater historical event was Christmas 1914, when they discovered red spots all over me and Dr Bean came round, as he frequently did whether we were ill or not, and pronounced, 'Measles'.

I was put ceremoniously in a front bedroom with a big bay window and a huge brass double bed. I had never had the luxury of being an invalid before. We northern children put up with colds, constipation and diarrhoea, chilblains, ear-ache and acne as being an accepted part of growing up. But measles was important. Measles was infectious. And so, joy of joys, a fire was lit in the little black grate, never having been lit in that same bedroom since I was born. The fire became my companion and confidante. No more were the shadows on the ceiling sinister ogres and giants, now they were brightly coloured Tinkerbells. There were pictures in the fire of golden caverns and palaces, and I wove stories aloud round them and into them. The firelight danced out on to the Christmas tree, the very first tree there had ever been in our house. It was the only time in my early years I can remember having a warm bedroom.

The three-foot tree, for that was all it was, stood at the end of my bed on a disguised upturned bucket, the baubles catching still more sparkles and spangles from the fire. There never was, and never will be, such a tree. With the chilling arithmetic of adult hindsight, I suppose that everything on that tree would not add up to more than half-a-crown, yet I can still feel the wonder of it all. There was a little white china basket packed with Cadbury's milk chocolate drops; a matchstick size white pencil on a silver cord (a relic I suppose from someone's dance card); a golden net of foil-covered chocolate sovereigns and half-sovereigns; dolls' chairs and table made out of mahogany conkers with backs and arms and legs woven with embroidery silk on pin supports. And, on top of the tree, the white and silver fairy doll never revealed that underneath the magic of the gauze there was a wooden clothes-peg with its wooden knob made-up to be a pink and white face, pipe-cleaner arms and wand; and a curtain ring crown. But the child of five never saw the peg, the pipe cleaners, and the curtain ring. She saw a fairy.

In my bed, apparently immune from measles, was our family rag doll, Kelly. How she got that Manx name I do not know, for she was begotten out of the coupling of a double cotton page of a rag book of printed dolls which my mother cut out, sewed, and stuffed. Kelly had more sticky kisses planted on her than any of the more elegant porcelain-faced dolls, and, pulled about as she was, she looked more distrait than distinctive. But she was the family favourite.

A few weeks before the VIP treatment of the measles bed, Kelly's life had hung in the balance. My sister Betsy, two years older than I, had ambitions for Kelly, and thought that she should be bathed, baptised and christened. Choosing the right moment, she crept up to the apple-attic ('At the top of the house the apples are laid in rows') and dunked Kelly up and down on the ball-cock of the cold water tank. So ardent was the baptism (complete immersion) that the ball cock and Kelly stuck down at the bottom of the tank out of reach of Betsy's hands. With tears and feet torrenting down the two flights of stairs, she wailed out: 'Mother, come quickly! I've drowned Kelly'. A soggy Kelly, many times her usual weight, was dragged out of the tank, squeezed through the wooden mangle, and laid out on the boiler lid of the black kitchen range to dry. Later, with my mother's deft hands, she was recoiffeured with rug wool, face painted from the tins of leftovers from home decorating and restored to years of loving life.

Although, looking back, I know my mother and father had different ideas about money, for my mother's ambitions for her children grossly exceeded my father's

Joy of joys, a fire was lit in the little black grate.

income, we never allowed lack of money to cramp our style, for, in every other way but money, we were rich.

We had space. Space for riotous games: hide-and-seek all over the four-storeyed house, space for creating and acting our own plays, space for writing, drawing/ painting, and singing round the piano, space for all our friends and relations, space to get away from them and read in solitude, space in the fields and gardens for wickedly dangerous games, space to climb trees, dig trenches, make hay . . .I think we profited too from good wholesome neglect — with time and space to make our own unrecorded mistakes without parental umpiring.

There were times, of course, when we were ticked off, nagged at, or brought to silent contrition. I only remember once being whacked — but that is another story a few years hence.

Children are not saints; nor are they little adults; they have minds of their own,

"I hate Filey, and I hate that little coccage, I want to go back to the Avenue."

and act with vicious or affectionate spontaneity. Girls' sadism is more subtle than boys', and they seem to hang on to their hates far longer. The four Hyde sisters were no exception.

Nancy, my second sister, six years old at the time of this episode — quite the gentlest of us all — must have been mightily provoked by my eldest sister, four years older, to bite her to bleeding point. After hours of Kathleen's tears and sulks, my mother exhorted her to forgive Nancy and be friends again. After a calculating silence, eyes screwed up in concentration, Kathleen stonily hissed her life-sentence:

'Very well, Nancy, I'll forgive you. But you'll never be the little girl that *didn't* bite Kathleen'.

Such was Kathleen's trenchant interpretation of the Lord's Prayer, which all children chanted every morning at the village school. I was only two at the time, and had not graduated to 'trespasses' and 'forgiveness'. But I do remember the bite and the blood.

A huge bonus in our up-bringing (rather too grand a word for the Topsyish way in which we grew up) was that we had open house. Our

The dresses in the top photograph had already been handed down from our Danby cousins and were then handed down through the Hyde girls to me! They never wore out.

friends called, chatted, stayed, played, shared simple unpartyish food, and went for walks. All our noise and aggression was diverted away from adults. As we got older, we joined the gang and measured ourselves against the 'dares' of our peers. Yet, however outrageous the games or the 'dares', only we were the victims: the cause and the effect. It would never have occurred to our parents that any child would be raped, mugged, assaulted or kidnapped. We were encouraged to believe that strangers should be greeted with a kindly word; that tramps needed food; and that all lame dogs should be helped over stiles.

We had simple but nourishing food, grown, collected, and delivered more or less unpackaged; wholemeal flour in sacks; brown sugar in strong blue paper bags; coarse oatmeal and porridge oats; unpolished rice; farm churned butter cut from the block and vegetables and fruit mostly grown in our garden — and later in the wartime allotments.

Oranges, bananas and nuts were birthday and Christmas treats brought home by my father from the stalls of Leeds Market. Beef was an everyday every week affair; it started on a Sunday as a crisp-on-the-outside-bloody-in-the-middle joint, gradually diminishing in various disguises to the Wednesday shepherd's pie. Chickens were treats, in our case put on the train by farming uncles for us to collect at Crossgates station the same day. Mutton, only rarely referred to as lamb, stews and hot-pots were family stand-bys, made from the stock pot of bones and herbs reinforced with the loathsome pearl barley. Cakes, usually madeira or seed cakes, were of the cut-and-come-again size. Rare treats were the sponge cakes with cream and jam — commonly referred to when we had visitors to tea as FHB — family-hold-back. Eggs came either from our farming relations or from our own Rhode Island Reds at the end of the garden, the cockerel Roderic Dhu ruling the roost. The phrase 'free range' did not need to be invented nor, of course, were eggs ever sized or graded. The hens were as free as we were.

Milk was delivered at the back door, without any thought of hygiene, from an oval portable metal churn with a pint measure ladle clipped over the side. We took our jugs, into which the pints and quarts were tipped to the door. The accepted practice was that the milkman then re-dipped the ladle to top up the pint. Our milkman had a devious way of going through the 'bonus' routine without letting the 'tilt' part with the milk. No weights and measures officers hounded the paths of salesmen then. It would have spoilt our family joke if he had been made to give full measure.

The milk was left in the uncovered jugs in a larder or a pantry. More pernickety people than we had lots of little net and beaded covers for jugs and dishes. I think my family were always so healthily ravenous that they got there before the flies.

There was no frenzied marathon supermarket shopping in our day. In fact, I can hardly remember my mother shopping at all except for the very rare occasions when we were taken to Leeds to buy new clothes or shoes. We children did the things-you-need-in-a-hurry shopping at the little village shop. The Leeds grocer — grandly described in gilded letters over his shop: 'Italian Warehouseman' — had a sit-down call every Monday morning and took down the order for the week. The next day his errand boy delivered the groceries, checked them from the list, sitting over his cup of tea at the kitchen table, then helped to put them away, before receiving his penny tip.

Bread, if not home made, was delivered from the baker's cart unsliced and unwrapped, not regimented into a 'Mother's Pride' block but individually wayward in its crusty top. The yeast man drove a neat pony and trap, and came to the door with his polished brass scales and weighed out the ounces from the hessian packs; the greengrocer and fishman called twice a week with a miscellany of seasonal local grown and caught goods.

Letters delivered by the postman three times a day (penny post!) were often exchanged for outgoing post with a friendly summing up: 'Ah see there's one from London, that'll be your daughter!' The cobbler collected and delivered our shoes and boots; the coal came in a ton load and was shot direct through the chute to the coal cellar after the metal lid of the coalhouse had been lifted. Firewood in bundles was brought round by the rag-and-bone-man, or rather a swapping operation of old clothes provided several months' kindling. His cry of 'Rags and bones' had to overtop the metal wheels of his cart and the clip-clop-clop of his horse on the cobbled road.

Another regular visitor, at dusk every day, was the lamplighter. We, like Robert Louis Stevenson, were lucky 'with a lamp before the door,' and so we watched him hook his long pole on to the little ring, pull it down to release the gas, and then with the beacon end of the pole set the gas alight. Later the gas lamps had a pilot light and only the ring pull was needed. Of course we knew the poem in A *Child's Garden of Verses* off by heart so a 'Leerie' was added to our family of familiars, just as the Bobby on the beat was our rather more awesome friend.

It was a simple recipe for simpler days. No junk food nor junk drinks — nor TV advertisements for them — no complicated expensive packaging nor foods standardised to fit the package. There were no garish plastic toys, no TVs, videos, computers, school buses ... and no child psychologists, juvenile social workers, probation officers and juvenile courts.

I wonder how much the expensive de-personalised commodities we think are necessities for our wall-to-wall carpeted life have in fact created the very problems they seek to solve.

All the same, how satisfying it would have been to endow my mother — and all the other mothers — with washing machines, central heating, electric irons, labour-less hot water, zip fasteners, disposable nappies, paper tissues and sellotape!

Little Miss Muffet
Sat on a tuffet

Eating her curds and whey

There came a big spider
And sat down beside her

And frightened Miss Muffet away!

The author's first acting part in the Driffield garden.

CHAPTER TWO

MY MOTHER

My mother was a 'joiner'. She joined every organisation which she felt would help to make a kinder, wiser and more peaceful world. She really believed that if working class folk had longer and better education they would end up reading works of literature, listening to or playing classical music, singing in choirs or joining William Morris craft groups and that they would all become 'beautiful people'.

Her resolute aspirations never wavered even though, quite often, they were at odds with the rather basic common sense of her Yorkshire friends and relatives. Even at 86, in the year 1959, she still truly believed that a Socialist Utopia was not far away. Perhaps that was why she never lost her good looks and that her lapis lazuli eyes shone with an undying faith.

At the beginning of the century she joined the Suffragettes; the Labour Party; the Fabians; the Workers' Educational Association; Leeds Musical Festival; the Literary and Philosophical Society, and the Anti-Vivisectionists. A few years later, when her reforming spirit wanted to go beyond this world, she joined the Theosophical Society, the Anthroposophical Society and the Society for Psychical Research.

Somehow she managed, between the bouts of what must have seemed tiresome domesticity, to work quite actively for most of these 'isms' or at least study the masses of serious reading which flowed into our home. She was sensible enough not to try to tidy everything away; in any case the stuff was there for reading: the *Manchester Guardian,* the *Daily News, Yorkshire Post* (passed on by relatives), *Women's Social and Political Union* pamphlets, the *Labour Record,* the *Clarion, Time and Tide,* and the Pethwick Lawrence's paper: *Votes for Women.*

It was the right time to be a Suffragette and a Socialist. What else could a thinking person be when women were exploited and excluded, factory hours were long, millions of houses had no sanitation? There was no national health insurance, no child benefit, and unemployment pay was thirty shillings a week. 'On the dole' meant joining a despondent queue of social rejects. So many benefits which we take for granted now were being fought for, long before the Second World War, by 'reformers' who would, by our present affluent social standards, be considered to be on or below the bread-line themselves.

Our household names were: George Lansbury, Arthur Greenwood, Philip Snowden, the Pankhursts and, in his earlier days, Ramsey MacDonald. These were the folk, it would seem, who kept hope alive. We joined with them boisterously singing the Red Flag, but perhaps more soberly:

'These things shall be: a loftier race
Than e'er the world hath known shall rise
With flame of freedom in their souls
And light of science in their eyes.'

The women who constantly recurred in our round-the-table talk were Margaret Macmillan, Annie Besant, Mrs Pankhurst and her remarkable daughters; the editor of *Time and Tide*: Viscountess Rhondda and Mrs Pethwick Lawrence.

If we, as children, were neglected — in the suburban housewife's sense of the word — we were ultimately enriched by our mother's breadth of vision, her mercurial mind and the way in which 'all things wise and wonderful' were magnetised to her and she to them. Her liberal idealism was a burning reaction against her own painfully restricted girlhood. This third daughter of a butcher-farmer father and a refined but narrow-minded mother, living in the West Riding village of Sherburn in Elmet, might never have blossomed had it not been for the vicar of the local parish church, whom I now know to have been the Reverend James Newton Earl. It was he who noticed that the little village girl, Annie, knew all the words of the hymns and crystallised them into pure song. I feel sure that he must have heard her mother snapping out: 'Annie, don't be so lazy; get your head out of that book and set the table!' It was the vicar who realised from what Annie read that she had language-in-the-head which she was too shy and too repressed to dare to speak. For no pay — and I imagine very little thanks — the vicar persuaded my grandmother to let him tutor her young daughter in his study at the vicarage. My mother described with awesome wonder what she felt on seeing a room lined with books, the big library desk and the silver ink-stand. There was a rose-globed lamp for *reading,* not the plain glass 'chimney' ones they had at home for sewing.

A boundless new world opened for her. Together, she in her dark serge dress and buttoned boots and he in his long black cassock, read aloud and revelled in the novels of Dickens, Scott, Thackeray, and George Eliot; the poetry of Keats, Coleridge, Wordsworth, Tennyson and Browning, and the plays of Shakespeare. 'Learning by heart' was an uncovenanted bonus which hardly involved a set learning process because the words were relished by the ears and cherished in the heart. Words became her personal treasures which comforted grief and proclaimed joy.

Sherburn Church, where my parents were married in 1900.

The Rectory, where the Reverend James Newton Earl taught my mother.

After the first meeting with my mother, the vicar was determined that Annie should go to college (a rare thing for women back in the 1890s) and so he patiently schooled her in mathematics, grammar, basic Latin, calligraphy and of course the Authorised Version of the Bible and the Book of Common Prayer. Nor did he neglect her singing for he heard Annie (excluded as girls were from the church choir) over-topping the choir boys as her voice rose to the vaulted roof of the church. So, in 1893, Annie Wainwright, a shy little country lass, was admitted to Ripon Diocesan Training College and into a haven of learning.

In those early days of the College the life of the students was closely woven into the life and music of the Cathedral. My mother's complete devotion and gratitude to the College and the Cathedral remained with her all her life. Canon Garrod, Principal of the College and a Canon of the Cathedral, cannot ever have had a more devoted disciple. He was still being quoted to her children fifty years after he had signed her beautiful gilded leather prizes. They are here now in my study embossed with the coat-of-arms bearing the motto: *'Nisi Dominus Frustra'*, the College's condensed version of the City of Ripon's inscription over the Town Hall: *'Except Ye Lorde Keep Ye Cittie Ye Wakeman Waketh in Vain'*.

I do not know what Canon Garrod would have made of her later dissension and deviation from the Church of England, but she never lost, nor departed from, the essential elements of Christianity which Ripon gave her, nor did she ever lose the musical and spiritual pulse of the Bible and the liturgy.

Looking at the inscriptions in her prizes, I notice one award for 'Reading Aloud and Repetition,' skills highly valued in those days of teacher training. How sad that nowadays the whole subject has been discarded yet it would seem to be a basic skill for a teacher to be able to communicate effectively and have the ability to spell-bind and hold the attention of the children whether the subject is pottery, poetry or politics.

As soon as the fifth child was out of a pram my mother became an ardent member of the Fabian Society and occasionally went off to the Fabian Summer Schools, leaving us in the charge of her sister, our Aunt Charlotte. Whatever experiences my mother had were multiplied in enjoyment by the re-telling to family and friends. Stories abounded, wise and witty words were reported of Shaw, H G Wells, Professor Tawney, the Webbs and Professor Joad. Some of these were not for young ears, and were told when we (or so she thought) were out of ear-shot. Children have remarkably good hearing for things they shouldn't hear, and we relished the gossip and stories of the sexual exploits of Wells and Joad. Thus we gathered, not without reason, that the Fabian Society was not all to do with creating a 'loftier race.'

My mother's on-and-off vegetarianism was always given a boost at these Fabian Society Summer Schools as the declared vegetarians had a good chance of sharing a table with Bernard Shaw. We girls were rather mocking about her 'pip and peel-water' diet, but looking back with hindsight, which is much more affectionate as one gets older, I think we were rather unkind and that she would, if she were alive today, have added the word 'Green' to her colourful life.

Ripon, the city where my mother, aunts and sister were at college.

My parents not only wanted to go on educating themselves, but they wished to give folk whose education had been cut short the opportunities for learning which they had missed. And so they organised a branch of the Workers' Educational Assocation (WEA) and worked with Dr F W Moorman, Professor of English Literature at Leeds University, to conduct the three-year tutorial courses. In those days the WEA classes were unique in giving further education which went culturally beyond the trades and crafts of the night schools, important and valuable as those were from a vocational point of view. Even though many of those who enrolled for the demanding three-year literature course had left school at twelve, they still fulfilled the conditions of written essays, orally presented formal papers and debate of a high order. It was, even for the most unschooled of the adult students, taken for granted that their elementary schools had turned them out at twelve with decent calligraphy, acceptable spelling, grammar and punctuation. So with the basic skills presenting no barrier, they were able to profit from the intellectual inspiration of Professor Moorman and enjoy not only his standard English interpretation of literature but his wonderful stories and plays in Yorkshire dialect.

We children were fortunate to grow up in an airy atmosphere of intellectual endeavour rather than intellectual strain and contortion. It was an age when artists were allowed to tell stories in their pictures, when plays could be 'well-made', when stories and novels could have a beginning, a middle and an end — and even a happy one. It was an age when music could have melody, and poetry could have rhymes and rhythm. Folk believed in the power of the narrative. Books were abounding, substantially bound and very cheap. It was an age of self-learning when men and women with only a few years of elementary schooling could still be short-listed and chosen for responsible adult jobs provided they had served their apprenticeship in the workshop, night school or library. Yet there were probably as many illiterates as there are now, but 'illiterate' is hardly the appropriate word for a first-class hedger, ditcher, thatcher, potter or reaper who took pride in his craft.

It was our custom every Sunday tea-time to set the large Victorian table for as many people as were likely to be there; we had complete freedom to ask anyone who was around to come to tea. Of course our parents too invited friends from church, chapel, WEA and over the garden hedge. An occasional visitor was the minister from the Baptist Chapel. When he came we all solemnly stood and sang grace:

'Let us with a gladsome mind
Praise the Lord for he is kind;
For his mercies aye endure
Ever faithful, ever sure.'

With our half-shut eyes, clasped hands, squeaky voices and suppressed giggles, we were always relieved that the united and generously resolved 'Amen' came after just one verse and we could tuck in.

I can see that table now with its utilitarian (but china) cups, straight, white and generous with a single navy blue border; two or three different patterns of tea-knives, the family size silver — but only plated — teapot covered with the purple, white and green satin tea cosy, a large slop basin, a huge bowl of lump sugar, with sugar tongs of course, and two immense jugs of hot water completed my mother's end of the table. Does anyone nowadays use a slop basin? sugar tongs? silver tea strainer? d'oyleys?

Weight-watchers would not approve of this almost entirely farinaceous meal: thinly cut white and brown bread generously buttered, home-made jam, Yorkshire tea-cakes or scones, Yorkshire spice cake — buttered of course, jam and lemon-curd tarts, rock buns, madeira or seed cake of cut-and-come-again size. Of course we did not have all those goodies at one meal. In fact, during the 1914 war, the bread was a dismal pale grey and, as sugar was rationed, it was a case of jam or butter, not both, and, if in luck, one cake or bun. But none of this stringency limited hospitality. Friends shared what they had, as indeed people learned to do in the Second World War. We sat down round about 5 o'clock, but the time depended on who called or stayed or chatted — there was simply no standing on ceremony.

Apart from eating, the main point about these teas was the *talking*. Talk was richer than the food and lasted far longer, for we rarely left the table before 7 o'clock. No-one had any inhibitions about bursting into song or quoting verse; in fact it was very often a song which moved us from the table to the piano, where we all gathered round the most willing or talented pianist.

When our parents had WEA seminars, we children were only tolerated as listeners, but Sunday tea was a linguistic free-for-all. I remember as a rather shy little girl of about ten thinking I might make a contribution to the conversation. The adults were rivetted in discussion of Oscar Wilde, and I latched on to the dramatic word 'prison' and piped up: 'Why did they send him to prison?' Before any of the somewhat surprised adults had conjured up an answer, Betsy, my twelve year old sister, with much more confidence than I, said 'Silly, he must have *stolen* something; they only send people to prison for *stealing*.' The adults were saved, but in retrospect I think it was rather unfair on Oscar. However, it was just the right time for my mother to signal that Nancy, Betsy and I should clear the table and wash up, which was a good chance to share a bit of juvenilia away from adults.

Just as my mother ensured that we were soaked in literature, so she endeavoured to steep us in good music. She really thought that if we went regularly to celebrity concerts, had tuition in playing the piano, sang part songs with her direction and were given practice time with a Bechstein, that one of us would become a concert pianist or a professional singer. Regrettably we fell far short of her aspirations.

However, she persevered, endlessly accompanying our singing and conscientiously taking us to concerts in Leeds Town Hall. Of course we sat in the cheapest seats which were benches in front of the huge organ pipes of the platform, giving us a good view of the backs of the orchestra but facing the conductor. I think the seats were sixpence each, but I can remember the wonderfully mobile faces and speaking eyes of Sir Thomas Beecham, Hamilton Harty, Malcolm Sargent and Sir Adrian Boult, and watching at close range the wizardry of Pachman's and Paderewski's hands at the grand piano.

But the seats were hard and symphonies are endless for the very young, and it was always a relief to stand up, to attention, for *God Save the King.* When Sir Thomas was conducting the orchestra the National Anthem became another performance with all the verses sung. Never have enemies been so confounded nor knavish tricks been so malevolent as they were under his belligerent baton. Then it was the long clanging tram-car drive home with my mother entranced, quietly humming and reliving the music, and I am sure feeling rather irritated that all her children wanted was the lavatory and food.

Occasionally we were taken to the Literary and Philosophical lecture recitals especially when famous poets talked about and read their own poems. We loved Chesterton's larger-than-life figure and exuberant delivery but we were rather baffled by Yeats' idiosyncratic incantation. Between ourselves we thought that we could say *The Blackbird* better than Drinkwater who had the oddest way of arguing with the metre and speech rhythms of his own verse.

When my sister Betsy and I, the two youngest girls, were still at the village elementary school, my mother was seized with the idea of giving us some compensating and cultural 'uplift' beyond the rote-learning which was the norm in the large desk-bound classes of the elementary school. So on Saturday mornings we boarded a tram car at Halton terminus, paid tuppence each to ride to Leeds and from there walked two miles to the Swarthmore settlement. Here enlightened Quakers made history, geography and nature study come to life. What a contrast to our village school: no desks, no ink-wells, no slate nor sweat smell, no 'down-the-yard' but bright curtains at the long low windows, rugs on which to sit for story-telling; models, contour maps, clay pots, weaving looms, great sheets of sugar paper for pastel drawings and poster paints. It was a children's paradise, and the charming lady in her Liberty smock with amber beads, soft voice, standard English speech and golden hair coiled over her ears seemed more like an angel than a teacher.

I did say we profited from good wholesome neglect but whatever 'ism' my mother was engrossed in, she always found time to read to us, or for us to read to her or read to one another. There were books all over the house, completely uncategorised, depending on shelf height and space rather than orderly bibliography. *Tristram Shandy* might be sitting on top of *In Tune with the Infinite* or the *Decline and Fall* might be rubbing shoulders with *Tom Sawyer.* Only the set of *Waverley Novels* and Arthur Mee's *Children's Encyclopaedia* had reserved seats on the bottom shelves. (The eight volumes of the encyclopaedias, bought when we all probably needed new shoes, had sparked off, not without cause, a gentle grumble from my father on my mother's extravagance.)

Hair-wash night Friday was a great story-telling time. There were no fancy shampoos then, at least not in our house, carbolic or Wright's Coal Tar soap were vigorously massaged into our scalps, always with the thought that we might — and we did! — pick up head-lice in the village school. After the militant wash we sat in the half-circle round the big kitchen fire, and built it up prodigally with great blocks of coal (£1 a ton in those days). In the oven, on the right-hand side, the bricks and the oven-sheets were heating which would later be wrapped round with pieces of blanket for us to take up to our beds.

My mother's part in the hair-drying was to brush and small-tooth comb each one of us until our scalps tingled and our hair gleamed. The certain way, we discovered, to keep the story-telling going was to *scratch*. This brought my mother and the small-tooth comb into attacking and hunting again, and the rhymes and stories went on and on to the accompaniment of brush and comb.

One night, I remember, my mother had read to us *The Pied Piper of Hamelin,* a painless introduction to Browning on whom my mother wrote and lectured. When she finished she asked us: 'What do you think happened to the children when they followed the Piper into the mountain?' Kathleen, the serious one, suggested that the Piper would have to stop playing and get the children some food; Nancy, who was always cold, asked: 'Would there be any gas-pipes or fireplaces?' Betsy, the tomboy, wondered if there would be trees to climb. I, the timid one, thought they would all be homesick. From this simple question, over the next weeks, a whole storybook emerged which we hand-printed, illustrated and bound.

Margaret McMillan

Because of my mother's passion for nurturing education for very young children she identified immediately with Rachel and Margaret McMillan who pioneered nursery school education in the slums of Deptford in the East End of London. Rachel and Margaret McMillan, with no grant, no public subscriptions, no private means and no funding from the Establishment but with enormous resources of imagination, energy and idealism, opened the camp nursery school in Deptford shortly before the First World War. These two sisters overcame all the obstacles of air-raids, mothers working late on munitions, fathers in the army, undernourished children, the vermin and squalor of the slums and 'death falling like hail'. It was to this scene of despair and hope that, at the height of the war, 1916, my mother sent my eldest sister Kathleen, to work in the camp school and to be one of the pioneer group of nursery teachers trained by Margaret McMillan and her staff. It is important to notice the word 'teacher' because the McMillans believed in total education for the under fives: 'Children need that very important kind of early education: *Nurture.*' Rachel and Margaret McMillan worked out, in detail, their altruistic principle: 'Educate every child as if he were your own'.

These 'happy few' students were in no sense just child-minders or nannies, but educated and accomplished teachers who were trained in the full understanding of the word 'nurture'. The children from these slummy surroundings were brought into a world of light, colour and fresh air. They were nurtured physically: bathed every day, given wholesome food, exercised and rested. Mentally: sense apparatus, sand, water, clay, questions answered with good talk and rich vocabulary. Aesthetically: inspiring music for dance and eurhythmics, rich use of language in talk, stories, poetry, verse and song, beautiful pictures, individual colourful overalls — and

Margaret McMillan in the garden of the Open Air Nursery School at Deptford in 1922.

Student-teachers at the Rachel McMillan Camp School College, Deptford, London. 1917. Pioneers in nursery education. Kathleen is extreme right.

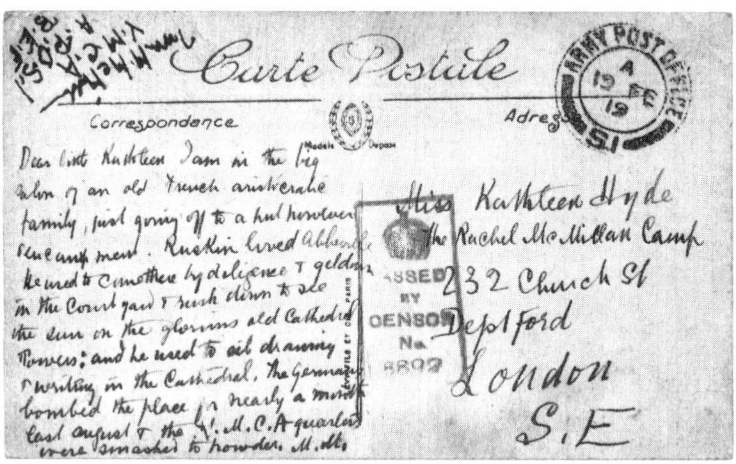

Carte Postale

Correspondance

Dear little Kathleen I am in the big salon of an old French aristocratic family, just going off to a hut however ... encampment. Ruskin lived Abbeville. He used to come there by diligence & ... in the Court yard & rush down to see the sun on the glorious old Cathedral towers; and he used to sit drawing & writing in the Cathedral. The Germans bombed the place for nearly a month last August & the Y.M.C.A quarters were smashed to powder. M.Mc

Adresse

Miss Kathleen Hyde
The Rachel McMillan Camp
232 Church St
Deptford
London
S.E

ARMY POST OFFICE S.1 19 FE 19

PASSED BY CENSOR No. 6892

Picture postcard sent by Margaret McMillan to my sister between the Armistice and the signing of the Peace Treaty in 1919. The card has been passed on by the censor of the British Expeditionary Force. Margaret McMillan was bilingual French and English and addressed various allied forces on education of the future.

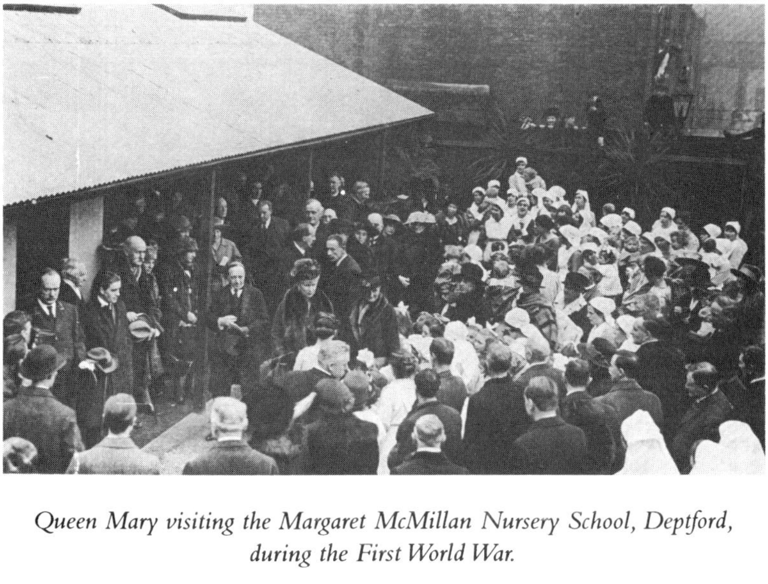

Queen Mary visiting the Margaret McMillan Nursery School, Deptford, during the First World War.

Spiritually: response to flowers, trees, birds, pets and people. It was holistic education.

The students not only carried out a working day with the children from 8 am to 6 pm, but used the children's sleeping time, evenings, holidays and weekends for their own study.

Margaret McMillan engaged staff with gentle voices, rich and flexible speech, charming manners and high standards in literature, music and the arts, yet who could cope with nappies, potties and the struggles of the under fives and be accepted by the Cockney mothers and fathers.

When the holidays came, Margaret McMillan received a deputation from her students-in-training insisting that they should remain at the school and not go home. They felt it was breaking trust to close the school at any time and so a rota was arranged to cover practically every day of the year, but Margaret McMillan insisted on her students returning home for holidays: 'Now that you love a few children, go and think of many ... you will make the world of tomorrow.'

My mother's belief in Margaret McMillan's work continued through many decades, my sister working with Jessie Porter to open nursery schools in the tough areas of Dundee and I identifying myself with the voluntary zeal of Jane Fishburn of Rochdale.

A regular visitor to the Deptford nursery school was Queen Mary, who came with as little official fuss as royal status would allow. She walked through the Deptford slums, with the children and parents within touching distance, and took a personal interest in the welfare of the children, their young teachers and even the jumble sales. It is sad to think that Margaret McMillan's pioneer work has been so feebly followed up by successive governments and that even the best of the present nursery schools fall far short of her high cultural standards.

The Rachel McMillan Training Centre
232 Church Street, Deptford
April 7th, 1920

Dear dear Kathleen

Thank you for the butter. It is delicious and it was nice of you to think of it for me.

How nice to think your dear parents are coming soon, at Whitsuntide. The camp must look its best on the day.

Tomorrow I am going to Oxford to speak at the Sheldonian and Miss Cole is coming down with me. Four Bradford teachers arrive on Monday for the new term. So you see the North is our great ally.

It has been a chill Easter, but the tulips are out at the camp and soon all the human flowers will be back to make it gay.

With love
Yours always
Margaret McMillan

This letter epitomises the closeness of Principal and students. Note that long after the First World War had ended, butter was still scarce and expensive, but the Hydes had their farms.

Theosophical Society

I think I was in my early teens when my mother became a theosophist and moved into a sphere of transcendental thinking rather than conversion into a religion. Certainly her theosophy tended to detach her from her family, at odds as it was with my father's Methodism and our school diet of routine Anglicanism.

Every Wednesday and Sunday Mamma was spirited away into the study of reincarnation, astrology and occultism while my father succumbed to the magnetism of the Reverend Leslie Weatherhead — the charismatic preacher and writer who not only filled churches in Leeds but the City Temple in London.

When my mother became President of the Leeds Theosophical Society, she worked in close touch with Clara Codd, Annie Besant and Krishnamurti and at the national conferences met and talked to Ghandi, Cyril Scott and Jung and other great figures of the New Age.

In addition to her theosophical teachings, Annie Besant, like other thinkers of her time, identified herself with the suffragist campaign. This made my mother's friendship with her even closer. But I sometimes wonder if my father suffered from some of Annie Besant's exhortations. She warned that well-educated women with high ideals of social reform would turn away from marriage. However, if the female élite did marry, she hoped they would choose men who did not expect women to fill their brains with domestic cares and the 'prattle of children to be the only satisfaction of their intellect'.

> *"Man shall grow tenderer and women stronger; man more pure and women more brave and free, till at last the race shall develop into a strength and beauty at present unimagined, and men and women shall walk this fair earth hand-in-hand, diverse, yet truly one-set each-to-each: A perfect music in noble words."*

Rather high-falutin' for a Yorkshire farmer's son who still carved the sirloin joint on Sunday with traditional 'men-served-first' ritual.

It was due to Anne Besant's influence that my mother directed her public speaking talents away from literature to lecture on the more baffling and controversial subjects of the occult world, hoping in so doing that she was carrying out the maxim emblazoned over the platform of the Leeds Theosophical Society:

'There is no religion higher than Truth.'

It was little wonder that we daughters (my young brother steered clear!) became so tolerant of *all* religions that we built up an immunity and never attached ourselves to any single one. Consequently though none of us ever felt out of place in the Church of England, Methodist or Baptist Church services, we have been very sketchy attenders. Even so, when nowadays I do go to church I find I can more than keep up with the regulars in remembering and relishing the words and tunes of their hymns and psalms. ('O sing unto the Lord a new song!') In spite of her travels into mysticism my mother never lost the common touch, and people in the village came

Annie Hyde with Annie Besant and Kirshna Menon, all speaking on Home rule for India.

to her for all sorts of odd reasons and with strange problems. One bizarre incident stands out in my memory but with the puzzle still unsolved.

A homely and unschooled woman from the village arrived one day with masses of paper all covered with strange handwriting. She was completely perplexed because the 'automatic' writing had flowed from her on to the paper without any reasoning or effort on her part, nor could she read what she had written. It was certainly not English. On examining it my mother concluded that it was some version of German but not the German of the 19th or 20th century on which she could have done a reasonable translation. The woman left the manuscripts and my mother promised to take them to the professor of German at Leeds University. This she did, but even he was nonplussed as the German on the manuscript was, he thought, the language of the 13th century. So the pages and pages of script were passed on to an Oxford don. Looking back on this incident I realise now how unquestioning we children were in accepting this strange phenomenon and giving the papers little more attention than we gave the *Yorkshire Evening News*.

But children *do* take for granted the circumstances and conditions in which they grow up and if you lived with my mother you accepted that an astral body was as tangible as the body of the postman.

During the Sunday evenings when Mamma was theosophising and my father was Wesleyanising, their youngest daughters had more material interests and invited 'best friends' in for sticky sweet-making evenings. Our Yorkshire prudence ensured that, even if sticky, we came out solvent so the entrance fee for our friends depended on their ability to filch, or bring from home, any suitable ingredients: sugar, cocoa, Nestle's condensed milk, desiccated coconut, black treacle, Lyle's Golden Syrup, butter, essences of peppermint, vanilla or almond, nuts and raisins; any one of these was grist to our sticky mill. It was lucky for us there were lots of hiding places in the attics though we did sometimes lose track of our finished masterpieces. Months after one of these gaudy nights, when spring cleaning time came round, my mother discovered a tray of grey green fuzz on the top of a wardrobe, which we probed and diagnosed as antique chocolate coconut balls.

The Theosophical Society did not entirely divorce my mother from her daughters because the Society's programme included much that was lofty in art, music, drama and dance. Of course, she arranged for us to 'join' and through this introduction three of us, Nancy, Betsy and I, became obsessive students of Greek dance and natural movement dance-drama under the inspired direction of Miss Cooke-Yarborough. I think these classes did more for our musical education than all the formal tuition we had received, for now symphonies and sonatas were remembered not just with our ears but right through to our *toes.* Another huge bonus was that Ann Whitehead, the great doyenne of voice and speech training, quite often joined forces with Miss Cooke-Yarborough in a combination of choral-speaking, mime and movement to narration and dance-drama. Our horizons of sound and movement were infinite, and we never begrudged the hours of practice and rehearsals which these perfectionists demanded.

Nearby in the Albion Hall, James Gregson opened the Civic Everyman Theatre in which he put on non-commercial plays with ambitious and dedicated amateurs as his players. Seats were free — apart from the conscience-jerker silver collection boxes — and, as in those days there were real silver threepenny-bits, it was possible for Leeds citizens to share a unique theatrical experience for the price of a Cadbury's whipped cream walnut. Of course my mother encouraged us to 'join' either as audience or performers, and so under the direction of these artists we girls, shivering in our mini Greek tunics, mourned, wept, intoned, droned, declaimed and danced our way through the choruses of *Oedipus,* the *Trojan Women, Antigone, Iphigenia* and *Electra.*

Through Miss Cooke-Yarborough, our little company gave performances in the gardens and halls of stately homes, occasionally before the Princess Royal (Mary) and other distinguished patrons of the arts but we also had the more demanding and nerve-wracking challenge of entertaining the blind, the deaf and the mentally handicapped. Miss Cooke-Yarborough was a severe disciplinarian and an aristocrat who schooled us not only in dance but into knowing how to meet people. 'Shyness is a sign of ill-breeding' was her compact creed, which she reinforced by showing that if one really listens and diverts thought away from oneself, then nervousness dissolves away.

One memorable performance in which we took part was the celebration of the Leeds tercentenary at Kirkstall Abbey; a pageant written and directed by the inimitable Nugent Monck of Maddermarket Theatre fame. We — Miss Cooke-Yarborough's students — were the Greek chorus, a somewhat tenuous link with the history of the Abbey it would seem, but Nugent Monck was an expansive man of the theatre who, in this production, encompassed everything from Dionysius to Queen Victoria. His erotic and compulsively rhythmic verse to which we moved had us in thrall:

'Had I clasped you but once in a virile embrace,
Just held you and felt my heart's throb to your throb,
Had I felt for one moment your breath on my face,
The high gods and low gods my life then might rob,
But I dare not have taken the love still unsaid;
Oh Nemesis, Nemesis, make my love dread,
For I'm but the wail of a soul that is dead!'

I write from a creaking old memory and it may not be quite accurate as we never saw this neo-Swinburnian outpouring in print, but it was heady stuff for young girls suppressed into Liberty bodices under their flowing Greek chitons. None of this fantastic pattern of life would ever have happened if our mother had been what was described in those days as 'a good mother': devoted, domesticated and dull.

No, as far as my father's farming family was concerned, my mother was not domesticated but 'bookish'. For most Yorkshire country folk the word is dismissive but my mother joined the farming Hydes with the same affection and enthusiasm as she joined everything else. She was loved by this extensive family and shared their delight in telling and hearing East Riding tales which she could relate with a dialect as earthy and salty as that of the farm hands.

It was true in Yorkshire estimation that my mother was not domesticated yet for all the school years of our lives, and even after, she made most of our clothes from the remnants and fents which she picked up with a sharp 'weather eye' in sales and markets; she conjured cast-offs into new life and knitted jumpers, coats, scarves, gloves and stockings. From the rabbit and hare skins which came from the farms, 'cured' by my father, she made her daughters little muffs and lined them with velvet; she machined on an antiquated Singer the curtains and bedspreads, and occasionally embroidered cloths for the tea-table. The weekly baking spread over the length of the long deal dresser would have stocked a baker's shop. She papered or distempered walls, painted the woodwork and stencilled 'Morrisy' art nouveau borders under the picture-rails of the high rooms. And like every housewife of that period she made jam in big stone jars and bottled fruit to see us through the year. What an awful struggle it must have been, especially for someone who preferred Browning to baking, to bring up children in the years of the Great War. One clear memory remains with me of Christmas 1917 when, I now realise, the horrors and the hardship of the war had brought so many people nearly to breaking point; I was eight, my sister Betsy ten, Nancy twelve and my eldest sister sixteen. My brother was still a baby in a cot having been born at the height of the war in 1916. Kathleen — our 'Sister Superior' as we called her — was in a bedroom on her own but we three carried on our custom of being three in a bed for Christmas Eve. After hanging our three pillow-cases at the foot of the bed, we huddled under the bedclothes to play our crazy tent game. As the most insignificant of the three I had the lowly job of being the central tent pole which meant painfully holding one leg as high as I could to make a bell-tent big enough for the other two to take the leads in the sheet-lined cone-shaped stage. I cannot remember any of the duologue as my whole being, especially my leg, was concentrating on when I could bring down the final curtain.

In the kitchen down below we could hear a continuous sound: 'whirr! whirr!, whirr!, click!, stop!, whirr!, whirr!.' On it went until the clock struck eleven, then all seemed quiet; our play was over and we could listen. Then silence apart from distant rustlings. The sounds changed to 'saw, saw, saw, chop, chop, chop, chip, chip, chip, s-s-s-s, z - z - z tap-tap'. It was now one o'clock, and desperately trying to keep awake, we fell asleep and didn't hear the clock strike again until six on a dark, cold Christmas morning. But we could get up. We weren't allowed to light the flaring gas jets but we had some matches and a candle, and trembling with excitement we made for our pillow cases which had fattened out in the night. But there, standing open on the floor each on four firm wooden legs, were three folding sewing stands. The bags, which closed up when the legs were put together, were each made of black satin lined with flowery cretonne: red for Nancy, yellow for Betsy and white for me. The bags opened four-square on their wooden frames with little pocket compartments for reels of cotton, needles, pins and scissors. The sounds in the kitchen were now understood: the sewing machine, the saw, the chisel and hammer. I was at the dithery stage of wanting to believe in Santa Claus but not being quite sure. That night I grew up an inch or two for a new belief struck home: a belief in my parents. It struck as crucially and clearly as the hall-clock striking 'One!' when we fell asleep but our father and mother went on, working against the clock to finish those three gifts and carry them up the stairs.

But I must not leave you with too domesticated a picture of my mother, for as soon as we could stand on our own feet she was able to take wing into the rarified realms of theosophy and leave my Aunt Charlotte to grapple with the more earthy jobs in life. This left Mamma free to accept invitations from far and wide to lecture and to meet folk of like minds. Children, I think, rarely consider that their mothers could 'turn heads' but looking back I think ours did. In those days we never heard the words 'sexy,' 'sexually attractive' or 'glamorous', yet I feel sure, my mother, in her artless gentle way, was all those things. It was evident from her pink and white complexion that 'God did all' for not a single cosmetic, nor even a pot of cream, graced her dressing table. In any case, dressing tables in ordinary Yorkshire homes were designed for a standing up critical check and not for long sittings of cossetting and cherishing. She rarely visited a hairdresser until in her seventies, but her fine head of hair — which turned at an early age from a rich Titian brown to snowy-white — made an unbridled halo round her head.

Now and again she had an exciting visit to Shanklin, Isle of Wight, to stay with her theosophical friend, a handsome bachelor. On her return we heard all about the laboratory where he developed his photographs of astral and etheric bodies. We could more easily appreciate the photographs of him and her in his luscious garden.

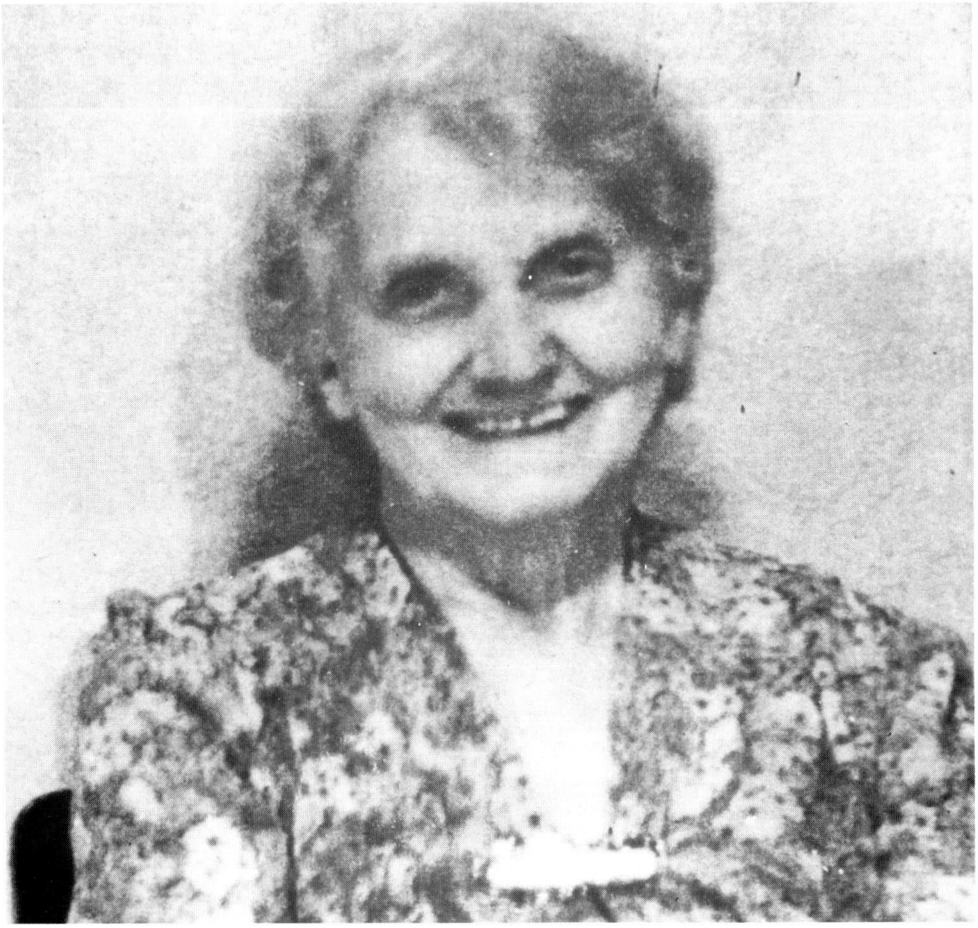

Annie Hyde aged 80. She died at the age of 86, frail in body but with a searching mind.

The whole relationship, we were told, was metaphysical and lasted for years, 'because', my mother said, 'sex never reared its ugly head'. A strange remark from someone who had borne five children and whose virtue was never doubted.

Now she has left this imperfect world, I do wonder if her theosophical beliefs of reincarnation have come true: if so, I do hope she has had a lucky draw, or an evolutionary up-grading, in this bizarre business of coming back to this earth. If she is still persevering to build a loftier race, I hope she is more cushioned than she was in this life. She certainly deserved to leave the cloudy hills and satanic mills to lie down in green pastures.

Christabel magnetising the crowd in Trafalgar Square to come to the House of Commons, October 11th, 1908.

Christabel and Mary Gawthorpe in Manchester, January 1909.

CHAPTER THREE
THE FARMING HYDES

Cockmoor Hall: a flash-back

My paternal grandfather, Francis Hicks Hyde, with his wife and their ten children — five boys and five girls — farmed at Cockmoor Hall, Troutsdale, high above the Pickering to Scarborough road. From Snainton a lonely bridle road climbs for three miles to, what was then, the only house. From there one can look out on one of the most magnificent and remote dales of Yorkshire. So high are its banks and so tangled its trees that the stream below looks like a thin silk thread of grey-blue.

It was said that when my grandfather wanted to summon the village shop at Snainton he fired his gun into the air and this brought the pony and trap not only to take the order but to provide, there and then, the 'possibles' which the shop-keeper knew by constant personal service might be needed.

About three miles beyond Cockmoor Hall, overlooking the great valley, stands a sturdy little school entirely on its own and 'not near nowhere'. It had to be so for it served four or five outlying farms including Troutsdale Mill, Basin How, Trouts Hall and Cockmoor Hall. As school children my father and his brothers and sisters walked on the high moorland road there and back every day in rain, wind, snow, hail or sunshine; children from the other direction took Mount Misery in their stride.

The village school mistress taught them all from when they arrived as five-year olds until they were twelve and were strong enough to have lifted the little school-mistress single-handed. But there was no question of that. She ruled. How she taught them all in that one room I do not know but my father, aunts and uncles were all turned out with copper-plate calligraphy and high standards of reading, spelling, punctuation and grammar. They had enough arithmetic to cope with guineas and farthings, chains and furlongs, bushels, pecks and quarts which were relevant to the economics of their day. Whatever they may have lacked in science or creative arts they were trained to be 'copers' and their further education sprang from the fields they tilled, the tools they wielded and the markets where they bought and sold.

At playtime, dinner-time and going-home time the hand-bell was rung by the favoured monitor, an unnecessary time signal as each child sat within whispering distance of the teacher's high stool. At 12 o'clock the 'looance' bags were brought down from the pegs, the kettle was put on the open fire, cocoa was made, grace was said and the children sat at their bench desks ravenously eating the pies and pasties

The bleak Cockmoor Hall stands high above Troutsdale (north) and Snainton (south). The beauty of Troutsdale lies beyond Cockmoor. The lovely little school received children who walked from remote farms, many of them six miles or more away.

brought from home. Some of them had already been broken into during the long walk to school so hungry lads tried to do a bit of bartering with those whose families were more generous providers. At 12.45 each child helped with the clearing up and sweeping. There was little left for the pig swill tub. For propriety's sake there were two outside earth privies carefully labelled Boys and Girls and next to them was the coal-house from which the boys filled the buckets and fed the open fire.

The only wall decorations in the school were the pink-pocked map of the world, a linoleum banner with the Ten Commandments ('I don't mind keeping eight of them' my uncle used to say!) and a forbidding portrait of Queen Victoria looking as if she approved of the verse they often sang:

'The rich man in his castle
The poor man at his gate;
God made them high or lowly,
And ordered their estate.'

But from all accounts the school was a happy place and so remote that the Inspector came only once a year and chose a day in the summer when he could have a good day riding on in his trap through the splendid Vale of Hackness down Forge Valley and back to Scarborough.

The Trek from Cockmoor to Fraisthorpe: 1896

What made my grandfather want to leave Cockmoor Hall is not quite clear but moorland farming is hard work and can be limiting. True there were arable fields round Cockmoor but they were neither large nor level. Fraisthorpe, south of Bridlington, on the flat plain of Holderness, offered extensive broad acres for growing wheat, oats and more especially barley. The grass was certainly greener and richer for dairy-farming and stock-breeding, and The Lodge, the new farm, sat comfortably in the centre of a neighbourly village.

It was in 1896 that the Hyde family carried out their trek. Anyone who knows that part of North Yorkshire will understand the arduous job of shifting a whole farm: shire horses, herds of cattle, flocks of sheep, hens, ducks, geese and all the ploughs, harrows, reapers, binders, scruffers and tools including the heavy Victorian furniture and crocks of a six-bedroomed house, without steam or motor power. It was my Uncle Dawson, the eldest son, unmarried, who loaded the last wagon of goods and stock and led from the rear.

Over the Derwent valley they rode and walked, never faster than the most reluctant sheep nor the sleepiest cow; over the fields of the Carrs and the Wolds to Ganton and Foxholes where they bedded down for the night. At five the next morning my grandfather stood on the high wagon and, after shouting his orders, called the family and farm-hands to prayer and they all sang the Doxology to speed them on their way:

'Praise God from Whom all blessings flow;
Praise Him all creatures here below,
Praise Him above, Angelic host;
Praise Father, Son and Holy Ghost.'

And then they fed the 'creatures here below' and tramped on to Thwing and Rudston, finally reaching Carnaby and the sea level plain of Holderness and Fraisthorpe.

We never heard how our gentle little grandmother and her daughters fared but I cannot imagine that my Victorian grandfather would make any concession to feminine needs.

Fraisthorpe

The village of Fraisthorpe must have been aware very soon of the squire-like attitude of Francis Hicks Hyde for immediately he sorted out the village workers he had inherited. The men he brought with him from Cockmoor slept in the big dormitory that ran across the top of the house. The Foreman, Wagoner, Wag Lad, Thoddy (or Third hand), Herdsman (or Bullocky) and Shepherd were regulars but I seem to remember Tommy Owt, a general handyman: a Jack-of-all-trades.

The farm kitchen at Fraisthorpe — with its big black iron grate of boilers and ovens, the eight-feet-long scrubbed table, the wooden benches, the red brick floor, the chiming wall clock, always fast, and the hams hanging from the ceiling hooks — was the pulsing heart of all activity. In it the cooking, baking, eating, sewing, washing-up and nursing all took place. But on Sunday evening the kitchen became the Chapel as it had always been at Cockmoor. It was not that there was any shortage of places in which to worship: Fraisthorpe and Barmston both had churches and a shared vicar. But they were Church of England and, although they were obligatory places of attendance as a parish duty, they were not, as far as my grandfather was concerned, places where he could pour out his Methodist soul. His allegiance was to Wesley. The village soon knew it.

On Saturday the kitchen was scrubbed and polished — for none of that could be done on a Sunday — and when the morning and afternoon services in the two Church of England churches were over, the harmonium and the lectern were wheeled out from the dairy, the long table was pushed into the centre of the kitchen, chairs from the dining room were added to the benches and the big Family Bible in the hall was opened out on the lectern for the readings. The one big Methodist Hymnal on the harmonium and the one held by my grandfather were the only hymn books. Words were known by heart or articulated, a syllable ahead of the congregation, by the energetic harmonium player whose duty it was to sing over the noise of the pedals and to keep an eye and ear open for anyone flagging in the hymns.

There was a sense of free-for-all in the services: the phrase 'non-conformist' was literally interpreted. The little congregation, released from the formula of the Common Prayer Book and fired by John Wesley, could sing lustily with a hot-line to

Fraisthorpe Church

Modern aerial view of Fraisthorpe to which the Hyde family trecked from Cockmoor in 1896. Notice the diminutive church in the foreground.

heaven. The villagers were on intimate terms with their God and their saints and were free to volunteer to preach, read the lessons or give testimony.

One Sunday in spring, after a month of devastating drought which was stunting the wheat and withering the grass, my grandfather led the farming worshippers in praying for rain. This they did in solos, unison and hymn singing.

On the Monday it rained; gentle generous drops giving heart to the soil and greening the grass. On Tuesday, Wednesday and Thursday it rained without a break in the clouds. On Friday and Saturday the wind and rain lashed the corn on to the ground and floated the straw in the stackyard. On Sunday evening water dripped from clothes and boots on to the kitchen floor. It was the foreman's first chance to speak publicly to his God. Holding his arms high above his head he raged in his rolling dialect: 'O Lord last week we prayed for rain but this is over doing it!' The rebuke evidently worked for they left the farm kitchen that Sunday evening in a benign red sunset.

The Carnaby station-master specialised in children's services but had little use for the 'Gentle Jesus, meek and mild' sops usually given to children. His faith burned with the fear of God and the Devil. Standing behind the lectern, his head nearly touching one of the cheese-cloth-covered hams, he chased the flies away as he threatened hell to the children who were squatting cross-legged on the red brick floor, looking angelic in their Sunday best.

'And tha'll go to 'ell as sure as I kill that fly!' he called out as he brought his fist down to demonstrate mortality. The fly flew off to the over-hanging ham and following its flight the preacher accepted defeat. 'Dang it. Ah's missed it; ther's chance for thee yet!'

On another occasion, when all the benches and chairs were filled with children for a Whitsuntide service, he tried out another hell-bent ploy: his forefinger wagging at three culprits: 'The divel is on a long chain, but he can reach you . . . and he can reach **you** . . . and he can reach YOU! To which the third boy, sitting as far away from the preacher as he could, called out: 'Bugger mu'd as well be *loose!*'

Testimony services were a significant feature of the country Wesleyan meetings. Anyone could stand and report on God's mysterious and marvellous ways. It was a chance for the women to have a say too and so on this summer evening, when it was easy for old Mrs Barmby to walk from her cottage to the farm, she was moved to heave herself from her seat and say in her slow trembling East Riding voice: 'As Ah sat on the privy seat this morning, Ah couldn't 'elp thinking 'ow fearfully and 'ow wunderfully we was made.'

My newly-married parents, standing near the hall door ready to escape when laughter overcame them, would never have patronised or mocked Mrs Barmby; they delighted in the old lady's earthy sincerity.

Although all the children in the village school and their parents were brought up to read the Bible, and to read it aloud, there were times when words were beyond their comprehension or pronunciation. One evening it was the wagoner's turn to read. Standing with his back to the roaring kitchen fire, the listeners packed shoulder-to-shoulder on the wooden benches, he began: 'The reading I've been asked to do (I wouldn't 'ave chosen it misen) is from the Acts of the Apostles, Chapter 13, verses 4 to 11'. With eyes glued to the hefty Bible on the lectern he read very slowly: 'So they being sent forth by the Holy Ghost departed unto ... S--S--.' He hesitated on 'Seleucia,' screwed up his eyes, looked heavenward, and finding the answer, levelled it at the congregation: 'Well I don't know the place so ivery time I come tiv it I shall say 'Sledmere' and on he went: 'departed unto Sledmere and thence they sailed to ... Cyprus. And when they were at ... Sledmere they preached the Word of God in the ... sighnagohgyews of the Jews.'

The first Monday in the month the kitchen became the surgery for it was on that day the doctor paid his visit from Bridlington. It was inconsiderate — and indeed could be lethal — if anyone chose to be ill on any other day in the month. They were a healthy lot and modest about disclosing details on the hidden parts of their bodies. Audible signs: coughs and colds, and visible signs: a hand caught in farm machinery or a swollen ankle were not difficult to explain. The old tended to live with more subtle, serious and chronic complaints.

One Monday a veteran retainer of my grandfather's was already drinking a mug of tea by the kitchen fire when the doctor arrived. 'Well, my good man' said the doctor, 'and what can I do for you?' 'It's mi knee doctor, it's proper poorly, it aches something chronic.' 'Well,' said the doctor, 'how old are you?' 'Why, Ah'll be 84 come Michaelmas — God willing.' 'Well' said the doctor, giving the right knee a friendly rub, 'I think it's just a bit of anno domini — old age, you know. 'Pulling his right knee away the man burst out 'T'other knee's t'same age and that don't ail owt.'

(Many of the Fraisthorpe and Auburn stories — and they are innumerable — have got into circulation and may have already been heard by the reader since they were often included in the broadcast talks of my cousin, Austin Hyde. I have relied on those present for my versions.)

One of the many Cockmoor Hall stories shared in letters and chats, since the first edition of this book, tells of a rather gormless shepherd struggling to make his sheepdog 'frame' in the gathering together of sheep to get them through the gate of the fold (the *yat)*. Shepherd had spent half his morning holding the gate open and yelling at the sheepdog. Time after time the dog lolloped through the middle of the flock and scattered them.

'Git away roon - rooned 'em up, yer daft divil', the shepherd bawled over and over again with earthy variations on 'daft divil'.

In desperation, Shepherd, whose arm was stiff and aching with holding the gate, bellowed, 'Coom back 'ere, yer bugger, and *thee* 'old t'yat an' ah'll drive 'em through missen!'

My grandfather died on 2 April 1910 and within a few weeks my grandmother had followed him and so ended the Methodist services in Fraisthorpe kitchen. Like it or not, from then on the village had to make the little church at Fraisthorpe their place of worship which was none the worse for an injection of non-conformity.

My Aunt Florrie cared for the lovely little church as if it were a treasured crib. The whitewashed walls, serene and simple, and the clear glass of the windows allowed God's light into every corner. There were never any contrived or elaborate flower arrangements but the slim silver vases always had clean water and fresh flowers. Every day, since only a bridle road divided the church from the farm, Aunt Florrie tended the homely flowers that spelt out the seasons: winter jasmine and winter aconites, snowdrops, crocuses, wallflowers and forget-me-nots, roses, sweetpeas and mignonette, sprays of unforced chrysanthemums and Michaelmas daisies followed by the holly and the ivy of Christmas.

The two dozen natural wood chairs were more than enough for the congregation which, except for special occasions, were often very few more than the 'two or three': the quorum approved by the Bible. A single bell, audible and visible for all the village, was, as children, our favourite toy. It baffled those who heard it on weekdays until repetition produced recognition: 'It's them bairns again', the villagers would say.

The harmonium, no bigger nor better than the one in the farm dairy, was strenuously squeezed into song by Aunt Florrie. Her handsome profile under her black picture hat, her floating floral chiffon, and slim patent-leather court shoes made up for the creaking pedals and the crotchety keys. She could have lured music out of a hand-saw.

'Strange how potent cheap music is,' said Noel Coward. It is equally true of tried and trusted hymns. Singing those familiar tunes and words is like eating hot buttered toast: it is homely and heart-warming and agreeably classless. Seventy years on, if I hear: *The day Thou gavest Lord is ended* I am back in Fraisthorpe church with the innocent wholesome country smell of rush mats, scrubbed wood, unregulated flowers, white linen and crochet altar cloth and slender beeswax candles — and see the men and their wives straightened and stiffened into their Sunday clothes, with their white starched collars drawing eyes away from well-worn cuffs.

After the service it was not difficult for the Vicar to have a chat with everyone. The question 'How are you?' was assumed to be genuine and needed answering: 'How are you, Mrs Barmby?' 'Eeh, I were badly but ah've 'ad a beautiful motion this morning!.'... And so on until each churchgoer's health and family had received a blessing.

A few yards' walk back to the house and there was a supper, not unlike the tea we had eaten an hour or so earlier, laid out on the dining room table. It was story-time led by Uncle Harry with a little judicious selecting of his tales in the presence of the vicar.

Clergymen enjoy stories against themselves, if by that one means the predecessors who have not hit it off with the village congregation. The visiting vicar the month before had broken the record for the smallest attendance: only six in the church; that is to say there were six when the evening service started: three near the front just behind the seats for the absent 'gentry' and three at the back — in the station to which it had pleased God to call them. In attendance was the churchwarden, my uncle's foreman.

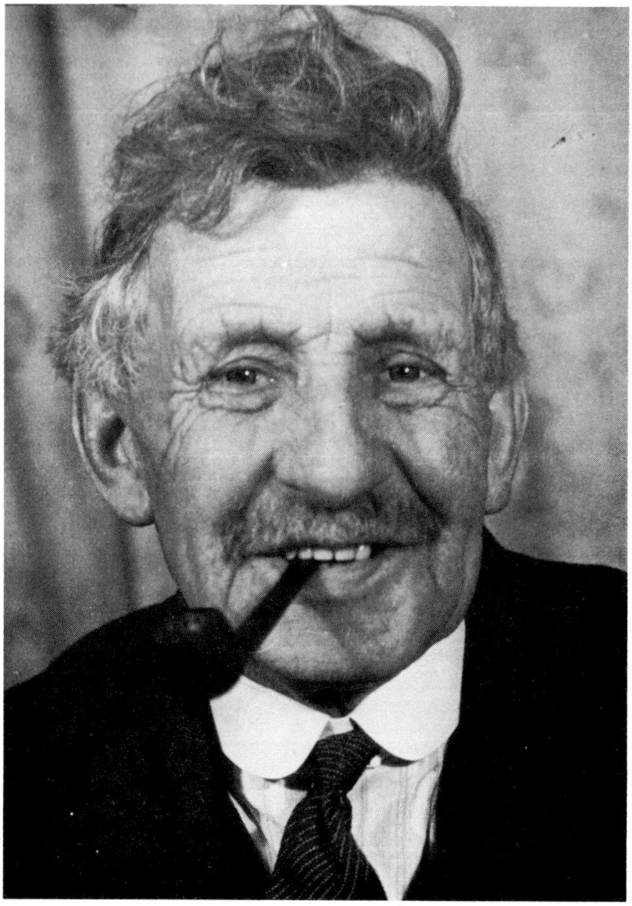

Uncle Harry Hyde of Fraisthorpe. 'Every wrinkle a furrow of fun!'

On and on went the sermon in a muted mono–tone until the sun had set and the church had darkened. Unseen by the preacher, one by one the 'few' slipped away home. The preacher, quite in the dark except for the two small altar candles, moved from the lectern for the benediction. 'And now to God, the Father ...' but only the church warden heard the blessing.

'Tell me, my man,' said the vicar peering into the dark, 'what happened to our congregation?' 'Well,' said the church warden snuffing out the two cand–les, 'them at t'back went out because they couldn't 'ear yer, and them at t'front went out because they could!'

Yorkshire country folk are chary of anything that smacks of affectation. They respect 'educated speech' but reserve their withering censure for the lah-de-dah. So the next story to be told at the supper table was of a 'locum' minister from the south who collected the odd fee while on holiday in Bridlington.

Thinking it necessary to talk down to simple village folk, he adjusted his sermon on the wise virgins to what he thought was the village's level of intelligence:

'As I came through your village this morning' he intoned pontifically, 'I observed a country woman picking fruit by the wayside and I said to her: And what, my good woman, shall you do with those bahskets and bahskets of fruit?' And she replied: 'I am going to preserve them for winter consumption.' This may not seem very funny to readers south of the Humber but it was hilarious to all those round the Fraisthorpe supper table hearing my uncle's clergyman's bleat.

Mrs Barmby, thinking that anyone who asked that question must be daft, would have said: 'Ther for jamming.'

Harvest Home before the First World War

Neither the kitchen nor the church at Fraisthorpe were big enough for the harvest festival; it had to be the granary — the place where we children put on our concerts with candles in bottles for footlights.

It was our job to strew straw over the granary floor for warmth and quiet ready for the harmonium to be carried across the stackyard and hoisted up by the cables and hooks which usually lifted the stacks of corn. The outside steps leading to the granary were scrubbed, the stable lamps hung from the beams and then Aunt Florrie covered the great wooden flour chest with a white crocheted counterpane to make a fitting altar. Benches from the kitchen, chairs from the church and the dining room were carried up the steps for this once-a-year congregation. Uncle Harry and the men picked out sheaves of oats, wheat and barley which would do credit to their farming skills (God being rather far back in their minds at this point). No fruit nor vegetables. That was only 'laiking'. Harvest to a farmer means *grain*. Aunt Florrie put her silver candlesticks, tallow candles and silver vases of tea roses on the altar behind the sheaves and beamed on Wag Lad and Thoddy for their shy efforts at corn dollies. Wagoner and Bullocky hung their more ambitious temples and angels from the beam above the altar. The bats hanging from the beams and the mice slipping through the straw were not out of place.

The Man born in a stable, who walked through the fields to Bethany, would have felt at home there. Everyone for miles around who had ploughed the fields, sown the seeds and battled with weeds and thistles, turned up for the harvest celebration. Two or three women, with baskets discreetly covered with linen tea-towels, slipped into the kitchen first with their offerings of custard pies, Yorkshire curd cheesecakes and spice bread before climbing the steps, patting their new hats into position, and choosing their 'good view' seats.

The service with the vicar — but mercifully without a sermon — relaxed into song. This congregation knew what they were talking about as they ploughed the fields and scattered the good seed on the land ... Whatever the social or domestic differences, all the workers down to 'Tommy Owt' were in concord as they sang:

> 'Come ye thankful people come
> Raise the song of harvest home,
> All is safely gathered in
> Ere the winter storms begin;'

The service over, the stable-lamps were unhooked from the beams and everyone trooped down from 'God's own temple' to the farm kitchen for the harvest supper with nothing stronger to drink than home-brewed ale or dark brown tea. The men loosened their ties and their tongues; the women found pegs for their hats and bustled around so that everyone could get down to the serious business of eating. Men assumed their right to sit 'square to the table' with the women in the wings waiting on. The family and relations made room by eating in the dining room and

Sacks of barley in a wagonette in Fraishorpe stackyard.

all the children had a free run from one room to the other. The doors of the dairy, larder, the harness room and the hall were open so that folk and food could be spread out for the 'spread'.

With the harmonium still in the granary, the singing both in substance and style became looser and my bonny was brought over the ocean to the tavern in the town and taken on to Dublin's fair city with few stops on the way.

But it had been a long day and gradually the kitchen was wrapped in an eiderdown of silence and sleep. A courting couple had already slipped away and, with passion to spend, had sauntered down the lane towards the sea. ('Harvest moon, up above, watch my loved one, keep my love ...')

We were too young to condone or condemn the out-of-wedlock out of bed-lock fumbling into the Sunday clothes. But the next day the straw hollow under the hiding hedgerow of the barley showed the shape, not of two, but one.

Back in the kitchen, the villagers collected their wives, their daughters and stable-lamps, and hovered about not knowing quite how to thank or say 'Goodbye.' Talk came down to earth: 'Neets are drawin' in; it'll soon be back-end.'

The living-in men moved towards the back staircase ready to hang their Sunday suits on the wooden rail across the sloping ceiling. 'It's been t'best 'arvest in my remembering' said Thoddy. It was the same summing-up every year. Old Dick who had kept very quiet, living the night away with his eighty-year old thoughts, snuggled his ancient fiddle under his chin and trembled his bow into:

'Now the day is over,
Night is drawing nigh;
Shadows of the evening
Steal across the sky.'

Although my uncle was the first one in the area to own a combine-harvester he enjoyed using the old reaper.

Fraisthorpe Lodge was affectionately smothered in virginia creeper.

CHAPTER FOUR
'A LADY AND A GENTLEMAN'

The Lady: Grandma Hyde

I wish I had known Grandma Hyde but both she and Grandpa Hyde died a few months after I was born and within a few weeks of one another. Perhaps it was as well she did not know her liberated grandchildren for I doubt if any of us could have lived up to her rigid Methodist principles and the impeccable way she ran her household and guided her children.

My father's mother, who left her village school at nine to pick up her education at home, later brought up her large family to be healthy, kind, alert, literate, sociable, law-abiding and capable. Her letters were a joy to look at and to read for they were written with a dip-pen in copper-plate calligraphy, standard English grammar, a generous vocabulary enriched with lively dialect, accurate spelling and correct punctuation. Family and village news was interspersed with homespun philosophy, and always she closed her letters with a reassurance of her love.

Her grandson, my cousin Austin Hyde, in a round-robin letter to his nieces and nephews wrote: 'I want all her descendants to have copies of extracts from the only two of her innumerable letters which have survived so that they may *'Look to the rock whence they were hewn'*. He goes on to say: 'Grandma Hyde never had any formal schooling after the age of nine but she was one of the best educated women I ever knew. Her education — which went on through life — was based on two books: her Bible and the Methodist Hymnal. She knew them both and quoted joyously and freely from each. Grandma Hyde believed in savouring good writing by, with and from the heart. Her nine children were each given a silver sixpence for every Wesley hymn they could recite or sing without the hymnal — a small fortune as the children were conditioned to be biddable!

There was quality and style in both her spoken and written English and her rich vocabulary spanned the down-to-earth day-by-day business of a well-husbanded Yorkshire farm and ranged through known-by-heart poetry to the aphorisms of great philosophers.

To two of her sons, who had left home to earn their living in towns, she wrote wise and warm letters to guide and protect them on their way. My Uncle Edmond received this letter on his 16th birthday. The owners of the cattle-feed mill in Driffield, to which Edmond was apprenticed, were heavy drinkers and unbelievers. From her place of worship, the kitchen of Cockmoor Hall, my grandmother penned-in her beautiful calligraphy — this letter:

Cockmoor Hall
Troutsdale
North Riding
Yorkshire
January 1896

My dear son Edmund

I do most heartily wish you many happy returns of your birthday, and pray that each succeeding one may find you more and more advanced in the knowledge and love of our Lord and Saviour, Jesus Christ, and that your path may be that of the just, shining brighter and brighter to the Perfect Day.

We often think and talk about you, father and I. We fear you are placed in a perilous position through the unfaithful proceedings of those with whom you have to do, but remember 'He that walketh uprightly walketh surely' and 'Earnestly strive to seek first the Kingdom of God and His righteousness' — and you know the promise added thereto.

The letter goes on to give shrewd and genial farm news, finishing with the constancy of her love for her son.

How Edmond managed to '*lay hold on life*' with the starkly contrasted ways of living is hard to imagine. But he did and later on when he married Selina, produced two sons and two daughters of rare quality and cheerful faith.

Grandma's kindnesses and understanding extended well beyond her family, living up to the Hyde/Danby tradition that *'no supplicant was ever turned from the door'*.

Most employers at that time took for granted the degrading hireling fairs at Martinmas when labourers were 'taken on' for a year at a pittance.

In the market the men, awkwardly dressed up in their Sunday suits, waited self-consciously hoping to be hired by a 'good provider'. But the bold and the shy little lassies were there ready to go into service away from the labourers' cottages where they had lived cheek-by-jowl with brothers and sisters crammed into insignificance.

The farm lassie's tasks would be legion, not only in the house but in the yard and amongst the animals. Her hours would be very long, rising early to clear the grates, light the fires and bring in water from the pump to the hobs and kettles. Her wages, paid annually, would be £5 or £6 for 51 weeks. Martinmas week was the annual holiday when she could, if she and her mistress chose, accept a 'fest', a 'fastening penny', probably half-a-crown, to stop again ('ageean') for another year.

In the following poem by Grandma Hyde her 15-year-old maid has agreed to stay on as she is devoted to her mistress and has become deeply attached to the babe she has helped to deliver. 'Ah' 'ings tiv a bairn' (she clings or hangs on to the babe). The 'noss' — the nurse evidently gave praise. The lassie's sister, Liza, having become a Leeds townie, brings her a little booklet of 'papier poudre' from which the maid takes a leaf and powders her face. Jim, the yard lad, pours scorn. He too is stopping on although offered a good job as Stubbins' Thoddy, third lad, because he is devoted to the newborn motherless calf.

A MARTINMAS IDYLL

Eeeh, ma wod! It's Mart'mas!
When Ah fost com' here
Ah were sure Ah'd finish
When Ah'd been my year.
Bud Ah's stoppin' on agean,
Missus ga' me t'fest.
Yistherday, i'd wash-hoose,
Wi'd bairn on her breast,
— An' Ah' ings tiv a bairn.

Eeeh, ma wod! Our Liza's
Getten wark i' Leeds.
An' she says Ah'd finnd a spot
As easy as finnd weeds.
She diz arn some money!
Dresses like a queen!
Liza says Ah'm daft-like.
Ti say Ah's near sixteen,
— Bud Ah' ings tiv a bairn.

Bairn was born i'April
Same day Cauf was born,
T'awd coo deed, da' missus
Lang luked wan an' worn,
She was bad an' all, though,
An' Ah felt reet flayed,
Noss said Ah did champion,
An' showed her hoo Ah cared,
— Bud Ah' ings tiv a bairn.

Jimmy, that's oor yard-lad,
Had to bring up t'cauf,
Left si young wi'oot a mum,
It's ower bad by hauf,
Jimmy's stoppin' on agean!
Tho' he could ha' gone
Ti be Stubbin's thoddy
If he'd ta'en it on
— Bud Jim ings ti'd cauf!

Lisa brought a beak wiv her,
She rubs her feace wi' a leaf.
It maks her look that bonny
'T'were o'most past belief.
She ga' me some, Ah used yan,
Took t'bairn ti'd coo-hoose door,
Jimmy'd just fetched cauf-stuff
A twea-three minute afoor
— He ings ti'd cauf,
Ah' Ah' ings ti'd bairn.

Ah taks t'bairn up ti'd cauf,
An' lets 'im stroak its head.
Ah taks a look at Jim,
An' Ah sees he's varry re-ad,
Then he says, "Thoo is a daft-head!
Ah thowt thoo had mair sense,
Than rub sike muckmant o' thi feace!"
An' he leaned over'd lahtle fence,
An' he - stroaked t'cauf
An' Ah - kissed t'bairn!
Wi' that Ah wipes it off,
An' says, "'T'were nowt bud fun!"
He's goin' ti Thwing ti-morn,
When he's fed t'cauf, an' done.
Ah's eff ti Thwing an' all!
He's helpin' wi my box!
He'll 'appen see me, comin' back,
Ah's bringin' t'bairn some socks!
Cos Ah clings tiv a bairn,
An' Jim, he ings tiv a cauf!

Cousin Austin and Uncle Harry had a wealth of stories about the farm lads and lassies at Martinmas. One which I remember happened very near to Fraisthorpe: A Wolds farmer arrived back home somewhat under the influence of the local ale imbibed in quantities on the Martinmas Saturday, bringing with him in the gig the newly-hired farm lass. His wife, all agog to see whether he'd brought a 'likely lass', watched the new girl climbing down from the high seat: 'Tak 'er back John! Tak 'er back! She'll nooan do — she 'ez lace at t'bottom of 'er bloomers.'

We were never conscious of the men being hired, for on the Fraisthorpe, Auburn and the Danby farms most of the men stayed all through the years we visited. They would, I feel sure, gladly accept the 'fest' to remain on farms where the farm hands were all well-fed and worked as a friendly team.

Grandma and Grandpa Hyde, the year they went to London in 1897.

Not all farmers had these high standards. One East Riding farmer, having eyed a hireling from head to toe, snapped at him, 'Well, yer can coom, but before ah fix it, ah'll 'ev to get your character'. With that he strode off to consult the man's previous employer. Returning, satisfied with the economic testimonial of 'Ees, all reet, with t'hosses and tonnups ...' he said: 'Reet, yer can coom, Ah've got yer character'. Slowly the hireling 'soomed up' his retort: 'Aye, and ah's got thine, and I isn't cooming!'.

The highlight of my grandparents' life was their first and only visit to London. Here is a part of a letter written by Grandma Hyde to her old friend, Mrs Pearson of Ebberstone. It is one year after the great trek from Cockmoor Hall to Fraisthorpe.

The Lodge
Fraisthorpe
East Riding
August 14th 1897

My very dear friend,

Your welcome letter this morning is another proof of the influence of mind, even at a great distance, for I had so many times lately been wishing to hear from you. We were talking about you last night and Bep has been talking of writing but as you know failed to do so.

I can scarcely think it is a year since we were talking and planning and preparing for coming here, and saying what a little time we had. It seems a very short time to look back upon, though so much has transpired since then — new places, new faces, new acquaintances, friendly people most of them, but that does not make us forget our old friends, nor make them less dear.

So you were a bit surprised at us two old folks going to the Big City? Well, not much more surprised than I was, and am yet. I never expected to get there, though promised a long time to go. However we thought every year we were getting older and it would be a more serious undertaking. Besides Cousin Annie was here and insisted on us promising, and then on the fulfilment of the promise, after many doubts and fears, and a few sleepless nights on my part, we made a start.

I have not regretted it in the least. I enjoyed it exceedingly and could cheerfully go again (though not yet) and would advise anyone and every-one to go, once, if they possibly can, for it is a most wonderful place.

*I had read a good deal about it, but no-one can form an idea of what is to be seen and heard: the constant bustle and crowds of people, buses, cabs, and almost every imaginable kind of conveyance, including '**motor cars**' — though not many of them,*

I enjoyed riding on the Top of a bus, had no fear whatever, (only before I went) though it was marvellous how they avoided running into one another, so many of them, Fancy, 14,000 horse-buses running daily, besides all other things. The streets were completely blocked sometimes.

Then to pass out of it all into Grand Old Westminster Abbey or St Paul's, where there was such calm solemnity; but when in there the noise of the city sounded like the sea roaring.

When looking on the astonishing works and designs of man, in all those splendid and gigantic works, I often thought the Psalmist might well say, 'Thou hast made him a little lower than the angels' and 'The inspiration of the Almighty giveth him understanding' — but I cannot tell you half I would.

[The letter goes on to give detailed information of the farm and its prospects and to extend a welcome should Mrs Pearson be able to visit them.]

The Gentleman: John Jackson
Royal Links

Grandpa and Grandma Hyde were contemporaries and close friends of John Jackson and his family and we all became related and friendly through their youngest son, Harry, marrying the Jacksons' beautiful daughter, Florrie. My mother told me that Grandma warned Harry, when he had set his heart on Florrie, that he would have to polish up his manners and speech if he were to be worthy of her. Florrie spoke 'high society' French and English having been sent to a finishing school in France. Although Grandma and my mother did not approve of the word 'finishing', as they both agreed that education was through, and for, life, they both adored Florrie who had as rich a sense of humour as her husband. They sparked one another off in genuine affection.

Auntie Florrie of Fraisthorpe looked and behaved like a friendly duchess - or rather as one expected a duchess to look and behave. Her father, John Jackson, our great uncle, whom we children called Daddy Jackson, was even more elegant and noble. I did not meet him often but I can see him now sitting on the lawn at Fraisthorpe looking like Old Jolyson Forsyte ('what a revel of bright minutes!'), his white starched cuffs revealing gold cufflinks engraved with the fleur-de-lys of His Royal Highness, the Prince of Wales (later King Edward the Seventh). Hidden under the well-brushed collar of his morning suit were gold collar-studs also given by the Prince. Even now, if I smell sweet peas and box hedges, Daddy Jackson comes to life sitting upright in the east coast sunlight, his finely manicured hands resting on the arms of the basket chair. I was fascinated that, even when a honey-bee alighted on his hand, he never moved.

When we all went inside for the lavish Sunday tea (farming and country folk dislike picnics, preferring to sit 'square to the table') and we children, having stuffed ourselves, asked if we could 'get down', Daddy Jackson always rose from the table, dabbed a large white napkin against his mouth, and ceremoniously opened the door for us. By habit and breeding he was a perfect gentleman; by profession he was 'a gentleman's gentleman', with his own servants.

It was the custom of His Royal Highness, the Prince of Wales, to engage Jackson as his personal butler-valet whenever he was a guest in one of the large country houses. This custom was carried on long after John Jackson officially retired and when Edward had become king.

It was no small undertaking to have this royal sybarite as a house guest but Arthur Wilson, a shipping magnate of some consequence, was also socially ambitious. Having a wife who was capable of rising to such an occasion, they both accepted the huge challenge and spared neither money nor effort in making Tranby Croft, their country home near Hull worthy of a Royal presence. The invitation appealed to the Prince as it was reasonably near to Doncaster where the famous St Leger race meeting was held on 8, 9, 10 September, an event always looked forward to by the Wilson family and a fixture in the Prince's calendar. Mary Wilson had already spent months in preparation for this royal visit for the smallest or most demanding whim of the Prince had to be satisfied and the whole entourage housed and fed. Even humble little Hessle station was red-carpeted the full length of the platform and decorated to look like a fête champêtre on the Riviera for the arrival of the Royal party.

Hostesses of Mary Wilson's social standing must delve into intricate details to ensure that invited guests are *persona grata* with one another but on this very special occasion invitations would be submitted to the royal household for approval. Lt. Colonel Sir William Gordon-Cumming's presence was never questioned for he was a personal friend of the Prince.

On the night of Tuesday, 8 September, after, of course, an elaborate and lengthy dinner, HRH, no doubt bored with the inevitable soirée, suggested a game of baccarat, a gambling game which Arthur Wilson had forbidden in his house and from which he had ordered counters to be removed .

Our family record by word of mouth was that the Prince asked the butler to go and ask the footman to set up a baccarat table — an embarrassing request in a house where the game was forbidden. A long table was improvised from card tables by Jack and the footman, then covered with a cloth and the chairs set around for ten players. Jack Wilson, the eldest son, needed no encouragement to play but Mary Wilson, like a true hostess, put on one side her personal principles and graciously joined in the game while her husband absented himself.

As the game proceeded, Jack Wilson, sitting at the head of the table next to Lt. Colonel Sir William Gordon-Cumming, noticed that he was shiftily moving the counters after the cards had been dealt and the stakes had been declared. Jack watched carefully throughout the evening and by the end was in no doubt that Gordon Cumming was cheating. Suspicion gathered strength after Jack had alerted other members of the family and two of the players; together they planned that they would keep a keen eye on play the following night. Preparations for the second night were more careful and the position of players skilfully arranged.

One interesting move in which John Jackson must have been either an onlooker or participant was the replacement of the card tables for a longer one and a more appropriate cloth found, a green baize one, to cover it. On the green cloth the obligatory baccarat white line was drawn in chalk, six inches from the edge of the table, all round, for the demarcation for the counters.

The surreptitious sliding of his counters by Sir William occurred again and four witnesses this time convinced the others — including the Prince of Wales — that Sir William was guilty. This was totally denied by the suspect together with a refusal to sign a document of submission which they prepared and presented. He stormed out of the room, demanding a private audience of his friend the Prince of Wales. Although this was granted it did not include any withdrawal of the accusation.

> [The whole three-day event was not only shadowed by this scandal but other troubles with the Wilson family. Arthur, the somewhat evasive host, was trying to cope with strike troubles in his shipping line docks in the port of Hull while his wife received the sad news that her brother had died.
>
> Nothing daunted, the Prince — and indeed his hostess —

decided that racing should not be abandoned but as a mark of respect black armbands should be worn! No doubt these would be transferred onto the black sleeves of the black evening suits for the final ceremonious dinner.

The documentary details of the military trial of Gordon Cumming and the long and scandalous civil court case in 1891 (in which His Royal Highness was called as witness), are a long and tortuous story admirably recounted in Gwendoline Attwood's book *The Wilsons of Tranby Croft.*]

Perhaps the reason why John Jackson was not called as a witness can be explained by a conversation he had with the Prince.

Knowing that his personal butler had been in attendance in the room both nights when baccarat was being played, His Royal Highness summoned Jackson to his side and enquired confidentially: 'What did *you* see, Jackson?'. Jackson's face wore its usual inscrutable calm: 'I saw nothing, Sir' was the reply of the perfect butler.

So, for discretion and impeccable personal service, John Jackson, on his so-called retirement, was the proud recipient of the gold cufflinks and studs bearing his own initials and the insignia of the Prince of Wales.

'Retirement' was a flexible state of affairs for the much sought after Jackson who could pick and choose the job he most preferred. In the event he chose only to accept a royal command and in between times enjoyed the comfort of his own home in Bridlington suitably staffed and conducted to his own high standards.

Daddy Jackson had only one boast which even we children heard: 'I have had the privilege of serving every crowned head in Europe'.

This was on the occasion of the Coronation of His Majesty King Edward VII and his beautiful Queen Alexandra on 9 August 1902, arguably the most joyous and magnificent of all coronations, certainly the one where the Kings and Queens of Europe still survived.

If discretion were relaxed and gold could speak, what a tale those engraved cufflinks could unfold!

CHAPTER FIVE
MY FATHER

When the Hyde family made their marathon trek in 1896 from Cockmoor Hall to the gentler and richer farmland of Fraisthorpe, my father was a young man working in Leeds, but came over to help.

If you lived on a farm in those days you were not a child for long. You very soon were 'another pair of hands' expected literally to pull your weight. There were cows to be fed and milked, horses to harness, sheep to be shorn, lambs and calves to be brought into the world and nurtured, hay to be cut and stooked, fields to be ploughed, seeds to be sown, corn to be reaped, hens to be let out, eggs to be collected, water to be carried from the pump to the house, butter to be churned, peas to be picked and shucked; potatoes, turnips and mangel-wurzels to be dug up and stored in 'pies' in the stack-yard and muck to be spread. Many of these jobs could be done, and done well, by boys and girls still at school.

Fathers and mothers were traditional teachers passing on to their sons and daughters the basic skills of rural living which they had learned from their parents. The Hydes had been farmers for centuries and were firmly welded to the Yorkshire Wolds, and assumed that their sons and daughters would inherit their farms and their skills and become part of the unchanged rhythm of farming life. But they wouldn't put it in such a high falutin' language: they might simply say: 'He's not much of a scholar,' schealmaister says, 'but I told him, 'There's no one better with 'osses.' Such was my father's early education, augmented by the village schoolmistress. It was she who knew, not only the children, but their parents and grandparents and everybody in the village from the parson to the postman. She was in step with the rhythm of farm life, knowing when it was not truancy but turnip hoeing that kept a child from school. She knew the insides of cottages and farms; which families were bookless and were therefore suspicious of book-learning. She knew which grandmas and grandpas, mothers and fathers could read to their children even if the only books were *The Bible* and *Pilgrim's Progress.*

'Teacher's Rest', as half-term was called then, may have been a rest for the teacher, but not for her pupils — specially chosen as it was to coincide with potato-picking, harvesting and blackberry gathering.

'Mixed ability' was not a phrase to be discussed at teachers' conferences but a fact of life; the school master or mistress coped not only with 'mixed ability' but 'mixed ages' with two classes: one for infants and primaries and the other for the nines to twelves. But what she taught was thoroughly 'dinned in. ' There were no educationalists around to challenge her rote-learning and her insistence on accuracy.

It was from the security of this rural life that my father was uprooted and sent to the city to earn his living. Even in those days it was an expensive business setting up a farm and my grandfather could only manage to do this for two of his sons: Dawson and Harry. Edmond was apprenticed to a cattle-cake-mill in Driffield and my father started as an office boy in the Commercial Union Assurance Society in Leeds.

He was not a self-pitying man but adapting to the soot and stress of Leeds must have been very hard on him. Whenever he could get back to the farm he did, saving up his meagre holidays and meagre wages to pay his train fare for the joy of working in the harvest fields for three weeks. 'I breathe deep,' he used to say, 'so that I can stock up with East Riding air for the winter.' Doubtful biology but commendable psychology.

Professor Moorman, who became a great friend, had my father in mind when he wrote this Yorkshire song:

'It's hard when folks can't find their work
Where they've been bred and born;
I allus thought when I were young
I'd bide 'twixt roots and corn;
But I've been forced to work in towns
So here's my litany:
From Hull and Halifax and Hell,
Good Lord, deliver me!'

But, of course, I did not know my father in those early days. By the time I emerged he had worked himself up in the insurance business to be an inspector; had, in 1900, wooed and wedded Annie Wainwright, bought a Bechstein for her wedding present, and between 1901 and 1909 fathered three daughters. After the war he became the manager of the Bradford branch of the Cornmercial Union Assurance Company in Swan Arcade.

Unlike most fathers of that period, he was adept at consoling babies, gently singing his home-made lullabies to the tunes of *The Methodist Hymnal*. By the time I came I think he'd run short of words because I was lulled over and over again to the tune of *Rock of Ages* to which he simply hummed:

Mee-O Mee-O/Mee-O Mee-O/Mee-O Mee-O/Mee ee-Oer Mee

Seven years later the same line and sounds were sung to soothe our young brother, and I have found it never failed to calm my daughter and grandchildren.

Most men of that period would never have been seen carrying a shopping basket but my father, as soon as he finished work at midday on Saturday, went off to Leeds market and bought all that he could carry from the acetylene-lit stalls. There he sometimes chatted to Mr Spencer of Marks & Spencer, but lacked the spare cash to take advantage of Mr Spencer's offer to take out shares when M & S launched out into the Penny Bazaars.

Other homely jobs my father undertook on our behalf were the daily dosing with Scott's Emulsion, the weekly dose of brimstone and treacle and the polishing of all our shoes — a job I think he enjoyed because he always sang to the rhythm of the brushing any song that would give a good shine:

'My object all sublime
I shall achieve in time
To make the punishment fit the crime
The punishment fit the crime.'

This tune is now strangely associated with Cherry Blossom boot polish.

Swan Arcade entrance gate to which my father had a key to get to his office. This photograph, taken in 1962, shows the scaffolding erected for the demolition.

His great enthusiasm was walking, and we were well and truly 'walked' from an early age ('Breathe in, shoulders back — step out') with two steps to his one in rain or shine. His favourite stopping place for us all to take extra deep breaths was the gap in the hedge where we had a clear view of Seacroft Fever Hospital. 'Breathe in deeply and you'll never need to go *there'* was his simple prognosis.

We never quite knew why he was not 'called up' in the First World War but perhaps four children at the beginning of the war and five at the end kept him home-based. Or was it the beginning of the sinister tuberculosis which put him out of action for many months six years after the first world war ended?

Like the Bisto Kids we smelt the steaming pie.

Whatever the reason he became a 'Special Constable', straight-backed and handsome in the not unattractive navy blue uniform. It was a friendly walking-and-calling job which suited my father. A chink of light meant a duty call on the offender and after a little help with the curtain or blind: 'You'll be all right now, Mrs Bleeze' was as far as my father got to martial discipline.

Daddy, like my mother, read to us but he recited or sang long narrative poems, many of which we came to know off by heart. We had a whole theatre of poetry with a stage peopled by *Barbara Frietchie, Barbara Allen, Sir Patrick Spens, Horatius, Thomas the Rhymer, Edward* and *Marie Hamilton* — the last three ballads spoken in a full-blooded Yorkshire version of Scottish.

My father also organised the conventional part of our somewhat bizarre religious education, alternating Methodist and Baptist chapels but also insisting on our attending every service in the tiny Fraisthorpe church when we were on holiday. Our Sunday School life was at the Baptist Chapel, which somehow was linked with the WEA. I think John the Baptist would have been startled had he seen our 'Total Immersions' clad from head to foot in black mackintosh hats, black mackintosh coats and black rubber wading boots, dripping and rushing to the vestry. We children enjoyed it as much as the annual pantomime!

Terms of endearment in Yorkshire are rather like four-leaved clovers; more remarkable than the three-leaved variety because they are scarce. I cannot remember any of us ever being called 'darling' — except by southern aunts — but my father was lavish with his own Yorkshire superlatives: 'little lamb', 'honey', 'my bonny bairn', and all four of us were his 'bonny lasses.' He spoke well and was critical of careless or inflated language or unchallenged platitudes. He disapproved of the maxim 'Honesty is the best policy', arguing that if one were honest only for subsequent insurance, it wasn't very commendable. He disliked hearing anyone recommend some fabric because 'it won't show the dirt'. My father's argument was blunt: 'No, but it's there'.

Although a simple man with modest ambitions and modest needs, he was in no sense limited by his large family or suburbia. Leeds United never had a more enthusiastic fan. As soon as our young brother Sonny reached the set target of ten he and my father went off together to the terminus and took the tram labelled Elland Road. Even if they did not always return glowing with victory, they always glowed with pride. Never in all the years of following Leeds United did one ever hear of hooliganism or violence, nor did my brother ever desert my father to join a gang. They would *discuss* the game all the way home and share it with all of us over tea.

Travelling to Leeds by train during the week was relaxed, sociable and comfortable; I think the LNER was as important to my father as his Liberal Club, for there he joined his card-playing companions in a compartment informally reserved for them by the station master. So lavish, in those good old steam days, were the railways in employing staff (though of course on very low wages) that there were always porters to fetch and carry; guards to wave flags and look after dogs, children, bicycles and prams in the guard's van; engine drivers and their mates; ticket collectors who knew all the trains — without a computer or a tannoy — and of course there was a station master who saw every train off and raised his top hat to visitors arriving at the station.

It was also the schoolboys' and girls' great meeting place. Many a calf-love affair depended on whether the girl or boy caught the 8.01, the 8.14, the 8.24 or the 8.32 and arranged to return home on the 4.40, the 5 o'clock, the 5.15 or the 5 .30. If the boy raised his school cap, pulled the leather strap of the window to lean out and opened the door for you and put your school satchel on his back with his 'walk you home' this was romance indeed. My trouble was that the boy I set my heart on travelled first class and I, of course, travelled third.

The unwritten law was that if one travelled on the same train as one's Papa (it was rare for mothers to go to work), it was never in the same compartment. Men had their newspapers, pipes, cigarettes, cards and their pals. We had our teacher and parent gossip, questionable jokes and our various cliques, and very often a bribed help with home-work.

In any case the adults would not have wanted to share a railway compartment with Betsy and her cronies. Poppy, at the same school and in the same form, had the confidence of the skilled raconteur. She also had pride of place in the gang as she had the distinction of being *adopted*. Betsy, not to be outdone by this one-upmanship, told everyone in the compartment that 'Hyde' was only her adopted name but that her real father was called 'Pèrenot', 'He', Betsy warmed to her subject, 'was a Ring Master in a circus. He left me and my mother — a tightrope walker — and went off to Australia'. Nobody argued with her nor even reported the crazy story to our parents but when challenged by Nancy to ask Mother if she could see her birth certificate, Betsy's rosy cheeks went as red as her school hat-band.

Sometimes the train conversation was raised by the presence of the two Armitage girls who wore their learning heavily having received most of it from their pontifical father. One morning the elder Armitage girl held forth on the Darwinian theory only to receive a retort as crashing as one of Poppy's hockey swipes: '*I'm* not descended from a monkey, if you and your father are!'

Excitement ran high when a porter or a guard walked the length of the train calling repeatedly: 'card sharpers on the train ...' My father used to tell us at home how the card sharpers operated and how their particular team had got the better of the smooth, well-dressed young man in spats and morning coat. Though how he expected to make money on a four-mile train journey one is left speculating; he perhaps had other 'con' ploys up his sleeve.

One of my father's regular train journeys on LNER was to the West Riding town of Doncaster. My sisters and I were especially interested in this journey because my father always brought back a packet of Parkinson's Doncaster Royal Butterscotch. This was one of the 'approved' sweets as Queen Victoria had given it her blessing away back in 1851, the year of the Great Exhibition. The neat foil-covered slabs of toffee were packed in white oblong packets which carried the Royal insignia, and we were told that 'scotch' was the 'scotching' or 'scorching' at high temperature of the best butter and the purest sugar.

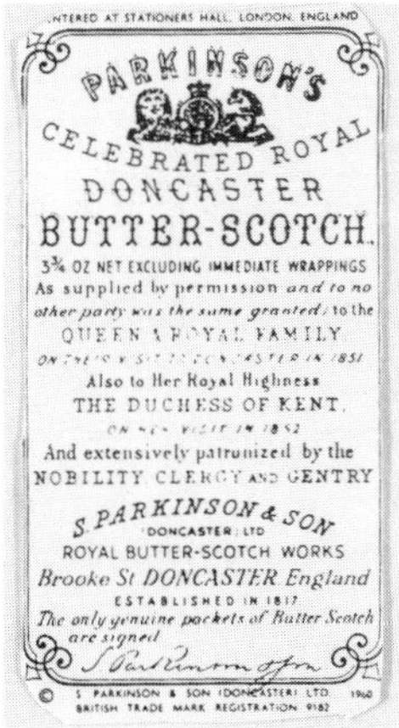

These were all 'approved' sweets.

One 'Doncaster Day' my sister Betsy and I decided to meet my father off the train to shorten the mouth-watering wait. As we were late and the train was early, we arrived just in time to hear it chuffing and puffing out of the station. Then we saw our father coming out of Mrs Danby's sweet shop with two white packets of Doncaster Butterscotch; we knew he had bought it there because otherwise it would have been in his well-worn leather Gladstone bag.

We were too embarrassed and let down to make any remark and he, bless him, offered neither an excuse nor an explanation. When we arrived home — after a rather stilted walk — he said quietly, while he was unwrapping the white packet, 'Well, never mind, remember Mrs Danby gets hers from Doncaster, and that's where this came from.'

(On what small incidents can one be disillusioned and one's trust be shattered. How cruel and narrow children are in their judgements!) Because we had so few sweets they figured large in our lives and were chosen with nerve-wracking care. Oh the agony of deciding how to spend that Saturday penny! Humbugs lasted — so did aniseed balls; sherbert in triangular paper packets with a liquorice straw to draw up the powder was fun but it was nose-tickling and its life was short. Terry's boiled sweets; acid and fruit drops, were parent-approved but were expensive at tuppence-ha'penny a quarter, delicious but boring if you only sucked and didn't crunch. Cherry-lips and dolly mixtures were fun because they were tiny, and one could win favour by handing them round with, of course, the caution 'Only one, mind'. Gobstoppers were 'verboten', so our experience of them was vicarious: 'Give us a go of your gob-stopper' a village child would say, 'and I'll give yer a suck of my liquorice'. We only watched the disappearing rainbow of the ping-pong ball-sized gob-stopper as it passed from one slavery mouth to another.

One Saturday, when I was about eight, I tried a new experiment. Spread out uncovered in a box on the counter — as many of the sweets were at Mrs Danby's — I spied some inch-long flat brown tablets on which was printed: 'Linseed, liquorice and chlorodyne lozenges.' In the box was a card: '10 a penny.' The word 'liquorice' I knew from the 'all-sorts' and the long black plaits; 'linseed' I knew from the seeds put into the cattle cakes at my Uncle Edmond's mill but 'chlorodyne' was a new word, magic and daring. I had heard the word 'chloroform' whispered between my mother and Dr Bean. Chloroform? Chlorodyne? What did they *do?*

Mrs Danby knew, without being told, that the order would be a penny: 'Those please, Mrs Danby' was the total conversation. Clutching my ten tablets in their little poke bag I went out elated with my very grown-up 'buy'. The printed phrase on the tablets went beautifully in tune to my skipped steps:

Linseed, liquorice and chlorodyne lozenges
Linseed, liquorice and chlorodyne lozenges ...'

I danced and sang all the way home with a child's airborne happiness ready to show off (though I did not know these words) my sophistication and erudition.

'Look at my new sweets, Daddy, I can *read* them! Will you have one?' Silently my father read the inscription: his smile crumpled into a frown. 'You must take them back; they're not for little girls,' and then more firmly: 'Take them back and ask Mrs Danby to exchange them for Terry's fruit drops.'

The tune, the rhythm, the magic words all perished. I dragged myself back across the field path to Mrs Danby's with a trudge of self-pity, and now, eighty years on, I have only to see or smell Terry's Fruit Drops to be back deep in the misery of that black Saturday.

Readers will have noted that we always called our father 'Daddy', whereas it would have seemed diminishing to have used the word 'Mummy' for Mother or degrading to have called her 'Mum'. There is significance here. Daddy tended to show or give all sorts of inconsequential things for easy assimilation, whereas my mother tried to hone and shape our rough-hewn little minds into literary collecting plates.

Visiting my father's office in Park Row, Leeds, usually included a long window-gaze into a confectioner's shop — in Boar Lane I think — called 'Eulah' where two massive steel arms — the height of the window — convoluted a thick skein of creamy butter and syrup. We were mesmerised with the grasping, catching, pulling and stretching of all that mouth-watering goo. Inside the shop an earlier concoction had been transformed into thousands of little round crunchy butter creams, neatly packed in white cartons with silk-tasselled cords for carrying. This my father exchanged for 6d and, of course, Betsy was 'the proudest tiger in the jungle' who carried it home.

Later, when Daddy became manager of the Bradford office, in the elegant Swan Arcade, our bonus treat was to go to Godwin Street and stick our noses on the window of Roberts' steaming-pie shop where every day and night of the year the huge meat and potato pie puffed out steam. It was a great *fee-fi-fo-fum* of a pie called 'Bertha' which, many years later, featured in one of J B Priestley's Second World War postscripts heard over the world by millions of people. This gave such massive publicity to the pie-shop that the writer and the owners had cause to regret it for all were pestered by 'gawpers'. However the pie kept on steaming until 1955 when the widowed Mrs Roberts retired, taking with her the secret of how 'Bertha' let off steam for 50 years!

For us it was one of the many wonders of our small but magic world and, like the 'Bisto Kids', our tip-tilted noses believed they were smelling a genuine pie.

We were too young to appreciate the 18th century elegance of the Swan Arcade; it was just very special to *us.* Mercifully we were all grown up and far from Bradford when, in 1962, this architectural gem was demolished — one of the many victims of Bradford's 'progress'. I am glad we did not witness its death.

A mile away, but half a mile from our home in the other direction, was a corner shop owned by Mr Allen, which we patronised when we were young adolescents. It was the very image of the little shop in Sawrey in which Beatrix Potter's Ginger and Pickles finished up with 'no money in what is called the till.'

Visits to Mr Allen's were only with the Avenue gang, led by two boys described by our neighbour Mrs Purdy as 'scamps' but dismissed by the parson as 'demons'.

The huge glass jar became a permanent extension of his arm.

Mr Allen was quite the fattest man I have ever seen, puffing and snorting over the exposed sweets and dribbling from his open mouth into the brass scales. His fat bottom was pressed against the jars and tins on the shelves on the wall behind the counter while his paunch bulged round the counter's edge. Any slight movement rolled the big glass jars of sweets to clank against one another. We children, I am ashamed to report, baited him wickedly: 'Can I have some of those, Mr Allen?' said Ken pointing to a jar on the very top shelf. 'We'll get it down if you can't,' said Archie. We tried every manoeuvre to serve ourselves and thus double our rations. Ignoring our offer, he pulled, pressed and finally fixed his step-ladder and dragged his huge weight high enough to grasp the jar with his fat flabby hands. With his back to us, we were able to grab a few of the sweets set out on the counter. By the time he was back to base, looking like a giant-sized pink blancmange, innocence smirked across our faces and the stolen sweets were out of sight in the boys' pockets or safely trapped by the elastic in the legs of our knickers.

The next stage in the operation was to watch Mr Allen pull out the glass stopper of the jar, push his podgy hand down to sweet level and then draw out his hand, made bigger by the clutch of sweets. One day, to our cruel delight, his hand refused to come out even when it dawned on him to release the sweets. Blood mounting, eyes protruding, mouth dribbling, nose running, snorts rising, he pulled and pulled and pulled in vain; the huge glass jar became a permanent hanging extension of his arm. We all, I am ashamed to say, scuttled out of the shop bent over with laughter, a bunch of horrid little sadists. We thought our parents had no sense of humour when we reported the tale. Typically our father quietly picked up a bottle of olive oil and set off in the direction of Mr Allen's shop offering, in a very practical way, to lend a more useful hand than the one imprisoned in the jar. A decorous silence on his return showed Daddy's disapproval of our callousness but later on, when we had been herded into the drawing room for a quiet read, we heard suppressed laughter coming from our parents in the next room.

I think that children of our class and life-style were given much more of their parents' time than children of the upper middle class or the aristocracy, although they usually had the devoted attention of a Nanny who took on the many-faceted role of *in loco parentis* nurse, teacher, moralist and umpire.

My father had more of the Nanny in him, I think, than my mother for he had the 'Martha' attributes (mindful of many things), my mother the 'Mary' qualities (worried about our souls!). It was very often Daddy who came to our aid and to him we called for help. Not only was he an uncensorious companion for his own children but an accepted pal of all the children in the Avenue. My mother told the story (with rather more jibe against my father than joy in his response to children) that she had answered the door to two little girls who asked: 'Can Mr Hyde come out to play, please?'

A child's life is prickly with indescribable fears: one of mine was *moths. I* was irrationally terrified of their thick sticky brown wings, their frenzied brawls round the gas lights, and their bloated bodies. One summer night when I had gone to bed

— window open, curtains drawn but not obliterating the daylight — I noticed not one, but about twenty huge triangular moths flattened out on the curtains. I screamed for help, not daring to get out of bed. Daddy came at once, and — not deriding or dismissing my fears — fetched a folded newspaper and went into battle. However much he slashed at the moths, not one fell down. After several aborted minutes he pulled one between his fingers to see if it were dead or in a coma. Then I heard: 'Well I'm damned!' 'Damn' was a word only used in extreme cases by my father, but he must have guessed that the little sadist who had cut out brown paper triangles and pinned them to the curtains was none other than his favourite little daughter, usually referred to as 'my bonny little Betsy'. As usual, she escaped punishment. Betsy was the tomboy of the family and tended to choose boys as her friends; the magnet was mischief rather than romance so she was constantly led astray.

One Sunday — a long boring endless Sunday (boredom, I feel sure, causes more iniquities in the young than deprivation) — Betsy and her friend and conspirator, Ken, decided to run away. No one seemed to notice their absence from Sunday School, but they were missing at tea-time and long after. When my father discovered that Ken was missing too, he knew that they were up to no good. Together the two fathers set off in the direction of Leeds while we huddled round Mother sick with apprehension and for some reason talking in whispers.

Seven o'clock; eight o'clock; nine o'clock chimed the big black marble clock on the mantlepiece. On and on walked Mr Turnbull and my father down the murky streets of Leeds to the infamous York Road. After a time they collected a burly heavy-helmeted policeman who shone his lamp on drunks lolling near the squalid pubs, on down-and-outs squatting outside the doors of the back-to-back houses, and guided the two fathers with his oil lamp between the dim guttering street-lamps. The little runaways, still armed with the fire-irons, a long poker and coal-tongs for any likely attack, but bereft of bravado, were found clinging to a street-lamp tired and hungry, having discovered the hard way that truancy was not the romantic adventure they had thought.

All the four mile walk back home Mr Turnbull, purple in the face, nagged and swore at his son: 'You'll get the biggest thrashing you've ever had when I get you back!' But my father squeezed his little daughter's hand in anguished silent relief and, true gentleman that he was, carried the heavy poker home.

Well, we never witnessed the caning that Ken received and we never saw him for a week, but Kathleen, Nancy and I rushed down from our bedrooms just in time to see my father take out from the bookcase cupboard and put into the little frozen palm, as many Cadbury's milk chocolate drops as it could hold.

Betsy's tomboyishness, rosy cheeks and flaxen curls endeared her to all the neighbours on whom, without invitation, any of us could call. Mrs Coultas, across the way, was one of Betsy's favourites, the visits no doubt encouraged by Mrs Coultas's iced buns. One day while Betsy sat there munching, Mrs Coultas said gently: 'Oh

'Betsy love, I wish I had your curls.' The bun was finished rapidly and off Betsy trotted with a hasty 'Thank you' and 'Goodbye'.

Half an hour later, the newspaper boy didn't just deliver the paper but rattled and rang until he got a reply. 'Is that your kid sitting on t'roof chopping 'er 'air with t'scissors?'

My father followed the boy to the side of the house, and there was Betsy framed by the sky-light sitting near the edge of the parapet of the high house, scissors only an inch away from her face and dangling her legs over the window-ledge. He daren't call out but rushed up the two flights of stairs to the middle attic, crept up behind her, thrust out his arm, clasped her round the waist and scooped her in. Betsy, completely shorn of hair on one side and curls dangling down the other, said: 'I was only doing what Mrs Coultas *asked* me to do.'

News always spread quickly down the Avenue, and very soon Mrs Coultas was in our drawing-room weeping: 'I never thought the darling girl would take it literally,' she said. My father had the sense to realise that it was a shock for Betsy and an unfair end to her altruistic gesture so he made her a soothing bowl of 'pobs' — hot milk with cubes of bread, a knob of butter with a sprinkling of nutmeg — and put her to bed. The next day my mother 'evened up' the coiffure to a crop. But Betsy's head grew curlier still, no doubt helped with the shot of adrenalin.

Unlike many parents of that period, ours did not believe in corporal punishment. I can only remember being seriously hit once, and I still smart at the injustice.

Until I was about twelve we each had a collecting box for Dr Barnardo's — a box I remember in detail. It was an optimistic size and covered with highly glazed pictures of the children in the 'Homes'. At one end was a gilt ring which one pulled to bring out a drawer until a flap shot up, disclosing the slit for the money, and saying: 'Thank you'. We enjoyed the fun of the drawer but rarely earned the 'Thank you'; our scanty pocket-money hardly inciting charity. We were therefore feeling guilty and apprehensive as the day for handing in drew near. 'Let's go and collect at the station' Betsy suggested with more confidence (cheek?) than I. We smuggled ourselves and our boxes out of the house and posted ourselves where the passengers had finished showing their contracts or giving in their tickets. 'Thank you!' 'Thank you!' said the box even for farthings and halfpennies. The rattle bolstered us and encouraged us to be more vociferous in our plea.

Then Papa and his train-friend came through the gate.

He didn't shout but went white with shame and anger, and we were pushed away from the station with a throttled 'I never thought I would ever see my daughters *begging*. You ought to be ashamed of yourselves!'

After the silent weepy walk home we were lined up in the hall, told to bend over and were walloped with the cane carpet beater and sent to bed. The 'bark' is considerably worse than the 'bite' of this weapon but our dignity and sense of justice were shattered. Because this action was so out of character, my father's behaviour on this occasion is mercilessly memorable.

Yet if he could do a kindly act he did, and never mentioned it. Harry, our healthy twinkly uncle, my father's younger brother, had the same dry humour, good sense of neighbourliness and dislike of officialdom. He was no letter writer so the installation, at long last, of a telephone in our house meant that my father now had a 'hot-line' for all the farming news. One night Uncle Harry rang up to say that the officials were coming down on their postman Ben as it had come to their notice that he took too long 'on the round'. Next Thursday the inspector was going to accompany Ben and check on his calls. 'Could you post a few cards and letters to folk in Fraisthorpe and Carnaby, to arrive Thursday morning?' 'Leave it to me, Harry,' my father grinned over the telephone, remembering that Ben usually had only two stops: Auburn and Fraisthorpe, where he always had a leisurely breakfast. The next day he took a long list of names and addresses to the *Yorkshire Post* head office in Leeds and ordered and paid for a paper to be sent to every one in the postal circuit. To the few who had a standing order already for the *Yorkshire Post* he wrote a card or a letter with a variety of names of the 'senders'.

Promptly at six on the Thursday morning, Ben arrived at the sorting office and set up the loaded mail bags as if it were an everyday occurrence. The bicycle for the inspector, red and gleaming with its empty carrier, stood waiting. At 6.10 am they both moved off. In and out of the Bridlington streets to the Quayside, then on to the cliff-top path Ben pedalled, twice as hard and twice as fast as his usual pace. On followed the inspector red in the face and breathing like a grampus, harassed by the path which frequently disappeared where the cliffs had crumbled, and which Ben knew so well. Four miles hard pedalling then into the farmyard of Auburn House, a brief nod and Good Morning to Miss Thompson the housekeeper, then on through the fields to Fraisthorpe, opening four five-barred gates for the inspector to puff through, a nod and a wink to the maid and a frenzied rush past the grinning Harry to every farm and cottage in the village.

'It's ganging te tak longer this morning with you, sir; I can bike faster when I'm on me own' Ben managed to say as he picked up his bike at a cottage gate where the inspector was resting. 'It's 10 o'clock' said the inspector. 'Doesn't anyone give you a cup of tea?'

'No time for tea, sir, on this job, but it gives me a good appetite for me dinner. We should be back in Bollington for us dinners. Wait 'ere,' suggested Ben. 'Yer see that farm t'other side o' t'wood about half a mile off? Well, I allus 'ave a fair packet for them. Yer can 'ave a rest; I'll do that one missen.'

Half an hour later Ben rejoined the inspector, who was not near enough to smell the ale which Ben had gulped down in the farm kitchen.

'We've nobbut a couple o'calls to mak now, sir; tha looks fair thrang. Ee lad, yer should do it ivery day — tha 'd er gotten used tiv it as I 'ave.'

Officialdom never troubled Ben any more, and the next day he said to my Uncle Dawson over his usual two fried eggs, rashers of bacon and fried bread: 'Well, I think I've earned me breakfast today.'

The cottagers marvelled for weeks at the generosity of the *Yorkshire Post,* and Mrs Barmby said: 'It's fost time we've had a daily paper — Ee it were good! I read ivery word on it.'

One day, in the early autumn when all the harvest had been gathered in, my Uncle Harry rang up with the bad news that a local farmer, whom we knew, had lost every stack of hay and corn in a devastating stack-yard fire: 'The trouble is, Fred,' my uncle said, 'he's had a bad few years and he's not paid his insurance.' After a brief silence of shock, my father said quietly: 'Tell him not to worry, Harry. It's been paid.' No one knew about this, and many other generous acts, until the gathering of the Hyde clan at my father's funeral. These occasions were the only full social meetings so lots of news was saved up from one funeral to the next, when, if the truth were told, the adrenalin rose and they also shared many a good Yorkshire story over the traditional knife and fork tea.

My father would not be described as 'musical' yet he had a savings bank of songs to draw on, never missed a local *Messiah* or a Gilbert and Sullivan performance, had a Yorkshireman's pride in the great resident orchestras of the Leeds, Bradford and

A major part of our education was in the Leeds Town Hall.

Huddersfield town halls, and paid for all his daughters to learn to play the piano and his son to have violin lessons for all their school lives — a considerable sum out of his small salary.

Our house, reasonably spacious by suburban standards, had only one bathroom, one lavatory, and no bedroom wash-bowls. On the landing — unusual in a house of this modest size — was a press-button electric rising bell, which, at seven o'clock each morning my father rang and called out: 'Kathleen, Nancy, Betsy, Coidy, Sonny, it's late!' Even after my two eldest sisters were away at college the same names were repeated day after day: 'Kathleen, Nancy, Betsy, Coidy, Sonny, it's late!'

I often wonder, now, how we all managed to be reasonably clean by eight o'clock in the morning. I do not remember any organised rota but I do remember my father's ritual shaving which he always carried out with the door wide open. I think, perhaps, it gave him more space for the thespian gestures which accompanied the slick sword-play of his cut-throat razor.

The stropping, soaping, scraping and wiping all had singing or speech accompaniments, and as far as I can remember, the ritual went something like this: with the leather strop hooked to the bathroom wall and held out with his left hand, he stroked the razor up and down with his right hand singing:

'When constàbulary dùties to be dòne
To be dòne
A polic̀eman's lot is nòt a hap̀py oǹe
Hap̀py oǹe.'

Up with the razor on the unstressed syllables, down on the stressed until the razor was as shining and sharp as the Gilbert and Sullivan songs.

A slower and gentler tune suited the shaving movement punctuated with the wiping of the lather and hair on to paper:

'On a tree by a river a little tom-tit	(shave)
Sang willow, tit willow, tit willow,	(wipe)
And I said to him: Dickybird, why do you sit	(shave)
Singing willow, tit willow, tit willow?'	(wipe)

The Pirates, Gondoliers, Mikado, lolanthe and *Yeoman* were all, at some time in the year, lathered into song.

Occasionally in a more serious mood he had visions of greatness and tried out snatches of political oratory, checking in the mirror whether his face was doing justice to the declamation of Lloyd George, Lincoln or Lord Grey.

> 'What is our task?' (shave and rhetorical pause to the bathroom mirror) 'To make Britain a country for heroes to live in.' (razor wiped and put in its case with a Lloyd George look of finality)
>
> or
>
> 'The lamps are going out all over Europe. We shall not see them lit again in our life-time.' (Short selective movements of the razor on the Englishman's stiff upper lip)

or perhaps:

'With malice toward none,	(razor in action)
With charity for all,	(wipe on paper)
With firmness in the right	(razor in action)
As God gives us to see the right	(wipe on paper)
Let us strive on to finish the work we are in.'	(razor carefully put into case with the eagle look of Lincoln)

Yorkshire folk, especially the men, are blatantly chauvinistic about their own county. My father's advice to any foreigner (and they had only to live over the border or the Irish Sea or the Channel to be that) was: 'Never ask an Englishman where he comes from; if he's Yorkshire he'll tell you, and if he's not he'll be embarrassed.'

Winter Saturday afternoons, as I have said, were reserved for Leeds United, but on summer Saturday afternoons the only place my father wanted to be was at Headingley watching Yorkshire play cricket. The Yorkshire and Lancashire match raised voices and temperature even when one of the teams was deliberately playing 'slow'.

This deadly rivalry between Yorkshire and Lancashire is neatly summed up in a story often told by my father and his nephew, Austin Hyde. They were both returning on the train from London following a conference of the Dialect Society. With them was a pedantic phonetician with suspiciously 'Received Pronunciation'. In the far corner of the compartment, a flat-capped, grizzled, stocky little man was ruminating while he carefully packed his pipe with Bruno tobacco. 'You know, Hyde,' said the know-all phonetician with an air of Professor Higgins, 'it's not just from speech that I can tell where a fellow comes from; I can tell just by looking at him. Then *sotto voce,* tilting his head towards the far corner, he added, 'It's obvious, for example, that that man over there is from Lancashire.' 'Well,' whispered my father, 'there's only one way to find out, and that's to ask him.'

'Excuse me, sir,' the phonetician enquired patronisingly, 'but are you from Lancashire?' Holding the bowl of his pipe in mid-air, the quiet little man turned the stem pointedly, like a gun, and fired his reply: 'Naw, ah'm not; ah'm from t'West Riding, but ah can 'ardly blame yer — ah've bin feeling badly all t'week!'

I was sorry that my father was not buried in Carnaby church yard in his own East Riding, where his father and brothers and sisters lie, but a funeral at Whitkirk Church in the West Riding pleased the locals who turned up in their dozens to 'pay their respects'. It was through this church yard, during our childhood, my father walked us to Temple Newsam House and where he paused at an ancient tombstone to read the mossy inscription aloud:

'The World's a City full of Crooked Streets,
Death is the Market Place where all men meet.
If Life were Merchandise which men could buy,
The Rich would always live, and the Poor die.'

As we came away from my father's grave, dug on the outer perimeter of the church yard, we passed two villagers, dressed like all the rest in their funeral uniform of black armbands on navy blue Sunday suits, and overheard one say to his mate: 'Aye, they've put Fred Hyde where he'd like to be, just 'is spot, reet next to t'cricket field. '

Whitkirk Church, where I was christened; my sister Nancy was married and my father burried.

The stone was one of our reading books.

We craned our necks to read the lofty inscription aloud.

Temple Newsam — our Sunday walk.

CHAPTER SIX
HIGH DAYS AND HOLIDAYS IN THE FIRST WORLD WAR

Six Pennies in my Pocket

The Ryecroft sisters, Gertie and Ada, were distant cousins of my father, so distant that no one ever worked out the family link. They were not exactly gentlewomen but genteel-women since polite poverty had made their whole existence pinched. Their meagre diet, their painful efforts to be lady-like, the urgent necessity of not growing out of their clothes showed in their pinched mouths, cheeks and waists.

They eked out their existence by 'proposing' themselves to any of the easy going Hydes — and that made up a score or so — who had open house. This they repaid by table-setting, washing up, mending, darning, ironing and minding children. They lived in a respectable but dingy Victorian terrace-house in a cheek by jowl suburb of Leeds, and used every possible device to make the best of, and disguise, their poverty.

Neither had been trained to do a job other than looking after aged parents who grew more demanding the nearer they grew to death. When — too late for Gertie and Ada to change their ways — the parents died, the two daughters went through the expected gestures of: 'bravely borne', 'passed away peacefully', 'sadly missed' and 'beloved father and mother', and added black armbands and black veils to their well-worn navy blue.

'It was thoughtful of Mother and Father,' said Gertie, 'was it not, to have kept up their insurances. It did mean we could give them a nice funeral.' (We only discovered after my father died that it was he who had paid the insurances, which included a small life insurance so that Gertie and Ada had at least enough to exist on.)

But there was one day long before I knew what was behind their tidy facade when Gertie and Ada — for we never gave these middle-aged friends a title — made a red-letter day for a little girl of five. It was December 1914, the first Christmas of the Great War, and my sisters had been invited to a party; I was too young, too small. The Ryecroft sisters arrived and said: 'Get your hat and coat on, child, and don't forget your gloves and handkerchief', and soon I was kitted out in my red knitted woollen coat, my rabbit fur bonnet and muff with their red velvet linings, buttoned gaiters and red knitted mittens fastened on to elastics up the sleeve of my coat.

'Guess where we're taking you!' Without waiting for an answer, they spoke as they often did in chorus: 'Marks & Spencer's Penny Bazaar! And here's a silver sixpence for you to buy all your Christmas presents. ' The chance of being the 'givers' and not the 'takers' made both of them glow.

My mother had praised their new hats though she knew that they had given their old navy blue felts a face-lift by turning up the brims into tricornes and putting eye-veils over the front. Giggling at their deception, Gertie explained: 'We found the veiling in an old box of Mother's and we copied the military style from a hat we saw in Matthias Robinson's.'

So the three of us set off for the tram. 'Please can we go on top?'
I could see the sparks from the cable, look into people's bedrooms, hear the click and ring of the conductor's ticket machine on his belt. After three miles of clanging and riding there we were, straight opposite the glass arcade. And I could *read* it! 'Marks & Spencer's Penny Bazaar.' Gertie helped me on 'Admission' but we all chimed in on *'Free'*.

My hands were hot and sticky with clutching my sixpence in the pocket of my muff; the fear of losing it obsessed me.

When at last we went in, having savoured every possible thing outside, Ada said, 'What about changing your sixpence?' It sounded threatening to me. 'Ask the shop-lady if you can'. She didn't need asking: ''Ow'd you like it, luv?' she beamed. ''Ow many pennies? 'Ow many 'ay'pennies and 'ow many farthings?' I was considered bright for my age so I couldn't let Gertie and Ada down: 'Three pennies, four ha'pennies ...' I hesitated, then I stumbled out: 'And the rest in farthings!'

Gertie and Ada beamed with pride and eleven bright gold new coins were in my hand. Too many to clutch. Far too many to spend! I pushed them into the red velvet poke in the lining of my fur muff. Gertie and Ada were just the right people for this store; the longer it took to spend sixpence the more their frugal minds were pleased.

Choosing was painfully exciting. The counters, tilted down from back to front, were packed — 'Don't ask the price — It's a penny!' There were cotton reels — enough colours for Joseph's coat — packets and books of needles from difficult-to-thread to crewel, pins on sheets, measuring tapes, coathangers, hairpins, hair tidies. 'No need to make your choice yet' said Gertie, lifting me up to get a better view. On we went: combs, hair-brushes, sponge bags, shaving soap, shaving mugs ... I chose a shaving stick in a wooden case which you could twist up and down. Gertie and Ada had to sniff their approval of the perfume. 'Lady-like' they agreed, which seemed odd for soap for my Daddy. It was wrapped up in brown paper, tied with string and handed over in exchange for my two ha'pennies. 'Ta, luv. Ta'Tah.'

On to the kitchen-ware: pots, pans, sieves, colanders, cups, jugs, teapots, slop basins...; it was mind boggling. I daren't touch even though Ada held me up so that I could. Instead I just pointed to a little white jug with purple violets and green leaves. 'Your Mother will love those colours' they both said in chorus. They peered underneath. 'Real china too.'

(It was much later that I learned that the Ryecrofts had told an aunt that my mother's Suffragette friends went 'too far' and that they thought parliament was not a proper place for women.)

Another penny bought an autograph album for Kathleen, with pages of pale blue, pink and green; a strap purse for Nancy with the other penny and a little black flat-iron for Betsy to iron her doll's clothes. And I still had four farthings in my pocket.

'Now my dear,' said Gertie, 'we think you should have the last penny to spend on yourself!' That crowned the day.

On to the counter of pencil boxes, pens, crayons, tubes of paint, rulers, waste paper baskets... I chose — and kept it for years — a shiny black hardbacked notebook with a metal pencil that fitted into a little groove with a *hundred* sheets for, it said on the outside, *Memorandum.*

'And now,' said Gertie and Ada in a chorus of conspiracy, 'we are taking you to a shop where you don't buy, you just *look*. I had never seen a 'looking-shop' before but as I was almost spent with spending, it seemed a good idea. I'm groping in my memory to try to recall whether in Briggate and Boar Lane the lamps had gone out because of the war. If they had I never noticed; all I remember is the dazzle of the toy-shop *The Pygmalion.*

Here were toys too high, too grand, too elegant and beautiful to touch let alone buy. The dapple-grey, red-saddled rocking horses towered above me. I could walk *into* the fully-furnished Wendy houses: there was a space to have a ride on a boat-shaped swing. A Noah's ark, big enough to hold 'all creatures great and small' — from an elephant my size to rabbits thumb-sized — seemed a very grand home for Mr and Mrs Noah ...

The magnificence was almost more than I could bear. The porcelain dolls, too superior to cuddle, flicked their long eyelashes up and down as if warning any would-be customer that they were designed only for good families.

A tall man came up to us in his black tail coat, grey-striped trousers, oiled hair and Kitchener moustache and addressed Gertie: 'Can I help you Madame?' 'No thank you,' said Gertie, 'we're just showing the child round before her parents come to buy.' Ada rubbed her hands nervously. 'Quite all right, Madam.' He bowed and glided away towards a lady in a velvet hat and fur coat...

Gertie and Ada had been whispering away above my head, but I did catch the last words: 'Let's take her; it's only threepence,' and I was whirled along into a cavern of snow-blue-white where the one and only Santa Claus beamed in the circle of white fur round his head. I was too excited and nervous to answer his questions but I came away with a parcel wrapped in red crinkly paper all tied up with silver ribbon. It was *mine*. This was not going in Ada's basket but into my muff. It was cold and blackly damp out in Boar Lane and the Town Hall clock boomed four times. The tram, trucks, carts and horses were deafening and I missed all of Gertie's and Ada's talk except: 'Annie did say we could ...' People seemed taller, heavier, darker, noisier ... as we pushed our way through to what I now know was Bond Street and into Fuller's Cafe.

The sheer bliss of that pale blue, pale pink, pale grey room, warm with tea and toast, remains haloed in my memory. Veils were lifted, gloves removed, and the neatest of little waitresses in a frilled white cap and bibbed apron wrote our order down: 'Tea for two and an extra cup for the girl; two slices of coffee and walnut cake

'Tea for two and an extra cup for the girl'.

for my sister and I.' (Gertie thought 'I' was more refined than 'me'.) 'A doughnut for the child; she doesn't like nuts.' As we weren't allowed to dislike anything, I couldn't understand Gertie's mistake. Had it something to do, I thought years later, with the simple fact that doughnuts were a penny and the Fuller's famous walnut cake was tuppence a slice?

Gertie — for she was the natural tea-pourer — half filled my cup with milk and then added hot water. Gertie and Ada manipulated minute pieces of their cake on to minute forks — an operation new to me — after making sure that my doughnut was cut into inch-sized pieces. They dallied luxuriously, making a little go a long way. They sipped their tea with their little fingers poised in air so that the flowers and the gold rims of the teacups were not hidden.

'Another jug of milk, please, waitress, and a jug of hot water if you please.' The Town Hall clock struck five. 'It's very homey, isn't it, Ada?' I didn't quite understand. It didn't seem a bit like their home as I remembered it nor even mine. There was a whispering between Gertie and Ada as they worked out whether they should give the waitress one penny or two. 'She's been very obliging with the milk and the hot water and so nice to the child.' It was an intense moment. 'Let's make it tuppence. I'm sure Annie wouldn't mind.'

Out in the dark damp cold, the newspaper men were bawling out: 'Late Night Final, Late Night Final...' and words I could not catch. 'Germans' ... was the only word.

But whatever Gertie and Ada heard it quickened their steps: 'No, we're not wasting a ha'penny on an Evening Post. We don't want any bad news today — not fair to the child. '

(The 'child' only realised years later that what the men were shouting out on that magical day in December 1914 — such a lavish and loving day — was 'Scarborough shelled ...one hundred dead, two hundred wounded'.)

Home. Tired and triumphant. I groped upstairs in the dark to hide my presents under the bed. Conversation stopped as it often did when I came into the room but I did notice — before they noticed me — Gertie's hand over my mother's and heard her say, 'That's your change, Annie, from the five-shilling piece' and Ada's slight soprano joined Gertie's cramped contralto: 'Thank you, Annie, thank you for a marvellous day!'

Bedtime. Dreams of Santa Claus riding a rocking horse in a snow-blue-light on a tram-car eating a doughnut ...

Daddy would return soon with his *Evening Post* under his arm.

Cows in the Kitchen

Because of the threat of air-raids in 1915 on the East coast, we did not go to the Hyde farms for our Easter holiday. Our parents were ingenious, economical and optimistic in the places they chose to compensate but how they came to decide on Crag Top Farm, away above Ilkley, is a mystery. It could hardly have been a *friend* who recommended it.

How we got to Crag Top has faded in my memory but there is no doubt that we walked, with all our luggage, from Burley in Wharfedale station.

My father believed in our *walking*, with little concern that small children had to take two steps to his one. 'Breathe in, two, three, four, five — out, two, three, four, five.' Our steps were paced out against the buffeting of the wind. On we struggled, up, up and up the winding three-mile cart track. 'Look over there,' he flung out his arm, 'there are the Cow and Calf on Ilkley Moor!' All I could see were a few bony cows sheltering near a stricken hawthorn and drystone wall. Not a calf in sight! 'We'll walk there tomorrow and you'll be able to sit on them and have a rest.' Sitting on a cow seemed frightening; sitting on a calf seemed heartless. My elder sisters, obviously with longer sight than I, thought they saw the cow and calf lurking behind a cloud over-hanging the little town of Ilkley below.

I did meet these solid animals the next day after a wild walk along the Ebor Way where I seemed to be blown from one gorse bush to the next. Those great rocks didn't look the least bit like a cow or a calf and the wind that whistled between them was not mooing but shrieking. Although it was late March, it had seemed quite warm on the station but up on the moor the biting wind seemed to have a grudge against us. It was the only time in my young life when I was glad to be wearing the Dr Jaeger woollen combinations, thick brownish knitted garments which encased body, legs and arms. It was much later that I learned that my mother had subscribed to the Dr Jaeger cult — of which George Bernard Shaw and Oscar Wilde were proselytes — of wearing wool next to the skin to absorb its noxious odours!

But I must return to Crag Top and take you into the farmhouse. We were used to farms of the Wainwright, Hyde and Danby families. There the fields of oats, wheat and barley were 'broad acres' proudly husbanded. Granaries, barns and stables stood four-square round the all-is-safely-gathered-in stackyards. Here at Crag Top, which was not a farm but a game-keeper's cottage, everything seemed to drop downhill, from the muck-yard which reached the front door to the scrubby runs for the hens, ducks and geese. Even the higgledy-piggledy pigsty was on a slope and everything that clucked, crowed, quacked, hissed and grunted was within hearing and smelling distance of the house. Fences had surrendered to the wind so that anything and everything could get through the gaps. There was no garden, not even an apple-tree, and any paint left on the doors and window-frames was blistered and cracked. It needed courage and prompt response to use the privy which had its natural air-conditioned gaps in the roof, walls and door.

After our daunting walk from the station, we were too tired and hungry to be critical and our mother, eight months pregnant — I now realise — with what was to be her fifth child, must have been longing simply to get her feet up. We children settled down on the two benches either side of the long deal table and, between ravenous bites, chased the flies from the bread and jam and craggy caraway seed cake. Tea was served — but that is too genteel a word — sluiced rather, from a huge enamel teapot (with handles back and front to make lifting and pouring possible) into enamel pint mugs. I was too busy picking seeds out of my cake to notice that the kitchen and the shippen shared the same top and bottom doors. Two steamy cows, their heads well over the half-door into our room, were plopping the end product of their cud-chewing on to the shippen floor. As the bottom door was several inches from the floor, we not only smelt but *saw* their uninhibited output!

We had fun at Crag Top, of course; children are bouncingly adaptable, and we sang all the nine verses of *Ilkla Moor baht 'at* and realised from first-hand experience why Mary Jane's lover would get his 'deeath o'cold'. The cannibalistic last verse, where we've eaten the duck that ate the worms which ate his body we bellowed into the wind.

Secretly, I think, we all counted the days — mercifully only seven — to the time when we should be tramping down, down, down that three-mile cart-track to Burley-in-Wharfedale station.

The time did come when a grandfatherly steam train chuffed and cherished us into Leeds station and another chuffed us home.

A six-year-old feels sensation without knowing how to explain it. If I had had the words I might have said that our modest Avenue house, seen with my new eyes, seemed spacious, gracious and loftily clean.

Nowadays, when I drive through Ilkley — as I often do — I 'lift up mine eyes unto the hills' and let the sybarite in me take over. Parked as near as I can to *Betty's* I then sink into its Edwardian comfort and order Earl Grey tea and toasted Yorkshire tea-cake. Raising a delicate china tea cup I drink a tea-total toast to the immortal Cow and Calf and think: 'Next time I really will give myself time to drive to Burley Woodhead, park my car, climb up Burley Moor to the Crag Top of my childhood and there meet George Greaves, its present occupant — a sheep farmer — who with electricity, modern plumbing and a Land Rover can comfortably take the wind and the heath, brother, in his Yorkshire stride.'

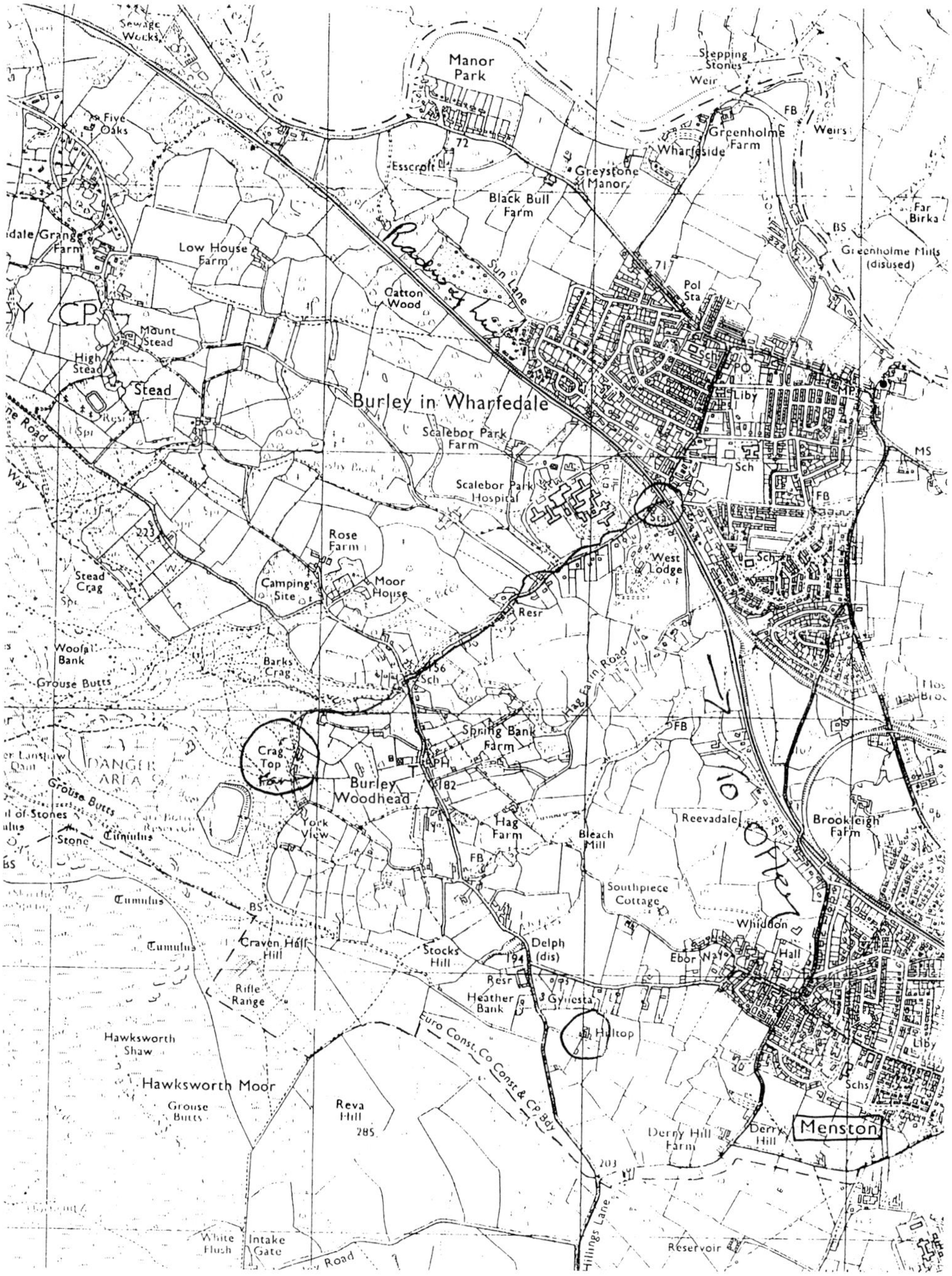

We walked, with all our luggage, from Burley-in-Wharfedale station to Crag Top Farm.

Cricket at Headingley

Cricket, in Yorkshire's golden age, was not so much a game as a religion. Husbands were known to rush their pregnant wives, temporarily exiled in another county, back into Yorkshire so that the son (or daughter) should have the right birthplace. No one, until very recently, could be in the Yorkshire cricket team — although he may have lived there for 20 years — unless *born* in Yorkshire.

Headingley was not just a cricket ground but a place of pilgrimage; a recovery ground, too, for all those boys who were 'too ill to go to school' on county match days. Hundreds of boys, happily settled in the stands, would push their distinctive school caps into pockets to escape identity and thus save their truant young masters, somewhere in the crowd, from glances of recognition.

In another pocket was the boy's autograph album ready to use as a passport to Paradise when he, at the end of the day, approached his hero at the pavilion. If the boy had been wearing his cap he would have raised it but being cap-less he lifted a reverential forefinger to his forehead, beamed his request for Sir, and returned in rapture, knowing that with Hutton's or Sutcliffe's signature his stock at school would soar.

My father's worship of the Yorkshire team outweighed his discipline as an employer. One afternoon his office boy knocked at the door and blurted out: 'I'm not feeling well, sir; I've got a bad headache; may I have tomorrow off?' Pause. 'I'm sorry you're not well, son; did you say you'd a *headache?* or is it...Headingley?' Blushes from the boy. 'A pity you won't be here tomorrow' said my father, 'because I'd thought of closing the office at noon and giving you all a half-day.' 'Eeh, that's good of you sir! Can I tell me Dad to bring me lunch to Headingley?' And then with a broad grin: 'I'll tell you what, sir, I'll be in at eight sharp instead of nine.'

Memory seems to bring the sun out and only once can I remember being at Headingley when rain stopped play. They were long golden days of sunshine when all the world seemed to crowd on to the Leeds trams bound for Headingley. Complete strangers discussed the weather, the ground, the players. No one ever considered that Yorkshire might lose; a draw perhaps or rain, but not defeat.

Hundreds of stories abound of the blatant chauvinism of Yorkshire supporters; the one in constant circulation tells of the man, neither Yorkshire nor Lancashire, who venturing to remark on the teams was told to 'mind your own bloody business'. My father's gentle faux-pas was to a fellow passenger on the tram: 'Which part of Yorkshire are you from, then?' my father asked after several minutes of shared appreciation of the Yorkshire star players. 'Oh, I'm not from Yorkshire. I'm a Salopian,' the man said with quiet pride which my father failed to catch. My father's lowered voice oozed sympathy: 'I'm sorry, sir ... forget it ... I shouldn't have asked.'

The finesse and glory of Yorkshire cricket was wasted on me, a young unathletic girl, but I remember how my sisters and I went in turn with my father and young brother, taking our air cushions and paper carrier bags stuffed with sandwiches and pasties to help the long day through. Of all the players, Herbert Sutcliffe was the answer to a maiden's prayer: tall, suave, hair cut and Brylcreemed to shine like black onyx and wearing immaculately creased cream flannels. He stood at the wicket, monarch of all he surveyed, checking, with bat upraised, that not one person moved in the crowd. Then he went into action imperturbable, majestic, poised and serene. I think the smattering of schoolgirls in the crowd were more impressed with his relaxed leaning on his bat between the 'overs' than they were with his flicks to the boundary. The game to me, who was so ignorant of its nuances, always seemed curiously slow, and I never presumed to join in the masculine conversation which was peppered with words as esoteric as those in French ballet: leg-glance, leg-break, short-leg, maiden-over, silly mid-on, hook-stroke, back-lift, off-drive ...

But I did absorb the atmosphere where the whole terrestrial and celestial globe seemed to be consummated into the bat and ball at Headingley. It was a simpler age when just 'being there' provided talk for weeks. It was an age when half-a-pint could last for half-an-hour's talk, when there were no exhibitionist huggings after each little triumph and no outer space masks protecting faces. There was, even through the rowdiest response, a seemliness and good humour impossible when sports are sharply cash-registered as they are now.

Strangely enough there was no resentment that the amateur 'gentleman' captain emerged on to the ground through a different gate from the professional players. The white roses on their caps seemed to preclude chips-on-shoulders.

Yet the whole day bristled with benign bellicosity. Yorkshire *had* to win. Dialogue was tough. At six o'clock, when the sun was reddening, a whole fleet of galleons, the golden tram cars, were lined up to carry that exultant crowd home to their Yorkshire teas of roast ham, home-grown salad, pies, pasties, spice bread and the ubiquitous ever-flowing custard.

From noon onwards the *Yorkshire Evening Post* and *Evening News* were hawked on the cricket ground, and in every street in Yorkshire; a new edition printed for every fallen wicket. My father collected his copy as we changed trams in Briggate so that he could see the last ball recorded in the 'Stop Press'.

Our high days at Headingley always ended, as they did with other Yorkshire folk, with a long, lush tea when the men of the family hogged the conversation. Every stroke, every catch, every wicket was analysed and adjudicated; Verity's wily bowling, Bowes' skittling of wickets and his equally devastating batting to boundaries, Sutcliffe's elegant sticking-power and Leyland, Barber and Mitchell assuring Yorkshire's invulnerability.

It was the county matches which magnetised the crowds at Headingley. Test matches were important. But not *that* important.

I must go beyond my commission of the first quarter of the century to a decade later when Neville Cardus merged his reports of cricket and music in the *Manchester Guardian*.

My mother, impressed not with the cricket but with Cardus's brilliant literary style, read out to my father a passage in which Cardus, in praise of Yorkshire, compared Woolley with an allegro by Mozart, and Macartney was described as a Mercutio performing a Queen Mab scherzo. My father nodded his head in agreement and then said: 'And that from a Lancashire man! You wonder what he'd have written if he'd been born in Yorkshire. I reckon he'd have been lost for words!'

CHAPTER SEVEN
A COLLAGE OF COUSINS AND AN ASSORTMENT OF AUNTS

Our Male Cousins

We were fortunate in our cousins on both sides of the family: the Danbys, the Hydes, and the Wainwrights.

The male cousins who added zest to our lives were all tall, handsome, gifted and affectionate. I recall with gratitude Horace Hyde's splendid baritone, his humour and his story-telling. Marrying into the Errington family added another dimension from which we all profited, for his brother-in-law, Sydney Errington, was an outstanding viola player and contemporary with Annie Wainwright in the Halle orchestra. *The Erringtons* — Horace's in-laws — were long established wholesale confectioners in Leeds who, of course, traded with the famous Yorkshire sweet manufacturers: Rowntrees and Terry's (both in York), Mackintoshes of Halifax, the Bassetts and Wilkinsons of Pontefract (licorice allsorts) and Farrahs of Harrogate Toffee fame. All of these firms — and of course the Quaker Cadbury's — are worthy of study, not only for their high standards of production but for their concern for better social standards and good conditions for their employees.

I have a special affection for Farrahs because the nicest of our relatives, including my father, very often brought home for us the familiar blue and silver tins. It all started with Mrs Farrah's making toffee on her kitchen range nearly 200 years ago and shrewdly finding good customers amongst the high society folk 'taking the waters' in the famous Spa. (Judging by the popularity of her toffee they can hardly have been on slimming cures.) When the toffee was being bought for presents to take home — to all parts of the British Isles and overseas — the paper poke would not do, and thus the elegant tin was designed and has remained the same ever since. Seventy-five years ago the well established prosperous firm was taken over by the Waddingtons of whom this generation are my close friends. (Their actress daughter has revived 'Farrah' as her stage name — a happy choice.)

Look closely at the letter from John Mackintosh to Joseph Errington for it has much to say. It was written in 1919, when, following the Armistice of November 1918 (the eleventh hour of the eleventh day of the eleventh month), Victory and Peace were formally celebrated in 1919. Although there were still serious shortages of food it seems from this letter that people were chewing toffee again. Reading between the lines one senses that the Erringtons had been having cash-flow problems but typical of the Mackintoshes, they had given, and intended to go on giving help.

Freddie Hyde, the 'Walking History of Scarborough'.

Austin Hyde when he was headmaster at Lady Lumley's Grammar School, Pickering.

Allan Danby, the inheritor of the Wolds Farms.

Horace Hyde in the First World War.

Sydney Errington, a cousin by marriage, who later was principal viola player in the Hallé Orchestra.

It is interesting to note the 'By Appointment' (Victoria), the simplicity of the one-word address: 'Halifax', the three numbers only of the telephone, the hundredweight as a standard measure, and the somewhat irregular format of the letter. In spite of the size and the prosperity of the firm, it would seem that John was doing his own typing. Or was the deal confidential?

BY APPOINTMENT
JOHN MACKINTOSH, LTD
MANUFACTURERS OF
MACKINTOSH'S TOFFEE.

TELEPHONES 817 & 818.
TELEGRAMS: MACKINTOSH, HALIFAX.
CODES: WESTERN UNION AND
A.B.C., 4TH AND 5TH EDITIONS.

Halifax

Sept. 3rd. 1919

Mr Joseph J.Errington.
41 Lowerhead Row.
LEEDS

P.S. We are sending you a 5 cwt. consignment additional to the usual 4 cwt. weekly. We may be able to repeat this in a few weeks time if you will write us.

Dear Mr Errington,

Thanks for Insurance Policy which we will take care of until you claim it again. Glad to know you are doing so nicely, and that you will soon be free from obligations, although as you say it is perhaps as well to get some funds in hand for trading and prompt payments. I think trade will be good for a long time yet, and you have a good opportunity to get well-established.

All I ask in return for the little help I gave is a continuance of the business friendship that has been between you and my firm for so many years.

With kind regards,
I am, sincerely Yours,

J Mackintosh

Managing Director.

P.S. I will see what can be done re bigger ration of Toffee.

Austin Hyde, a regular visitor to every Hyde house and farm, was the greatest influence in our childhood and our growing-up. As he was many years older, highly gifted and of exemplary character, we were somewhat in awe of him. In his student days at Leeds University we were 'open house' for all his boisterous friends. Children tend to remember the quirky things, so 'Billum' stands out in my memory because he could play the piano with his feet! One cannot imagine now that a gang of students would be kept entertained all evening singing round the piano every song in the Scottish Students Songbook from 'Little Brown Jug to 'Gaudeamus Igitor'. But they did and were genial in teaching the young Hyde girls to sing 'in parts'.

Later, when Austin became a senior English master and gradually became an authority on Yorkshire dialects, one marvelled at his easy flow from 'Received Pronunciation' of Standard English to a whole range of North, East and West Riding speech. (In the Castle Museum in York in the thirties, if one pressed the buttons for all three recorded examples of the dialects, it would be Austin's voice, significantly varied, which spoke all three.) Uncle Dawson and Austin were great buddies bonded as they were by their fanatical Methodism and their general appreciation and knowledge of local history and the homespun yarns.

Austin, very soon in his career, became a county hero as a speaker and writer but was also nationally known as a regular broadcaster. During the First World War we saw less of him but his air force uniform made his rare visits significant. Woodhouse Grove School welcomed him back after the war as second headmaster. By this time our mutual first cousins, Henry and Alan Danby, who had been boarders at the Grove before the war, had left.

In fact Woodhouse Grove School featured strongly in our lives and as it was a short railway journey from Leeds to Apperley Bridge, we had many 'see-you-behave-well' visitations. Many sons of our parents' friends were Grovians, not least my first boy friend. The tradition was continued by another cousin, Horace's son, John Hyde, who still keeps me posted (as a retired member of staff) of fascinating Grovian news and celebrations.

Today, as I was writing this addendum for this second edition, I was handed a cutting from the Bradford paper showing a photograph of a slice of history. A chestnut tree from the Grove grounds, so old and precarious it had to be chopped down, has been carefully sliced to reveal nearly 300 years of ringed history. The Woodhouse Grove School forestry officer has printed a significant item of British history on every ring and thus created a unique teaching tool.

But to return to Austin's final years when he settled in Pickering as headmaster of Lady Lumley's Grammar School. He used to point out in his talks on dialect and linguistics that his pupils knew that the King's English — and later the Queen's — was appropriate for school, church and travel but that their home and country speech was also the King's English — but the King was Alfred the Great!

The north moors of Yorkshire and the Vale of Pickering, where Austin and Jessie finally made their home, gave him his zest for bee-keeping and extended his circle of friends beyond his schools, church and lecture halls.

Woodhouse Grove School Staff 1912. Austin is 4th from the left on the back row.

Of the numerous letters I received after the publication of the first edition of *Life in a Liberty Bodice,* many, who did not know me at all, knew Austin through his plays, lectures, sermons and broadcasts.

I am particularly indebted to the Reverend Thomas Hicks 'clover friend' of Austin's who shared a site on the northern moors .

He enclosed verses in which he described the unique service he conducted on the moors as a last tribute to Austin. I have based my own verses of this ceremony on his information but included a reference to Austin's best known poem 'Dapper t'owd Mare' — one of the last of the shire horses on Auburn farm.

F. Austin Hyde

The Last Post sounded by the Reverend Thomas Hicks and friends

We scattered his ashes where bees suck the clover
In a broken-down sheepfold; his earth-life was over:
Will Clement, Bill Lupston, Tom Hicks and the rest
Gave the bee-keepers' tribute: 'Clover's the best',

Committal with curlews, lark's sky-song of prayer,
Ashes blown high in the strong moorland air,
Ling quickened our thinking, for some of us there
Recalled Austin speaking his: 'Dapper t'owd Mare'.

Secure in his Faith, he'd made a request
That his ashes be scattered on land he loved best —
'Then I'll meet my Maker, My Father and Guide
Freed from my body', said F. Austin Hyde.

Freddy Hyde, another first cousin, was a press journalist of a very high order and a correspondent for the BBC. Young reporters, learning their trade, had an exacting mentor, for he demanded that no personal or confidential matters should ever be disclosed and that all facts should be checked and accurate before they went to press (Shades of C P Scott of the *Manchester Guardian).* Every cub reporter had to show that he had a set of finely sharpened pencils for the precision shorthand which Freddy expected.

He was known locally, not only as the *Gentleman of the Press,* but also as *Scarborough's Walking History* for there was nothing old or new that did not find a place in his observant mind and ready pen.

Unlike the other male cousins, who had laughing eyes, he was not gregarious, preferring rather to spend quiet leisure hours watching the sea birds on Bempton cliffs. We much younger cousins never knew him well for he did not find it easy to talk to children — he had none of his own.

Sadly, but predictably, his well-bred, well-heeled wife, Kathleen, very soon became bored with him and escaped whenever she could to ride to hounds or go on riding holidays. The 'away' fixtures grew longer and more adventurous, including safaris in the non-touristy parts of deepest Africa with her secret lover. When she returned to Scarborough, it was to her old family home or close friends. But as she had a soft spot in her heart for her Yorkshire-bound husband she engaged a competent housekeeper to oil the wheels of their elegant house in Ayton. Kathleen had *cordon bleu* standards of cookery so, wherever she was, she contrived that Freddy's refrigerator was richly loaded.

According to her sister-in-law, if Kathleen were unable to deliver food in her own car, she made sure that whole menus were sent from Scarborough to Ayton often by *post.* One home-made masterpiece was a fish pie — no ordinary one but a gourmet concoction of Scarborough's best seafood — sent through the parcel-post and delivered to the door by the postman!

But the way to Freddy's heart was not through his stomach for he was a temperate man in every way. He refused to listen to any criticism of his wife and never invited sympathy for his loneliness. He went on for years, alone, quietly reporting, listening, watching cricket and the sea birds. He and his errant wife never divorced but met briefly at decorous intervals.

I am glad Freddy died long before fax machines, mobile telephones and shrieking headlines. To him they would have been anathema.

He could well have been one of the unsung heroes in Gray's *Elegy* ...

'Far from the madding crowd's ignoble strife
His sober wishes never learn'd to stray;
Along the cool sequester'd vale of life
He kept the noiseless tenor of his way.'

[I have taken the liberty of changing Gray's plural into the singular for this occasion.]

An Assortment of Aunts

Because my mother and father were equally at home and at ease with the down-at-heel and the well-heeled, the earthy or the aesthetic, and did not presume to criticise or patronise their fellow men, they were both highly respected and loved.

Consequently, we had an abundance of *aunts*. There were, of course, those aunts we inherited and those we adopted or accumulated. The inherited aunts tended to be cosy, rural and wide-hipped; the adopted aunts (called AA for short) were drawn towards my mother, and she to them, through the magnetic passions of socialism, suffragism, education, music, literature, theosophy and the freedom of India. The inherited aunts brought presents of butter, cream, eggs, cakes and crocheted d'oyleys. The adopted aunts brought books, journals, Pre-Raphaelite prints, song sheets and mind-jerking word games like Lexicon and Kan-U-Go.

All of them gossiped; the inherited aunts of cakes, clothes, curates and courtship; the adopted aunts of free trade, free love, free verse, Fabians and fraternité.

As there were four Aunt Annies in the Hyde family, each one was called by her surname: Aunt Annie Andrew, Aunt Annie Swann, Aunt Annie Danby and my mother — Aunt Annie Hyde, who all were aunts to about twenty nephews and nieces. The other inherited aunts were a mixed bag: Auntie Bep, Aunt Selina, Aunt Alice, Auntie Florrie, Auntie Lizzie, Aunt Charlotte and Aunt Maggie. Two of these will not come on the scene until the farm chapter, but Aunt Charlotte and Aunt Maggie, two idiosyncratic spinsters, you will meet very soon.

Aunt Hannah needs to be put apart from the rest although through marriage she was — one could have wished otherwise — one of the family.

There were one or two others on the Hyde side who never quite surfaced and were rarely mentioned; I suspect that they were outlawed for some carnal cropper discreetly hushed behind the 'not-in-front-of-the-children' screen.

Aunt Carrie and Aunt Annie Lloyd

We saw Auntie Carrie and her sister Annie nearly every day as they lived in one of the towered houses which flanked the entrance to Morritt Avenue.

Carrie had a conspiratorial sense of fun, an infectious chuckle and had all the nonsense verse of Lear, Belloc, Carroll and W S Gilbert and other quirky writers at the tip of her neatly-controlled tongue.

But it was Annie who bathed our grazed knees, found us new shoelaces, wiped tears away after her Bible reading of Joseph-thrown-into-the-Pit. It was Annie who ushered us into the bathroom and gave each of us a crisply ironed linen guest towel for our grubby hands. It was Annie whom we once found crying while she was picking raspberries in the spinster-cherished garden.

Carrie's beauty to me was in the exquisite pattern she made with her lips and her crystal-clear eyes. Whether it was in light-hearted gossip, racy rhymes, profound or magical poetry or her spell-binding stories, she was a magnet. We were her 'best-beloveds' in the *Just So Stories* (which, through requests for repetition, we knew off-by-heart) we, with her, went to sea in a sieve, gyred and gimbled in the wabe, went up the airy mountain, down the rushy glen and pushed back tears on:

She lived unknown, and few could know
When Lucy ceased to be
But she is in her grave and oh,
The difference to me!

I remember the lovely and loving three grace notes on dĭffĕrĕnce and how she sustained long smooth breves for the iambic stresses in:

I wìsh I wère where Hèlen lìès

The whole *Golden Staircase* and *Golden Treasury* were known by us through her, for, like Walter de la Mare's *Martha:*

Her small dark lovely head
Seemed half the meaning
Of the words she said

Aunt Carrie

Little did I think that forty years on I was to hear first-hand, during our round table tea-talk in Twickenham, de la Mare's own appreciation of his *Martha* and share experiences of unforgettable 'spell-binders' including the spells cast by W J himself.

The frustration now is that a few lines of some crazy catchy verse will come into my mind — with no apparent association of ideas — and pester me until I've found the rest of the verses, a pursuit which tends to draw in other well-versed ageing friends. Why — never having said or heard such a verse for over 70 years — should Aunt Carrie's *bel canto* voice be heard again saying:

The gingham dog and the calico cat
Side by side on the table sat
'Twas half-past twelve and what do you think?
Nor one nor t'other had slept a wink

And yet I could not remember one line more nor the name of the author. By some strange synchronisity, the phrase 'calico cat' had been teasing the memory of my friend Moyra Platts — another octogenarian whose frustration ended with her enquiry through *This England* resulting in 136 copies and the author's name, Eugene O'Field, dropping through her letterbox for over two years!

How amused and amazed Aunt Carrie would be to know that her round-the-fire or bedside stories and poems have been relayed through the generations and that *The Old Woman who lived in a Vinegar Bottle; Epaminondas* and *Little Black Sambo* have been told over and over again into my grand-daughter's eager ears.

Children lose track of their childhood as the adults do of theirs but we were agog when Carrie announced that she was to *marry* and that we were to have, for so it turned out, a very jolly Uncle Jack. The 'grapevine' running in and out of the houses of The Avenue never had so much gossip, for Aunt Carrie was at the age in that period to be dubbed 'on the shelf'.

What we children were shielded from was Annie's hurt for she and her sister had lived all their lives in the family house inseparable through childhood, adolescence and their spinster-teacher careers. And now Carrie was to share her bed with a *man* in their family house!

Such things were not talked about in front of children but in my research for this book I discovered that, not long after Carrie's marriage, Annie was certified insane and committed to Menston Asylum. Did anyone ever think that she, who was so fastidious and well-read, would be wearing the sacklike uniform of that grim asylum for 20 years, and that she would be buried there?

All I recall was overhearing my mother whispering to my father — 'I always take Annie a new Swiss lawn handkerchief; that is all she asks for. She tries to keep it but as she is not allowed to have anything of her own it is swept up into the communal laundry and never seen again. She's asked me to bring Browning's poems to read to her (there is nothing wrong with her brain) but how can you say *How good is man's life* ... to someone in Menston? Of course I'm not allowed to leave the book with her ...'

There is much more to this tragic story but if it is to be told it cannot be in the recall of an innocent Yorkshire childhood.

Auntie May Hutton

We children never met our Auntie May Hutton; she lived in Devonshire — a distant land as far as we were concerned. All the close bonding with her was through the post; I suspect that my mother never pressed her to come and stay, thinking that our noisy, servant-less, somewhat haphazard house would not be her scene.

Auntie May like many of her generation was an inspired letter writer. Deep affection, indeed many-splendoured love, was shared between my mother: 'Swallow' and May Hutton: 'Brer Rabbit.' From their college days together and through the rest of their lives, they dove-tailed in their ideas and joys, and we, because Auntie May never married, became her children too.

I have only two survivors of the letters written on the paper bearing the purple, white and green motif of the Suffragettes. Yet she wrote every other week.

Beverley House
Chagford, Devon
23rd December, 1913

Dear Swallow

Here's wishing you all a happy Christmas and prosperous New Year. I had to send to town for the things, as there is nothing here, and I haven't been over to Paignton or Torquay as Her Majesty is in the Riviera for the winter. I usually stay with her a bit about this time. I think the sweet shop must have got squashed coming because Owen's are usually very careful. I do so hate having things that look as if they had "had a past" like the mysterious lady in the melodramas. Give the one who gets that the box of chocolate or something else as well. I wouldn't send it, but I know children like messing about with such toys.

I have sent to my bookseller (hem!) to post you on a book you will, I hope, like if you haven't read it. If you have, send it back and I can find you something else "spicy".

I am sorry you didn't get over this summer, but I expect you to let me know, when you have an opportunity; let me know at once. If April is fine Chagford is beautiful from April to end of October. Of course in any rainy month it is "demd damp, moist, unpleasant"; still I think it is beautiful then, but you can't get out. You can see a range of tors from our garden, beginning with Cawsand Beacon. I think Swallow (I don't like bragging) but I rather think you will gasp when you see that there view!

As for your clothes, it don't matter. We are not overburdened with "Chagford chuckies" as callers, and our friends who come over from Paignton don't care twopence what you have on, but they jolly soon find out what you keep inside. I should never under any circumstances be anything but proud of you.

Many thanks for paper, and letter; it was very interesting. I wish all our women were out of prison; things couldn't be worse than they are now. I do wish it were all over.

With best love to you all, and best wishes for a happy time.

I am, Swallow dear,
Always yours
Brer Rab

My mother's long looked-forward-to visit to Chagford and the tales she told on her return made us able to boast to our friends of our familiarity with Devonshire, true though it was that we only knew it through blurred sepia snapshots and my mother's clarity as a rapporteur. Little did we realise then the apprehension she felt as she prepared for her visit.

The reference to the Queen also made my mother think that the confidence and security established in their mutual heart-to-heart, mind-to-mind correspondence might shrivel a little in the formal light of the social round. These women could never have behaved pettily, sharing as they did the agonies of their friends and colleagues in the cause of Votes for Women.

Auntie May writes on the Suffragette writing paper:

> *'Elsie Howey is in prison again. I am so sorry Elsie got caught; they are always so horrid to her in prison. She is one of those people (especially aggravating to the elementary specimens who officer such places as prisons) who possesses an inviolate calm which nothing can disturb or even touch. They, these officials, feel instinctively that she possesses some strange power which baffles them, and so ---- well you know how such are treated in this world.'*

Deep loving friendships existed in those days with regular exchange of long letters between women of like minds.

It was customary too for girl-friends and sisters to share beds. Except in our dormitory on the top floor — where we had three school type iron bedsteads — all five bedrooms had double beds. This was as true in stately houses as it was in cottages. Twin-beds were a nineteen-thirties innovation stemming from the Heals & Gordon Russells return to natural wood and the reaction, but understandable, clearing out of Victoriana by the avant garde.

Bedded together as girls were it never occurred to anyone to use the taboo word 'lesbian'. I had picked it up in print in my very late teens through illicit reading. We never *said* the word. In our mini-media a 'lesbian' was as remote as a cyclops!

Although Yorkshire folk had a chauvinistic way of writing off 'The South' and an assumption that everywhere south of the Humber was not 'real England', they were when I was young a little in awe of 'Southerners'. We endowed Auntie May with a halo of glamour because she lived in Devonshire in a house which could look over the moors to 'Widdecombe' — (another name to conjure with because we were on singing terms with Uncle Tom Cobley) a house which ran on oiled wheels: smooth running made possible by the presence of staff and the absence of children. As holidays for us were always within range of Scarborough, Filey or Bridlington, the very word 'Devonshire' was as exotic as far Arabia and as romantic as Illyria. The song *Glorious Devon* was a favourite in our round-the-piano repertoire, and we sang it with idolatrous fervour and vicarious pride, an unusual gesture for folk born and bred in Yorkshire:

'Devon's the fount of the bravest blood
That braces England's breed,
Her maidens fair as the apple bud,
And her men are men indeed.'

Auntie May had a genius for choosing and sending, exactly at the right time, gifts for five children whom she only knew through photographs and my mother's vignettes. She never sent dolls or frilly clothes but rather games and books which demanded some enterprise and effort on our part. One hefty Christmas book, I remember, was called *Boxville* — crammed with ideas, plans, measurements and instructions for making a whole village out of cardboard boxes. It really only needed intelligence and glue to construct it and space to leave it set out in all its evolutionary progress. The ingenuity came in the latter stages when we pinched anything we could find from the kitchen or the garden to give it life; lentils thrown on to a glued roof made passable pantiles; dried sage or thyme for the lawns and garden paths; cut up loofah — pinched from the bathroom — for trees; silver paper from our Doncaster butterscotch for pools and streams; coarse oatmeal for the ploughed fields; butter beans for cobbled yards; brown sugar for sandy roads and hay for straw-thatching.

All this happened in the middle attic which was our playroom. Nobody was concerned if we were sticky or had patches of paint on our hands and faces. We had freedom to make mistakes, freedom to argue about possessions and achievements, freedom to use up every bit of our physical energy.

Auntie May never saw the results of her very practical child psychology, but we never needed a child guidance clinic!

And then it was Easter when she sent books rather than eggs; splendidly tough hard-backed and illustrated volumes — now collectors' pieces: *Secret Garden, Water Babies, Robinson Crusoe, Treasure Island, Peacock Pie, Uncle Remus, Uncle Tom's Cabin* — over the years a whole world of reading.

Another Auntie May present which kept me busy for weeks, and which taught me quite a lot about foreground, middle distance and background in landscape drawing, was a shadowy stencil picture-making outfit. Trees, hills, fields and mountains took shape and relative prominence according to the pressure one made with a dry sponge charged with powder from a charcoal block. These impressive pictures, ranging from deepest clerical grey to misty white, were then framed with black passe-partout and given to long-suffering and tactful aunts and uncles as presents. Where they put them after their kindly comments I don't know, but everyone in those days subscribed to the idea that presents — even from adults — should be home-made.

Of course we wrote formal little letters of thanks to our aunt, but none of us had the words to tell her — nor did we even know until adult hind-sight sharpened our sensibilities — that she gave us far more than could ever be contained in a brown paper parcel.

Auntie Annie Swann

Somewhere, somehow, and with someone, Auntie Annie (who was my father's cousin and a 'Hyde') had changed her name to 'Swann' but we children never heard much about her husband Frank or any other male in her very self-contained life. To call her a 'widow' would have diminished her and she was far too spirited to cling to her daughter. She had been, after all, a Matron of a hospital.

Like Auntie May there was a certain aura about her as she also came from 'The South' — indeed from Worthing, which became a joke word long before we met Miss Prism in *The Importance of Being Earnest.*

Once a year Aunt Annie Swann came to stay, and perfumed the whole house with Yardley's Old English Lavender Water, Houbigant face powder and Bourjois rouge. Whether it was natural good health or good humour or sheer artifice, Auntie Annie Swann always emerged looking like a cheerful cherub. Her strawberries and cream skin — pearly grey marcel-waved hair, topped by a purple velvet bow like a kingfisher poised for flight — her rustling silk ruched dresses of lavender or purple — her lavender sprinkled lacy handkerchieves — did not quite equate with the *Sporting Pink,* which was her newspaper.

Suspended from her silver chatelaine belt was a huge pocket purse of the same silk as her dress, in which she kept her silver flask of brandy, her crystal bottle of violet coloured smelling salts and a hard-backed, glossy black note book and its corded pencil.

This secret note book and the *Sporting Pink* utterly engrossed her until about 11 o'clock when, having made detailed notes on 'form', she put on her elaborate hat, decisively jabbed two long hat pins into the crown, put on her cape, pulled and stroked her many-buttoned kid gloves, and set off for her 'constitutional'. I think her 'health-walks' — though we never questioned her whereabouts, nor were we invited to accompany her — were to get to the nearest telephone or the nearest bookie. When the glow in her cheeks went beyond the Bouriois rouge, then we could be pretty sure that she had backed a winner!

The removal of hat and gloves was a private matter carried out with decorum in the intimacy of her bedroom; she then regally descended the stairs and, returning to her upright chair, sat perfectly vertical and nodded off, only altering the angle of the purple velvet bow on the top of her head. Perhaps the twitchy smile and the flickered eyes came from a dream where her chosen filly galloped past the winning post of the St. Leger!

Were the forty winks the result of a secret swig from her brandy flask when the long kid gloves had been removed? I like to think that the cognac was not just a medicine, but a consolation for disaster and a celebration for her triumphs.

A residue of my father's Methodist upbringing was that we were not allowed to play gambling games likes Snakes and Ladders or Ludo on a Sunday. Auntie Annie Swann had no such Calvinistic inhibitions so when she stayed with us the rule was waived and she became our ally.

I think all the cheery gods were on her side as she managed with her deft hand to throw up more 'sixes' than any of us and seemed to alight at the foot of a ladder rather than slither down a snake. She was invariably first to get rid of all her dominoes, too, matching the white dots like a magnificent bird of prey. We didn't mind her incredible luck because, as soon as the game was over, she dived down into her poacher's pocket, pulled out a poke of black and white striped humbugs, and chuckled, 'Goodies for losers!' What splendid child psychology!

Even now, if I see a game of snakes and ladders, my nose tingles to the memory of Auntie Annie Swann's cognac and lavender which, for a week or so every year, gave our Wright's-coal-tar plain-living-high-thinking home a sumptuous ambience.

Post Script

My sister Betsy, who died in 1989, kept in touch with the aunts far more faithfully than I ever did. When sorting out her papers I found these verses written, I should think, about 1930:

A Swann Song at Christmas

'What can I give dear Aunt Annie Swann?
(The rest of my presents are posted and gone)
I've given her scarves and slippers and mittens,
Toys for her budgie and bows for her kittens.
She looks so benign with her fine silver tresses,
Old lace and lavender, purple silk dresses;
I wish I could give her something to treasure,
Brandy perhaps? Would that give her pleasure?

Oh now I remember, I once went to tea
When she had the radio on for Aintree,
And gentle Aunt Annie had nothing to say
'Til racing was over on Grand National Day.
And so, dear Aunt Annie, I'm now sending you
A token for Sporting Pink, all the year through.
So pick out the winners; let 'Pink' be your mascot
For Cheltenham, Newmarket, Aintree and Ascot!'

Aunt Hannah Wainwright

The Wainwrights had a tradition of good stock farming going back for centuries and I am indebted to Don Bramley of South Milford for having tape recorded my cousin Walter Wainwright, aged 86 in 1974, talking about Hall Garth Farm and the other of the 30 farms in and around Sherburn-in-Elmet in what Don describes as the 'good old days'. Walter was a lively raconteur who appreciated not only good husbandry but the ancient history of Sherburn as part of the Kingdom of Elmet.

In his book: *Fragment of Local History* Don recalls that the village centre was once 'Sherburn Boys' Endowed School' founded and endowed by Robert Hengate in

1619. Readers of *Pepys' Diary* may recall that Pepys called at the school on his way to York in 1623. But it is Sherburn Church — handsome and decorative — that dominates the village and the country round, standing strikingly pale silver grey, high up on its own green hill.

Aunt Hannah, Walter's mother, was a harridan She of course was inherited; we would never have chosen her for adoption.

She ran my uncle's farm in the West Riding, in the village of Sherburn in Elmet where my mother was born, with a tight-lipped grudge.

Visitors were rarely taken beyond the kitchen to the parlour, a room with an uninviting smell of Sunlight soap, mothballs and the family Bible. Aunt Hannah certainly did not create an atmosphere in which 'parleying' could flourish and any conversation she had was stingy and for adults only. Children were always targets for her barbed comments for they were always in the wrong: 'Can't you see the floor's just been scrubbed?' was a typical greeting after we arrived having walked several miles of the 20 mile journey.

Through constant nagging, mistrust and penny-pinching, the red of her lips had totally disappeared; in its place a hard straight line curved downwards at each corner like a portcullis through which affection and humour could never pass.

Aunt Hannah conducted a non-stop battle against dirt, and kept her willing and warm-hearted daughter, Blanche, no doubt significantly christened, and her little scullery maid, Lizzie, constantly scrubbing and scouring. Steps, window sills, gates, pillars, flag-stones — even the water-trough with the pump — were all scrubbed and whitened. Every churn, jug, bottle, teapot and cup was 'scalded', even though every drop of water had to be boiled on the kitchen range or in the copper kettle on the hob. Red-tiled floors were scrubbed every day then covered with newspaper, only removed when the maid's hessian aprons were changed for white afternoon 'pinnies'. Carpets, rugs and mats were hung up on the miles of clothes line fastened to the trees in the orchard and mercilessly attacked with a cane carpet-beater — a weapon which served the dual purpose as a 'walloper' for children. The 'living-in' farm men didn't risk Hannah's tongue, and meekly got rid of their mucky clothes and boots in the wash-house before daring to set foot on the kitchen floor.

Any villager who dropped below Aunt Hannah's unforgiving standards was tartly written off: 'How she's got the face to go to church with all those clarty pots in the sink, I don't know.' Cleanliness was not just next to godliness, it took precedence. I can think of only one hymn which might have parted Hannah's tight lips into song:

> 'Whiter than snow, whiter than snow;
> Wash me and I shall be
> Whiter than snow!'

Why my mother should ever have sent us to Aunt Hannah for a *holiday* I shall never know — but 'sent' we were. We carried a strange piece of luggage — a Japanese hamper: a large oblong box of soft straw with another box of similar, but fractionally larger, size which fitted right over it. Thus it could be clamped down or raised up according to the needs of the number travelling. On that particular day it was well down as it only had to hold the skimpy summer wardrobe of two little girls, aged ten and eight. Though not heavy, it was a clumsy piece of luggage, and I remember how scratched our legs were by the time we had walked the three quarters of a mile to the station.

We found a third class 'Ladies Only' compartment with a 'lady' in it (for that was always the instruction) and sat on the edge of the seat, hands on the basket ready to get out at each station, though we had memorised the sequence of stations before we left home. I suppose the journey was *not* more than eighteen miles, but infinite to us. 'Mind you behave yourselves!' called out the ticket collector with a grin after he'd told us the way to the farm. We didn't realise then that everyone in the village had Aunt Hannah weighed up and that he was not the only one feeling very sorry for the two little Hyde girls.

Hot, sticky and scratched after the walk from the station, we stood in awe on the whitened doorstep: 'So you've come then,' Aunt Hannah said with a flat West Riding snap. We followed her in silence up the back staircase (the front staircase was kept polished up for 'best') and into the large, low-ceilinged bedroom, crisply cool with its frosty white basin and jug on a pale grey marble wash-stand and white counterpane on a huge high brass bed. What was the composite smell? White Windsor, white linen, white mothballs, white shelf paper, dark green oilcloth and rag rugs? Children cannot analyse atmosphere, but, looking back, it would seem that such a room could never have known passion, conception, birth. Death more likely. Yes, it was a room in which an undertaker would feel professionally at home. 'Get your things unpacked,' Aunt Hannah snapped.

She took out our beautifully laundered white cambric dresses and longsleeved cotton nighties which my mother had ironed and goffered with such care and shook them out with a sniff. 'Not what I call white, but what can you expect living near Leeds. '

Within ten minutes of meeting her, and with not many more words, she had demolished our family, our home and our confidence. 'I suppose you'll be wanting some tea,' she said grudgingly, after which it was a surprise to find lavishly buttered bread on plates with linen d'oyleys, big brown eggs and deep apple pie and cream. 'You'd better get to bed before the daylight goes; I couldn't trust you two with candles.' So in the dimming light in the clean cold bedroom, we stood at the wash-stand having a token face, neck and hands wash, and climbed up into the big brass feather bed. 'And don't be late up! It's market day,' was her loveless good-night.

The *God is Love* text over the bed neither convinced nor comforted us; we just counted the strokes of the village church clock as if each was a knell of doom. Next day it was a great relief when Aunt Hannah with her husband, and the wagoner, and little skivvy 'under orders' packed the wagonette with the trays of eggs and the freshly churned butter and drove off to market. Without her the farm revealed its delights, not least the stack-yard, which came right up to the back door. We peered into shippens, stables, granaries and dairies, and drank in the strong nose-tingling farm smells, then into the orchard and hoisted ourselves up a gnarled apple tree and came down clutching sharp green ridged Keswicks. (Where have all the English apples gone? Why are all the apples we buy now the shape and size of the blue trays?)

Crunching the apples, we returned to the yard near the house and leaned against the haystack, reducing those apples to the barest core, the juice running down our chins and on to our white 'pinnies'. 'See who can throw their core on to the top of the stack!' Of course Betsy did; I didn't. 'Look, there's a ladder on that side; let's climb up.' Then we remembered that Aunt Hannah had left our dinner with the farm men's on the long deal table in the kitchen. 'Let's take it up to the stack and have a picnic.' Not easy to carry plates of bacon-and-egg pie and rhubarb and custard up a ladder, but in two goes each, up and down the ladder, we did.

The sun had been there before us and made a kindly hollow of comforting warm hay. We forgot our homesickness, feeling a little cherished at last. Not one crumb of food nor drop of juice was left from that secret feast, and after a few minutes of 'I Spy', the hay smell and the afternoon sun drugged us to sleep. I do not remember how long we slept; what I do remember with sickening recall was a screech which pierced into our ears and paralysed us. 'What the hell are you brats doing up there? — I'll teach you! ' Without another word, still wearing her bonnet and cape, Aunt Hannah strode off to the shippen where the huge black bull was chained. Dragging the snorting rearing animal, the chain clanking on the cobble stones, she finally tethered him to a post only a yard or two from the stack.

In aggressive silence, her fist clenched menacingly towards us, Aunt Hannah stormed off into the house and banged the door with a finality that shut us out forever.

Round and round that haystack, to the end of its tether, the bull raved and butted, while we clutched one another. We could hear both our hearts like twin drums. The hay which had glowed and comforted us seemed chilly now, damp and prickly. Even the sun had abandoned us. We were totally alone in a dark cold circle of paralysing fear.

It seemed the middle of the night, but it was only about eight o'clock, I think, when we heard our uncle's voice arguing with Aunt Hannah's malevolent screeching. Ranting on, she followed him to the back door and rasped out, 'Well, you get the brats down and pack them off to bed — no food for those two little devils.' I think Uncle Will would have liked to have dealt with us more kindly, but he, poor man, had been conditioned over many years to accept that his wife always had the last word.

So without a glance toward our aunt, we went candle-less to bed without tea, without supper — without love.

[Children's judgements of adults tend to be based on one or two memorable incidents; I am assured by a Wainwright first cousin that Aunt Hannah mellowed with age into a rather sad and kind old lady.]

In a dark cold circle of paralysing fear.

The next day was the village spectacle of a Wainwright pig-killing, a regular occurrence to keep the Wainwright butcher shops in Sherburn well stocked. So horrific is that memory that I have tried to seal it away — the hanging of the squealing pig, the naked belly, the swinging and crunch of the axe, the long bloody split spewing out the entrails and the unearthly shriek ... I ran back to the house sobbing, hands over ears and eyes, leaving the gang of men and boys gloating.

There was no comfort in the cold white counterpane in which I buried my head. 'Was there a God for pigs?' I wondered as I looked up at the text over the bed. 'What was He doing to let this happen?'

Tea-time brought no more comfort. 'What's all that blabbing for?' 'Why haven't you eaten your pork pie?' Aunt Hannah's mammoth masterpiece dominated the table.

Later I understood why mother (born a Wainwright) had two diet codes: a meat-eating one for all the farming fraternity of the West and East Ridings and a meat-less one for her theosophical and anthroposophical friends.

I must not leave you with an unfair picture of the Wainwrights of Sherburn for Blanche, Aunt Hannah's daughter, was a buxom plump-cheeked young woman filled out with laughter. She was generous, motherly and capable, often taking on the role of nannying her younger cousins. It was understandable that she visited our free and easy home far more often than we visited hers and, having lived a restricted rural life, she enjoyed being a conspiring ally in taking us on jaunts to Leeds. There

Three Wainwright cousins visiting us in their splendid hats.

we often met and visited our other Wainwright cousins in Leeds. Amy and Anne Wainwright, more quietly behaved than the Hydes, were as talented as they were good-looking and added much to the musical life of our family.

Amy was hauntingly beautiful with gleaming dark hair, delicate complexion and features, deep blue twinkling eyes and long dark lashes. It was she who summed up for me the ephemeral word: *beauty* — a foil for my plainness. Her unforced resonant voice echoed her gentleness and she relaxed warmly into genuine listening. Her piano accompanying for her sister, Annie, playing the violin, was lovingly unintrusive. Annie, more complex and enigmatic, played like an angel but I did not hear her public playing until I worked in Manchester and went regularly to the Hallé. I was mesmerised by her fingering. The only irritant was my mother's constant comparison of the amateur efforts of her untalented daughters!

But by now we were all grown up and it was time to forget our mother's oblique criticisms and realise that perhaps when we were not there she had praised us with equal fervour.

Aunt Charlotte

Charlotte, my mother's sister, had never married but she never let us forget the suitors whom she had turned down — or so, with repetition, had she convinced herself.

My mother sitting between Lizzie & Charlotte

Spinster aunts — since few had been trained for any career — were always on call to mind the house, look after the children, feed the cats, water the plants, attend funerals, visit hospitals, act as midwives, have the children to stay in the holidays, and deliver the parish magazine. Aunt Charlotte did all those things and many more from her strategic little cottage in the High Street of Sherburn-in-Elmet.

Now that we were all in the second or third stage of our schooling, my mother wanted to return to teaching, not only to earn some money to help to pay for our higher education, but, I think, just as pressingly, to unshackle herself from domestic chores. She had, after all, done it for eighteen years.

She schemed with Aunt Charlotte to join the family as our housekeeper, as their mother, my grandmother, had died leaving Aunt Charlotte free for the first time in her life.

I remember my maternal grandmother only vaguely as looking like the portrait of Whistler's mother: tall, thin and gaunt, serene and austere, sitting in a straight-backed upright chair, summoning her daughter with a rap of her tall stick. Many years after Grandma died mother told us without emotion or self-pity a horrific incident in her young life.

Grandma Wainwright's black-bonnetted church-going did not seem to prescribe, 'life more abundantly' but rather a liturgy of, 'thou shalt nots'. Although not a professional singer my mother sang with radiant accomplishment and received invitations to give recitals, not only in Yorkshire, but in historic houses in Scotland.

One night when she was giving a song-recital in the prestigious Queen's Hotel in Leeds, her mother hearing that she was singing in a *public house* summoned the farm-labourer groom to accompany her on the train from Sherburn in Elmet to Leeds. As in her book, no gentlewoman should ever be seen in licensed premises, she ordered the groom to go straight into the music salon and bring out the young mistress at once. The beautiful innocent nineteen-year-old girl was dragged out to the station where my grandmother had waited. The three travelled the twenty miles back to Sherburn in the thunderous silence of the conspiring train.

After my grandfather died, and some time before I was born, my grandmother and Aunt Charlotte settled themselves into a little end-of-terrace stone cottage which shared a high stone wall with the village school playground. 'Will yer throw us t'ball back?' a faceless voice would shout from the playground side of the wall, and I with my yard-length body and my half-yard-length arm would try to pitch the ball eight feet high. Those aborted efforts should have forewarned me that ball games were never going to be my forte!

Of course Aunt Charlotte groused when the balls knocked her lettuces and pea-sticks down, for her burgeoning little garden was her pride and joy. There were regulated rows of aspiring raspberry canes and unregulated stragglers on the ground of hide-and-seek strawberries; there were holly-hocks trying to look over the playground wall and camomile clinging to the ground; there were night-scented stocks and day-scented pinks and bulging onions which looked as if they didn't quite know whether to stay in the basement or go up to the ground floor. And she, a bonny russet-cheeked country lass, made gallipots of raspberry, strawberry, gooseberry and rhubarb jam. Oh, those heady smells from the frothing scum in the big brass pan and the testing spoonful of jam shrinking and stiffening on the saucer to say 'Ready!' She waxed papers to put over her bottles of wine-sour plums (a Sherburn speciality) and kept a trio of demi-johns corked against the ooze of her sloe gin and elder-flower wine.

Of course she knew, and was liked by, everyone in the village, and it was more than likely if you stopped to chat and were asked to stay for tea that the jam on your bread or in a sponge cake had come, so they would tell you, 'from Charlotte'. It was through Aunt Charlotte that we acquired Lizzie, a girl from the village, who became the only resident maid we ever had and who stayed with us in the Avenue for many years. It was Lizzie who brought the three of us (Nancy, Betsy and Coidy) to stay with Aunt Charlotte to sleep in the heavily scrolled mahogany bed, big enough for three. When Lizzie had finished 'seeing us in' her mother called to ask if there was anything we needed and said: 'Why not let the littlest bairn come to us?' And so it was that I became 'the proudest tiger in the jungle' selected by Lizzie's mother and given a room of my own in their friendly little cottage near the church. There in the tiny bedroom with pink roses peeping in through the dormer window was a two foot wide bed tucked under the sloping roof, which I knew my head would almost touch when I sat up. The walls, ceiling and even the across-the-corners cupboards were all neatly covered with wallpaper festooned with pink roses, blue bows and grey trellis. It was a perfect little hat-box. I felt like David Copperfield when he saw Peggoty's upturned barge:

> 'If it had been Aladdin's palace, roc's egg and all, I suppose I could not have been more charmed with the romantic idea of living in it. '

I, who was so easily homesick, felt comforted in that neat little box because it was just the right size for a small girl with big fears, and Lizzie seemed permanent and protective.

Lizzie had learned a lot from her mother and my Aunt Charlotte; all those really valuable things they never taught at school like lighting fires, making spills out of newspapers, melting the candle-ends down to make new ones, toasting tea-cakes at the kitchen fire, pouring the dripping out of the roasting tins and leaving just enough to make the big square Yorkshire puddings crisp and shiny brown on the outside and light, deep and airy in the middle. Aunt Charlotte brought all those delicious country ways with her when she came to live with us in 'The Avenue' — or so we thought.

It had not really dawned on us that our country aunt would be drawn to the city as the tide is drawn by the moon. She loved the new electric lights, the clanging trams, the shop windows, the myriad sounds of the criers, the drapers' stores where the money-to-pay and the money-for-change was shot along the wires high above the counters to and from the counting house. Within a few weeks — when country timidity had been exchanged for urban jauntiness — she was on nodding and name terms with all the local shopkeepers, and had worked out exactly how to get her best two penn'orth going into Leeds by tram and how to make her money go a long way at Marks & Spencer's (no longer a penny bazaar).

Her real undoing — or 'doing' if one is measuring evolution with the yardstick of liberation — was her discovery that peaches, apricots, pineapples and pears could be bought in *tins.* From then on the tin-opener became her friend and her secret weapon.

Like all the country folk of that period she had been brought up to believe that there was something feckless — even immoral — about buying things 'ready-made', but I think she revelled in cocking-a-snook at the maxims of her thrifty mother and relaxing into towny insouciance.

Much to my father's chagrin her stand-bys became John West's Canadian tinned salmon and Bird's custard. My mother was much too happily occupied with her teaching and her 'isms' to notice that there were no longer any sticky porridge and gruel pans; instead there were big showy packets of 'Shredded Wheat', 'Grape Nuts', and 'Force' which pleased all of us hugely with their pictures, coupons and free gifts. The beef tea, which always had been made from endless boiling of shin bones was now conjured up in seconds with a flip of a teaspoon into the Bovril or Marmite bottles. Oxo cubes — a new experience for Aunt Charlotte — coloured and flavoured gravies and soups.

Not for the liberated Aunt Charlotte the tedium of bread-making. She preferred a little jaunt to the Thrift Stores, the Maypole or the Co-operative bakery where big white crusty loaves could be bought for fourpence wrapped in 'will-do-'til-you-get-home' tissue paper. All in all she became a dab hand at short-cut cooking and baking, and even bought slab-cake instead of making her eggs and butter rich Dundee. Sunk standards indeed!

For my father, brought up round a creaking country table of home-made bread, pies, cakes, buns and pasties, farm-produced meat and vegetables and locally caught fish, Aunt Charlotte's housekeeping was a small fracture in a married life which had started off so romantically and continued so joyously when we were very young.

Yet we owed Aunt Charlotte much. To us she was not an irritation, but FUN — a grown-up with whom we could have the kind of badinage and persiflage not tolerated by other adults. This of course led to appalling disrespect for her which, with mellowed hindsight, I blush to recall. But our aunt's quirky humour and her sprightly spirit absolutely ensured that she could hold her own.

Her spare pepper and salt hair was filled out with 'pieces' which quite often ended up, not on the thinning patch of her crown, but in incongruous places. How Neb our Welsh terrier, managed to get hold of one of these pads we never knew, but Aunt Charlotte's tussle with the 'dratted dog' stretched the hair out from its compact circular shape into flying streamers and made us all take sides, having no shame in wanting Neb to win!

One of Aunt Charlotte's many odd hobbies was making bee-wine. Where she got the original 'bees' from was a mystery, but these floating beads of yeast rising and falling in a bell-jar of water seemed to magnetise her into meditation. She would sit at the kitchen window-sill for hours — or so it seemed — simply mesmerised by the bees' tranquil movement. No one seemed to drink the wine but herself; we much preferred her sharp-and-smooth, sweet-and-sour raspberry vinegar.

Wine-making in Aunt Charlotte's book was not a domestic chore but an adventure, a gamble and a challenge which fitted in well with her new life, especially as we had cellars and attics where bottles could explode without ceilings needing re-painting. Her star turn was rhubarb wine: no laborious picking or stoning, just great thick red stalks which could be brought in armfuls from the garden. All that was needed in preparation was a wash in the flat stone sink to flush away the Leeds grime. (I wonder if it was this carbon which made rhubarb such a prolific plant for five or six miles in and around Leeds?)

At Aunt Charlotte's, wine-making was an adventure.

Then the mangle-rollers were slackened to give the space usually needed for blankets, and one of us would be employed turning the massive mangle wheel while Aunt Charlotte guided the foot-and-a-half long sticks between the rollers. Down the juice fell into the tub below. It was of absolutely no consequence to Aunt Charlotte that, just the day before, our socks, jerseys and woolly knickers had all been shot down into the same tub. The greatest blessings both for her and for us were her salty wit and her waggish fun. She had the Yorkshire country-woman's knack of shrewd economic comment — much harsher and more crude in the West Riding than in the North and East: 'daft as Dick's hat-band', 'daft as a brush', and when thirsty: 'I'm spitting feathers'.

When I was inveigled into 'signing the pledge', joining the Band of Hope and paying for the little white-ribbon enamelled brooch, which was the outward and visible sign of my avowed temperance, Aunt Charlotte entered in her housekeeping book: 'Coidy's beer account ... 2s.6d.'

Anyone who could pour out rhymes, tell dialect stories and mimic the neighbours and relations was a welcome addition to our household, and we children egged her on. Her rather feckless dusting and polishing suited us, too, as it let us off the domestic hook. Although she had scant schooling, she seemed to know all the poetry on which we had been nurtured, but she preferred irreverent parodies. To add to our jumble of church and chapel-going music, she delighted in putting new words to the tunes which all of us had in our memories for ready recall. Her silly lyric to *The Church's One Foundation* was one of the many that she could produce in her breezy, wheezy voice on the slightest cue:

> 'She wears her silk pyjamas in summer when it's hot:
> She wears her flannel nighties in winter when it's not;
> But sometimes in the springtime, and sometimes in the fall,
> She slips between the bed-clothes with nothing on at all.'

Harmless stuff, but not very uplifting!

One of Aunt Charlotte's games, however, took us into adult life, and is still a favourite party game. A first line of a well-known poem (and remember how many *were* well-known) was called out and we all set to work with pencil and paper to write a line to complete it as a rhyming couplet.

Some survivors are:

Scott's: 'Oh Young Lochinvar is come out of the West;
He's travelling north so he'll need a thick vest'

Campion's: 'There is a garden in her face;
No produce yet, but watch this space!'

Wordsworth's: 'I wandered lonely as a cloud;
No wonder I was in my shroud!'

Each evening, when our Mother came home from the loftier and more genteel realms of English Literature in a High School, we had to slip into a higher gear. She quietly steered us into piano practice and homework while, I suppose, dear dotty Aunt Charlotte opened another tin or went with a watchful eye to check her rhubarb wine!

Aunt Annie Andrew

Whenever my Aunt Annie Andrew came into a room a light went on. She sparkled her way through the first few stages of her life: first as an adopted sister of the Hydes at Cockmoor Hall; as a fellow-student of my mother's at Ripon College; as a witty head teacher; as a ravishing bride to the ebullient Percy Smith (a technical school-teacher); as a VAD nurse in the First World War, and most important of all, as the perfect, and most popular aunt. As far as we five children were concerned, we always thought of our Smith Aunt and Uncle as childless but there were hushed references to 'Frank' whom, we gathered, was killed in a motorcycle accident. But this was one of the many taboo subjects — 'Not in front of the children'.

Aunt Annie Andrew

I suppose we profited from her childlessness. Her spirituelle qualities were wasted, I would have thought, on her sensual husband who, even on his modest teaching salary, was more at home with horses and hounds in the field or on the racecourse than with ladies in their drawing rooms.

Aunt Annie Andrew was a joy to the eye and the ear, for like my Aunt Carrie she cast a spell as a story-teller. Whereas I was bewitched with the intricate mobility of Aunt Carrie's lips and the magic of her voice, Aunt Annie Andrew's eyes zig-zagged like lightning, synchronising with her racy speech. She was an irresistible raconteur. Every major or minor incident provided her with a script and she had a shrewd Yorkshire economy in summing people up.

Aunt Annie Andrew as a VAD Nurse in the First World War and as a Teacher in the Twenties.

One day I remember during the Great War she arrived in her VAD uniform with her collecting box, selling flags for the Red Cross. Dabbing tears of laughter from her eyes she reported on her last donor — a neighbour of ours: 'You know, Annie,' she chuckled, 'she wouldn't give you the skin off her rice pudding; she gave me a threepenny bit for her flag and asked for tuppence change!'

Aunt Annie Andrew wore all her clothes with style and epitomised the phrase: 'well turned out'. It was she who nudged my mother into buying a rare new outfit and introduced her to 'the best tailor in Leeds'. She would arrive with a swatch of fine West Riding worsteds: 'Feel this,' she would say, 'that'll never sit out.'

This choosing and handling of West Riding fabrics in the great days of the Yorkshire woollen industry was a characteristic of all men and women who grew up within smoke-distance of Leeds, Bradford and Huddersfield. Even now when I am buying a cloth coat or suit I rub the fabric between my finger and thumb to test its quality. But if I were thoroughly mill-minded and linguistically wedded to the West Riding, I might approve the cloth with a guarded superlative: 'Aye, it'll do.'

Aunt Annie Andrew was the authority in the family on 'costumes' for that was how all suits were described then. These were not bought 'off the peg' but were skilfully created by the Jewish tailors in Leeds, most of them living in the back streets round Sheepscar and Barrack Street. Measuring, fitting and refitting were serious affairs and no Jewish tailor worth his matzo would want to put his skills into inferior fabrics. So the customers chose and bought their worsted, gaberdines, serges and baratheas with eyes and fingers anticipating the judgment of the Solomons,

Jacobs and Samuels who would be transforming the cloth into sculptured costumes.

Like nearly everything else in that age, clothes were made to *last.* The details were impressive: canvas and linen inter linings, dust braid on the edge of skirts, carefully honed bone buttons — sewn on with waxed thread never to drop off — hand sewn hems and revers and heavy silk-satin linings finished off with a label bearing the owner's name or initials. To the one finger-tip length coat two skirts were made — an economic and sensible idea as skirts had to stand (or sit!) more wear and tear than the jacket. These costumes were intended for outside wear — shopping or paying calls. When the women returned home they changed out of their costumes and blouses into a working frock or a tea-gown depending on their social station.

After two or three years of fairly regular wearing when the fabric was losing something of its original pile, the prudent owners had their skirts unpicked, turned and re-made so that the off-side matt surface was now uppermost and ready to face the next sitting.

If I seem to have digressed from my Aunt Annie it is deliberate for she was, as I said, the authority on tailors and tailoring and had a genius for discovering a Weinberg or a Rothenstein, hidden away in a modest little house, who had *haute couture* standards but gave north country value for money.

It was our dear generous cultivated aunt who picked up the cue that books all around us (the Everyman Classics for example), commendable as they were, seemed rather solid for a regular diet. And so she good-naturedly tuned in to our young low brows. What a joy all those outsize glossy hard-backs were: *Chatterbox, Girls' Friend, Rainbow* et al., the Angela Brazils, the Elsie Oxenhams all so toughly bound and backed that they stood the racket of being lent to all our friends or used as valuable swaps.

Aunt Annie's bubbling chatter and prodigal Christmas and birthday gifts lighted up all the years of our childhood, and as she lived only a few miles away we could count on her regular visits. Then, one year, when I was about 16, no Christmas books arrived. The gap which should have been filled by the latest rampageous novels was too big to describe. Depression descended. And there was no Aunt Annie Andrew during the whole Christmas holiday to fill the house with laughter.

A letter to my mother followed in which she wrote with Dickensian exuberance about the death of Great Uncle William; the vast rectory in which he had lived alone for years and the village where he was both Rector and Squire.

Aunt Annie had a ready quotation: writing from William's study she noted: 'where moth and dust doth corrupt' and added: 'everything in the room had stopped, like the watch and the clock, a long time ago.' She swiftly created the scene: the worn Aubusson carpets, the faded tapestries, the pile of stale sermons, the blackened silver, the undisturbed veiling of cobwebs, the dust-sheeted rooms and the dust-covered study.

The Reverend William Smith (nephew of the inventor of the steam plough seemed to be his claim to fame) died intestate and without any close family; thus his nephew,

Percy, whom he barely knew, became the undisputed heir to the estate: a feudal composite of farms, cottages, manor house, rectory and school.

The weight of all these possessions — for neither my uncle nor my aunt had the desire nor the aptitude to become lord and lady of the manor — changed my aunt from a happy-go-lucky generous chatterbox into a worried fretful woman. Gradually the humour sizzled out of her talk and letters. Bitterness seeped in. There were no more presents for the Hyde children.

Pandora's box had not only spilled out riches but suspicion, fear, mistrust and confusion. Uncle Percy's house, cars and cigars became larger, his ties and suits louder, his drinks stronger and longer, his race meetings more frequent and further afield, his gambling more risky, his face coarser, his belly more convex and his nose more incarnadined. He was, we understood from other folk 'good company' but my aunt had always been agreeably husband-free when she visited us.

Years of light-hearted spending from a light purse, and the freedom of spirit which only the unencumbered can know, made dear Aunt Annie Andrew unable to cope with uncovenanted possessions. Her eyes still flickered restlessly but her pulled-down brow and darkened sockets crushed every glance into despair.

Ironically, like their benefactor, Mr and Mrs Percy Smith also died intestate (still in their red brick suburban villa) before they had time or inclination to benefit themselves or to choose their own beneficiaries.

The closest relative was Maggie, Uncle Percy's sister, our maiden aunt whom my uncle had always dismissed with derision.

Fate deals some quirky hands.

No one must have been more surprised than the fanatically frugal Aunt Maggie when she found she was holding every ace card in the pack and had become, in late middle-age, a woman of considerable property.

CHAPTER EIGHT
THE SMITH FARMS AND FORTUNES

A flash-back introducing Aunt Maggie Smith

Before you are introduced to Aunt Maggie and hear how she used the Smith fortune, you must hear of its strange beginnings and Uncle Percy's unexpected inheritance.

In the 16th century the Smiths of Buckinghamshire farmed in Broughton near Newport Pagnell, then the main family home. In 1637 they bought Church Farm at Little Woolstone and much later, in 1882, they acquired land and farms in Egginton.

William Smith, born 1814, was no ordinary farmer, having been totally in charge of his father's other farms at Woughton and Linford at the age of 14! On the death of his father, in 1837, he inherited the ancient family home, Church Farm, and from then on directed his imagination and energy to producing maximum crops from his quite extensive farmlands.

It was typical of Bill Smith's resource and sagacity that he realised how many hundreds of tons of horse manure dropped on to the London streets behind hansom-cabs, carriages and drays. So he arranged that 5 hundred tons of the stuff should be transported on barges every year and be delivered to his own private wharf on the Grand Junction Canal quite near to Linford Lodge, another Smith farm.

Many eminent Victorian engineers were furthering the use of steam power: the railways, the woollen and cotton mills. The mining industries and the potteries were all becoming heavily industralised. William Smith, an independent thinker, had long felt that the plough drawn by horses did more harm than good to the soil. The ploughshares sliced down below the sub-soil and the horses packed the soil into a solid mass which blocked the life-giving action of air and water. In the first place he experimented by designing and creating a 'cultivator' and had these manufactured by James and Frederick Howard. Following this in 1855, he created the Smith steam plough which was manufactured first by Fowlers and then by Howards.

This 'smasher' of Bill Smith's led him into a very stormy life involving him as it did in masses of correspondence and conflicts with the 'establishments'. William's had always been a strong voice in agricultural politics; it was said that when he raised the wages of his farm labourers he ordered other farmers in north Buckinghamshire to do the same. And they did. Later on, however, when his workers thought that these new-fangled machines imperilled their jobs they threatened their employer with destruction of his crops.

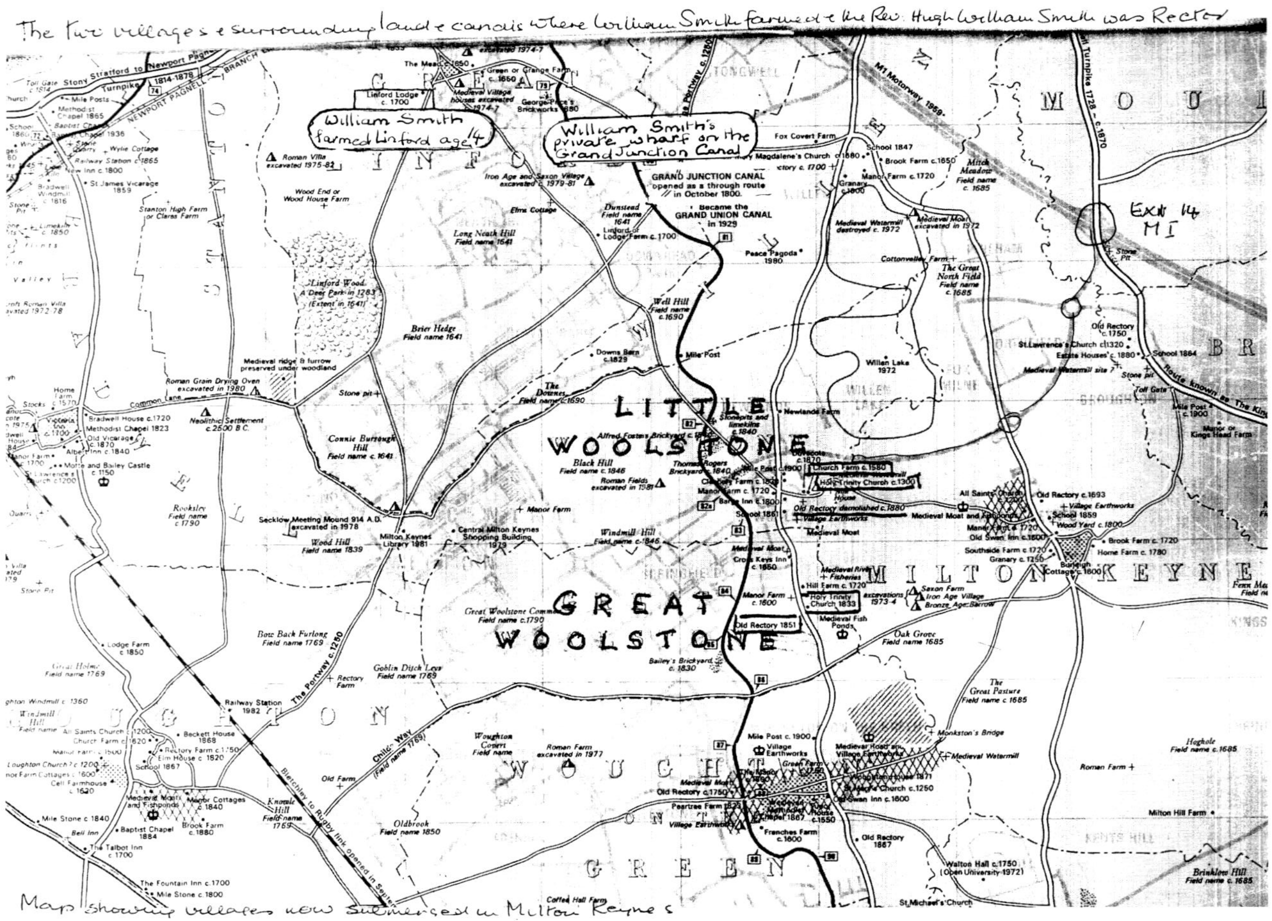

Map showing villages now submerged in Milton Keynes; the three villages where the Smiths farmed for three centuries and the two rectories where the Reverend Hugh William Smith was also the squire.

WILLIAM SMITH'S SYSTEM OF STEAM CULTIVATION.

Engraving showing the steam-plough and cables in action and the four different types of plough which it powered.

William Smith's steam plough displayed in the Rural Museum of Reading University.

Meanwhile, between 1858 and 1862 hundreds of sets of steam ploughs, winding drums and cables were sold and sent all over the British Isles and overseas but not without strife. Cheshire Royal Agricultural Show exhibited one of the ploughs in 1858 but the following year the Salisbury show refused to have the machine demonstrated as, they argued, it was not a plough but a cultivator.

So frustrated and disillusioned did William eventually become that he decided to finish with arable farming forever. To this end he put all his cropland to grass (richer, greener, lusher grass could not be found, fed as the soil had been with London manure) and then he followed this act with a 'curtain' to his final drama. Quietly and secretly he built, almost touching his house, a great mausoleum in which he put his original Fowler plough, winding drum and cables. The machinery was totally entombed for the building had no doors, no windows, no ventilators, no spy-holes. And so it remained, well into the 20th century, for 60 years.

One marvels at the lack of curiosity of the tenant farmers who took over Church Farm that they never probed into nor speculated on what the building was hiding. Not until 1926 did anyone show the slightest curiosity but, when a few bricks crumbled away, the tenant farmer, Mr Heady, broke down one wall of the freakish building. Not realising the historic interest of the machinery, he left the building open to the ravages of air and damp. For 30 years the equipment which William Smith had saved and protected for posterity was corroded with rust. A rescue operation was organised by the new tenant, Mr Griffiths, and, with the roof and walls demolished, William Smith's 'folly' was craned away to be restored and put on show at Bedford in 1958.

Even in his old age William Smith was still a fighter opposing various establishments, not least the Royal Agricultural Society. He died at the age of 86 just at the dawn of the 20th century. His tombstone, almost invisible I am told, in the graveyard at Egginton — 12 miles from his birthplace of Little Woolston, carried this inscription:

> 'In memory of William Smith who died October 17th 1900 aged 86 years also
> Louise Martha his wife who died March 20th 1903 aged 72 years'

A childless couple. His only 'child' the steam plough, is sadly not mentioned, and the weeds and weather have almost obliterated him from memory.

The 300 year old Smith estate, which had increased through Bill Smith's ingenuity and energy, passed to his newphew whose life contrasted greatly with his farming uncle who had left school at fourteen. Hugh William Smith, after graduating at Pembroke College, Cambridge, returned to Woolstone and became the Rector of the two parishes (Little and Great), which had been combined in 1855.

We have little information on Uncle William's bachelor life at the Rectory as I suppose that he and his nephew Percy had little in common, the 'godly' and the 'ungodly' rarely meeting.

On the morning of Wednesday, 16 December 1926, when the Reverend William Smith was being driven by his groom, Henry Lee, a motor-car caused the pony to shy and to throw the Rector on to the kerb, resulting in fatal head injuries.

Church Farm. The Smith family resided there since 1637.

The Rectory at Woolston, Buckinghamshire. Home of Rev. William Smith until he died in 1926. (Photograph 1991, author on garden seat.)

Ironically it was his nephew, my uncle (William Clarence Henry Smith — known as 'Percy') who was summoned to come from Leeds to the hospital at Newport Pagnell to identify the body. Hundreds of parishoners, villagers and farmers of North Buckinghamshire could have done this with sincerity and sorrow but blood, when it comes to inheritance, has its own powerful osmosis, and Uncle Percy, therefore, became the sole beneficiary, inheriting not only a substantial part of the two villages, but farms well beyond.

The headmaster of the tough Junior Technical School in Leeds quickly resigned his job and, with no inclination to live the life of a country squire, was quite content to let his wife, our dear Auntie Annie Andrew, wear herself out clearing up and disposing of hundreds of years of accumulated treasures, jumble and junk.

Aunt Maggie Smith

Whereas Auntie Annie Andrew's eyes flashed and whirled like strobe lighting, Aunt Maggie's small black-boot-button eyes were continually blinkered by the hen-like movement of her eyelids. So often had the lids flicked up and down that her eyelashes had either popped off or were cropped to the roots.

Maggie aged nine collected rents from her lawyer father's and grandmother's grim properties in the mining town of Swadlincote.

Mostly one would describe unmarried aunts as 'maiden' aunts but this was too gentle a title for Maggie, christened Frances Louisa, who could more properly be described as a spinster aunt. She was designed from the top of her tightly netted hair to the tips of her black-button boots to be impregnable.

It was from the Smiths' house in Roundhay, Leeds, that Maggie visited us and it is only in the last years that I discovered her strange upbringing in the mining town of Swadlincote in the East Midlands — a place utterly unconnected with any of the contemporary members of our family. Her father, we are told, was known in Swad–lincote as 'Lawyer Smith' but never practised. He evidently lived on the income from rents from various small properties.

Why Maggie rejected — or was rejected by — her own immediate family we do not know, but as her mother died when Maggie was four she was adopted by her maternal Grandmother Lacey. The old lady and the young girl became utterly dependent on one another. Grandmother Lacey, like Maggie's father, also seemed to own some depressing property in the clay and coal mining town, and Maggie became a hard-working little adult at the age of nine, educated at home.

One of Maggie's duties to relieve her grandmother was to collect the rents from the miners' cottages. Every Friday night Maggie put on her bonnet, serge coat and buttoned gaiters and, armed with the rent book and carpet bag, she knocked on the doors to collect the half-crowns. Sometimes there was a peep behind the lace curtains and the little girl would be left on the doorstep in the quiet dark because the money had run out. Mostly Maggie was made welcome and on good days, if the mining husband had not been drinking, she would be invited in and given a biscuit or a rock bun to put her on her way.

It was quite usual for families with ten or more children to live in these grim two-bedroomed terrace houses. The youngest baby slept in a drawer pulled out from the wooden knobbed chest in the kitchen; the older children slept literally like sardines: head to toe, toe to head so that at least four could occupy a double bed. There was no mains water, just one stand-pipe down the back yard where the earth closet and the midden were also shared by eight cottages. Coal-clogged pit clothes and the miners themselves were washed in the cold little wash-house which jutted out in the back yard.

But Maggie got used to this, and only noticed the bright fire (for each miner received a ration of coal — true it was the inferior stuff but at least they could keep warm) and the black-leaded shining grate with its highly polished brass fittings. Poor they were but they were proud.

It was a strange and lonely life for a young girl. Even as a woman there seemed to be no filial or regional connection with her brother, Percy.

He and his wife did visit Stanhope House occasionally but Uncle Percy's double-cream life and Auntie Annie's genius for friendship could hardly be contained in that penny-pinching little villa with its everlasting aspidistra and its bread and margarine teas.

So different were the two Smith sisters-in-law that, as far as I can remember, they never visited us together. There would have been, one might suspect, a conflict of up-staging; Auntie Annie elegantly costumed would probably be carrying as a gift a blue and silver tin of Farrah's Harrogate toffee but Aunt Maggie in her eccentric clothes would, no doubt, be carrying in her carpet bag her crochet and her returnable 'empties'.

The most memorable of Aunt Maggie's visits was on Empire Day in 1919, the year when peace was signed after the Great War. On that day she sublimated whatever hidden passions she might have into an orgy of imperialism. On the flounced hem of her long white cambric skirt she had loyally threaded red, white and blue ribbons in and out of the insertion band, leaving flying colours at each side to flirt with her ankles. Her panama hat, browned through several summers, sported a broad band of

Stanhope House, the grim Victorian residence where she lived, married and died.

red, white and blue corded ribbon with streamers gaily following the line of her unyielding spine. Nipping the finger-tips of her gloves, she pulled them off synchronising the movement with the command: 'Children, gather round the piano; I want you to sing Rule Britannia to celebrate our glorious H'Empire.' When Aunt Maggie was being particularly imperious she scattered spare Hs on to unsuspecting vowels.

Dr Thomas Arne surely never intended his tune to be pitched so high but with Maggie's cracked soprano and our childish trebles we positively splintered Britannia years before the 'wind of change' blew her into the wings.

Aunt Maggie could not have realised until she got home — for she rarely removed her hat in our presence — that while she and the piano were relentlessly ruling the waves, Betsy, singing behind Maggie's hat, had plaited the three streamers in an uplifted pigtail.

When our aunt rose from the piano stool, her eye caught the pelvic-level hem of Betsy's gym-tunic: 'If I were your mother,' she blinked, 'I would crochet a five-inch hem and sew it on to that skirt,' and added, evidently thinking the Hyde girls needed a few guide-lines, 'Modesty and Manners, girls, Modesty and Manners,' each M having its decorous eye-shutting emphasis.

Aunt Maggie's repertoire of songs included a few Victorian ballads with a moral tone, and as if to justify her own spinsterhood, she blinked and gargled her way through the Gypsy's Warning:

'Do not trust him, gentle lady,
Though his voice be low and sweet,
Heed not him who kneels before you
Gently pleading at thy feet.'

As we grew older we were reluctantly drawn into our aunt's frugal foibles. Her suggested walk to Crossgates meant returning her collection of jars and bottles for a penny each, out of which, with a little bit of luck, we might receive a ha'penny. Even when she came into her fortune this habit persisted so we were quite surprised when we each received the strange sum of £120 each.

My Auntie Annie and Uncle Percy Smith, as I have indicated, died without any intention of making Maggie an heiress but, as blood is thicker than water — and our side of the family was on the watery edge — Maggie found herself becoming the landlord of a substantial part of the two villages: Little Woolstone and Great Woolstone, in north Buckinghamshire, now almost obliterated in the vast metropolitan city of Milton Keynes.

Though still watching the farthings and pennies in her everyday life and being very stringent with herself, she treated her newly acquired wealth with Quixotic abandon. The tenant-farmers who had for years paid their not inconsiderable rents to Great Uncle William, Uncle William and later to Uncle Percy must have listened with jaw-dropping amazement when their new landlord, Miss Smith, *presented* them with their farms and all debts were cancelled. Strange that a woman, who, as they say in Yorkshire, 'would not give you the skin off her rice pudding' should part with property which had been in the Smith family for centuries and moreover would have given her a sizeable income. She never moved from the house where she had spent all her life in the industrial Midlands — three counties away from her inheritance and light years away from the lush farm-land life of Buckinghamshire. Unlike Aunt Annie Andrew, Maggie had no intention of letting her good fortune become a burden, so she devised ways of reducing her capital to a sum more in keeping with her needs.

One such gesture had bizarre consequences. She announced in the local paper that any church or chapel which got in touch with her would receive something to its advantage. Vaguely, I suppose, she had reckoned on the Churches of England, the Methodists, the Baptists and perhaps the Roman Catholics.

But not, not the six hundred!

We heard that they turned up in droves; Latter Day Saints, Jehovah's Witnesses, Plymouth Brethren, Christian Scientists, Unitarians, Congregationalists, Evangelicals, Seventh Day Adventists, British Israelites, Pentecostals, United Reformed Church and the Salvation Army ...

All must have thought 'God moves in a mysterious way His wonders to perform.' None was refused. All received a cheque. Considerably more, we understood, than any of her family.

Aunt Maggie had always had a weakness for men in uniform so her charity stretched out to Boy Scouts, Boys' Brigade and Territorials, and all soldiers who defended her beloved H'Empire. This possibly was how, very late in life, she came to meet one of the soldiers-of-the-Queen (Victoria, of course) and to our amazement announced that she intended to marry Captain Cyril Collingwood. Cyril, we learned much later, was one of the eight men chosen by Baden-Powell to spread the gospel of scouting and to train them as BP Army Scouts. Apparently Cyril became a personal friend of BP, and in 1891 joined his army. In 1895, now a captain, he was sent by Baden-Powell to Coomasi to raise a levee of natives for the Ashanti War. After serving in the Boer War and later the First World War, he used his cavalry experience as a riding instructor in the engineering industry. During the Second World War, when Cyril was in the Fire Service, a direct hit on Bolenbroke Hospital resulted in a miraculous escape from death. Cyril lost an ear and was referred to in Swadlincote as the one-eared Captain.

Maggie, now turning 70, and with the gypsy's warning forgotten, walked up the aisle of Gresley Church in full white wedding regalia on the arm of her 74 year old bridegroom.

There had been some mystery surrounding Cyril's personal background. No one seemed to know whether he was a bachelor or a widower nor how, prior to the marriage, he had come to be living in Maggie's impregnable house. No one knew where he was from; he was certainly a complete stranger to Swadlincote. One suggestion was that Maggie had met him when she was staying in her brother's house in Leeds and that Cyril was engaged as the gardener. But, as far as the vicar was concerned, it was necessary to know whether there was any just cause or impediment why these two septuagenarians should not be joined in holy matrimony. All this was resolved when it was established that the wife whom Cyril had left had since died. It was with some relief that he polished up his medals and buttons, took the mothballs out of his uniform and could say unfalteringly at the altar, 'I will'. As the wide-hipped bride and the one-eared bridegroom came out of the church, a strange conversation took place. Aunt Maggie spotted her near neighbour lined up by the church path: 'I hope we don't have any family,' she blinked through the cloud of white veil. One cannot help but conjure up pictures and dialogues of their honeymoon. One could say it was a marriage of convenience but at times, I was told by the neighbours, it seemed remarkably inconvenient for both.

It did, however, bolster up Cyril's miserable little war pension, for he had, as they say in Yorkshire, 'only to hang his hat up'. Cyril and Maggie continued to live very frugally, he with culinary standards closely related to a boy scout's billy-can and she with her skimmed milk and Saturday night market throw-out vegetables, but they launched out for various military celebrations. Once a year Cyril joined the remnants of his battalion to walk proudly with other veterans of the First World War. ('At the going down of the sun and in the morning, we will remember them'.)

On one such occasion Aunt Maggie invited my sister Nancy, by this time married and living in London, to join her to watch the huge military procession round Hyde Park. They worked their way in and through the crowds until they found a place,

The East Window in Gresley Church donated by Frances Collingwood Smith

Detail of inscription at the base of the window.

with a thousand others, where they could line the roads. And there, my sister imagined, they would both stay put for an exciting but relaxed hour.

She had not reckoned with Aunt Maggie and Nature's insistence. 'I must go to the lavatory', said Aunt Maggie, whose voice was fortunately drowned by the approaching drums. 'And you must accompany me to carry my parcels.'

Just as the magnificent procession of cavalry and infantry was approaching, with clockwork-timed military bands, Aunt Maggie dragged my sister through the cordoned barrier and out into the road. Dumbfounded police were helpless. Sergeant majors bellowed slowing-down orders. Drum-majors marked time.

All that my embarrassed sister wanted was for the road to open and swallow them up, and she prayed that Aunt Maggie would not have ideas of returning to their original spot.

Maggie, back in Swadlincote, boasted to the neighbours: 'I had a splendid view. Right on the top step of the public convenience!'

Postscript

Maggie was never defeated by official–dom. She kept solicitors, accountants, executors, vicars and councillors firmly in their place. Having quarrelled with the vicar of Swadlincote Church (where she had been a member all her life), she transferred her support to Gresley: the Church of St George and St Mary, and there, apart from a few stormy church council meetings, she managed things well. If you visit this beautiful church you will find near the base of the bell tower a brass plaque which reads:

'The three bells of 1639 were repaired and re-hung in this belfry in 1958 through the generous gifts of Frances Louisa and her widower, Captain Cyril Collingwood.'

Move into the nave and you will see the great east window which Maggie endowed. The Parish Magazine of 1957 contains this tribute:

'Mrs Collingwood died before the east window was completed. To the former's generosity we and future generations are deeply indebted as we shall realise later in the year when our new east window is put in. We cannot help feeling regret that she did not live to see her gift beautify the church.'

Cyril, the white bearded soldier, did see the window ceremoniously installed. Maggie's will had ensured that all her bequests were faithfully completed.

If you retrace your footsteps back from Gresley to Swadlincote you will find in the centre of the town the Collingwood Centre for Old People. It is full of lively over-sixties sharing their coffees, teas and dominoes. Here, it might also say on the sign-board, is all that remains of the Smiths of Buckinghamshire and the rich lands farmed by them for over 300 years.

Aunt Maggie was the last of the line. From childhood, when she went rent-collecting, through her single state and single-minded middle years to old age, she had the confidence to make up her own mind. Most of us lay waste our powers getting and spending and, in the process of doing so, we dither.

Not so Aunt Maggie. She never dithered, never consulted anyone for advice, but firmly and self-confidently paced herself, taking into her stride years of habitual thrift, through to the final years when, without any change of living, she graduated into being benefactress to the town, but was described by everyone as 'mean'.

Yet folk, who were neither kith nor kin, must bless her for her prompt and kindly, sometimes dotty, dispensations. She moved with the times, but the times were, without any doubt, totally her own.

CHAPTER NINE
THE FARMING DANBYS

A flashback introducing Aunt Annie Danby

Generations of Danbys, aristocrats and the more humble yeomen and tenants, have farmed in the North Riding of Yorkshire going back, one might surmise, to the Danes from whom they got their name. The village of Danby, and Danby Low Moor, in the North Yorkshire moors look down into Eskdale and east to Whitby where the abbey stands sentinel high above the sea. It is wild and beautiful country, too hilly and windswept for arable farming, so it was in the Vale of Pickering and the Yorkshire wolds, never far from the sea, where my ancestors the Hydes and the Danbys farmed.

It is in the Yorkshire wolds that we summer visitors experience the great stretches of golden corn rippling in the wind and the broad acres of green which merge in the far distance to the blue of the sea and the sky. One horizontal sweep of the eyes can encompass an undisturbed arc of horizon; the little farming hamlets, huddling to the south of their protective dark green coppices and gentle hills, do not break the view. Even the stone walls, the fences and the hedges leaning away from the wind add to the feeling of liberation. Striding between the giant pieces of patchwork, the white chalky roads bounce their light back into the air and move, as the shadows of the clouds move, over an orderly but emancipated landscape.

If inter-marriage weakens the human stock, there seemed no evidence of this in the in-breeding of the Hydes and the Danbys. In 1895 Annie, my father's eldest sister, married a first cousin: Richard Danby. It was from Cockmoor that the bride wearing a comely dress of dove-grey silk drove down in the gig with her father to the little church of Ebberston, the village where the Hyde and the Danby lands almost met. The bride's and the bridegroom's mothers — Grandma Hyde and Great Aunt Annie Danby — who were sisters, prepared the simple wedding feast in Cockmoor Hall and both welcomed the guests as they descended from the broughams, wagonettes, gigs and traps. It was a marriage sealed with affectionate kinship and the promise of a long life ahead.

But it was not to be. Richard Danby, healthy, energetic and of impressive stature — already tenant-farming in Scamridge, Ebberston, Welldale and Foulbridge — was suddenly struck down with Bright's disease and died at the peak of his farming career on 28 January 1902 at the tragically young age of 39. Having inherited from his father not only the farms but the knowledge and wisdom to get the most out of

Welldale Farm, Snainton, was the major farm of the Danbys and in close contact with Cockmoor Hall nearby. Richard Danby's mother, my Great Aunt Annie stayed on long after his death and handed out gold half-sovereigns to her grandchildren.

'Through all the changing scenes of life'

Great Aunt Annie Danby

the land and out of his men — without divesting them of their strength — he had become a highly respected farmer and a well-loved employer. In his early thirties he served his community on the Scarborough Rural District Council, the Scarborough Board of Governors, the Scarborough Board of Guardians and, of course, the local parish council. Like the Hyde and Danby grandfathers he upheld and served the Church of England but gave his heart to Methodism.

He died leaving two sons, Henry and Allan, and two daughters, Doris and Mary

Widowed Aunt Annie Danby with her five children. 1904.

(four little 'steps' aged one to five) and left one child in the womb of his stricken but courageous wife, Annie.

Three days before he died he summoned the labourers on the home-farm to his bedside. Ten men, clutching their caps and some pushing back tears, stood round the massive mahogany bed while their master struggled for breath. He then thanked each one in turn for all they had done and assured them that they would not lose their jobs. Turning to his old shepherd, who had never worked for anyone else except the Danbys, he whispered: 'John you are like me, a man of few words. You have been a good servant and put your heart into the job. But now John we must both make our hearts right with God.' Then turning to the others he said: 'Keep the farms in good heart for your sons and mine.'

The obituary notice in the Scarborough Post filled three columns, and in it they spoke of him as a large-hearted farmer, a Liberal Christian, upright, kind, honourable and conscientious who made any wilderness blossom as the rose.

The two-mile white road from Snainton to Ebberston became a slow-moving river of black led by the hearse pulled by black plumed and be-ribboned horses. Black funeral carriages followed by wagonettes and gigs, painted black for the occasion, were driven by men in black top hats, their women-folk black-veiled to shroud their grief. Behind and on foot followed hundreds of villagers from nearby and distant farming communities wearing their flat caps, Sunday suits and black arm-bands. It was easy to tell which were the Danby farm-men; the six bearers and other workers, thirty or so, following the horse-driven vehicles, all had their work-worn hands covered with new black gloves and had new black ties round their high stiff collars. My aunt, gathering the team of men together the day before the funeral, expressed her thanks and her faith in their loyalty for the future and then she quietly equipped them with the outward and visible signs of respect and sorrow: the black gloves and ties.

The three maids, in a trap newly painted to shine like Whitby jet, felt protected from the January cold in their new black beaver hats and their caped face-cloth coats, a gift from their mistress. 'She always thinks of others,' Alice, established as one of the family, said to the younger girls. Pride and sorrow were in harness as they drove through the village where every blind was drawn.

Ceremony is a sheet anchor in the stark desolation of grief, and three months later Aunt Annie and her four children, all still in their mourning black, were again in Ebberston church for the christening of the fifth child — a girl. The long white ancestral christening robe drew the light to the centre of the small black circle of family and god-parents — a lacy waterfall flowing with promise and hope.

On his death-bed Richard Danby had expressed a wish that if the baby were a girl she should be called 'Edith' — the name now solemnly repeated by the god-parents and the vicar and duly recorded by the registrar. But already 'Edith' had been discarded — a cold unfriendly servile name my aunt thought — and from the first suckling of the bairn at her breast, she had — prompted no doubt by the onomatopoeia of the busy lips — called her 'Babs', the name which has remained with her for ninety years.

All this was before I was born but Richard Danby was kept alive for all of our family as the key character in the continuing Danby saga through the widowed Aunt Annie and the fatherless family of five. Richard's good husbandry (in every sense of the word) ensured that his farms and family continued to flourish through the succeeding generations but sadly there are no grandchildren now to inherit the farms.

My aunt punctuated her long widowhood with orderly decisions on farm strategy, neighbourly needs, correspondence and gifts to relatives, quiet acts of charity, anniversaries and the upbringing and education of her five children.

The village of Snainton, richly endowed with fertile land had no such endowment for education. It was traditionally assumed by the villagers — and their children subscribed to the idea — that book-learning could finish at twelve or at the latest fourteen, and then strong lads and lasses could get down to the 'real' jobs on the farm. 'It's nobbut laiking', was shepherd's blunt summing-up of schooling. My aunt's

Richard Danby of Welldale age 39 — the year he died.

mental and physical horizons stretched a little beyond Snainton so the boys were sent to Woodhouse Grove School near Bradford and the girls to Ravensworth in Scarborough, as boarders, though the girls' school was only half an-hour's train ride away.

By the time war broke out in August 1914, Henry and Allan had left school to be apprenticed as farm pupils to learn, at first hand, from two respected Wolds farmers, the standards set by their father. The girls were nearing the end of the Christmas term at Ravensworth when, without warning, Scarborough was shelled from German warships in the North Sea.

Here is a letter to my mother from her nieces after the shelling of Scarborough, Wednesday, 16 December, 1914:

Snainton
Dec 18th 1914

Dear Auntie Annie,

Mother said that we should write to tell you that we are safe from the shelling and are now at home from Ravensworth.

Would you like to hear what happened? On Wednesday morning, we were just getting dressed in our dormitory when there was the most terrible noise and the whole building shuddered and cracked. Some of the windows were broken and our jugs and bowls rattled and one broke on the floor. We went down to breakfast and stood behind our chairs while Mrs Saunders said Grace and Prayers. We could hardly hear her for the noise. Then before we could sit down we were told to walk down quietly (!) to the cloakrooms in the cellars where we put our hats and coats on. No breakfast!

You remember that our school is next to Scarborough Station. Well, Mrs Saunders has a key for the gate to the platform (to let the day girls have a short cut from the trains to the school). So she sorted us out in the cellar into two groups and took everybody from the school and put them on the two trains that were standing ready to go. We were on the 9.30 Pickering train; the girls who lived south went on the York train from the other platform. None of us had a ticket! By 10 o'clock we were in Snainton station; the others puffed on to Pickering. What they did there we have yet to hear!

You can imagine how surprised and pleased Mother was (as she had heard the dreadful noise) and she and Alice made a huge breakfast for us in the kitchen with a roaring fire. It is very exciting as we shall not go back until after Christmas.

But someone will have to go for our trunks and tuck boxes as we were only allowed to bring what we stood up in.

Our postman (who always knows everything!) says that the school is to be closed and he has heard rumours that Mr and Mrs Saunders have found a big Hall in the country where Ravensworth will go and Mr Saunders will find somewhere for the Greystone boys.

Mother has booked a box for your family and ours for the Pantomime in Leeds so we shall all meet in the New Year.

A Happy Christmas to you all!

Your loving nieces,
Doris, Mary and Babs

XXXX times 3 for our cousins.

This letter from Aunt Annie Danby to my mother followed a few days later:

Snainton
Nr Scarborough
Dec 24th 1914

My dear Annie,

The girls have already told you of the German's attack on Scarborough from the sea. News keeps filtering through of the casualties and disasters but we have so much anxiety here at home that I have not been able to get in touch with Scarborough friends and relations.

Shortly after the girls came back from boarding school, Babs was taken desperately ill with an inflamed appendix which burst before our doctor could get a surgeon. The operation (Sunday, 20th) was done by Dr Godfrey (the surgeon) on the kitchen table and he has engaged two trained nurses from the Berkeley Moynihan nursing home in Leeds to stay in the house. The worst, we hope, is over but with three doctors in and out of the house and two nurses in residence it is like running a hospital.

I told the doctors that nothing must be spared to save my darling Babs' life. But how fortunate we are that I could say that. One dreads to think of poor folk with similar disasters unable to get the help they sorely need.

The day before the shelling (Dec 15th) I sent off on the passenger train to Crossgates the usual box of the girls' clothes. It is so useful that your girls are just that bit younger. Am I right in thinking they are 5, 7, 9 and 13? How quickly they grow up! Mine 12, 13 and 14! (Could someone collect the box, dear; there was no chance to let you know it had gone.)

Annie, my dear, I am so sorry that I shall have to cancel the Pantomime booking at the Theatre Royal. The doctors say that Babs will be an invalid for six to nine months and that she must not return to school until the September term.

But we must all be thankful for what we have got and pray that this dreadful war will soon be over.

Henry and Allan are happily settled in as farm pupils for two years' training: Henry with Mr Ullyot of Gembling and Allan with Mr Wride at Little Kelt. It is money well spent as they are both prepared to work hard and are 'framing' as Yorkshire folk say. Their Father would have been proud of them. But Henry is determined to 'join up' if the war is still on next year. I dread to think of it, Annie; he is so young but I can't say that to him. He will find Foulbridge farm in good fettle when he takes over at 21. Harry, as always, is helpful and is on the lookout for a farm for Allan.

I am sure you and Fred will have a joyful Christmas with your happy little brood but you may not get this letter to wish it so until Boxing Day.

Forgive my not sending the usual Christmas hamper but I know that with your loving heart you will be praying for us as we do for all of you.

Ever your loving sister-in-law,
Annie

PS

I hope that the navy-blue garments (gym tunics, hats, blazers and coats) fit in with your girls' uniforms. Sorry I had no time to remove the red badges on the blazers and the hatbands. Mrs Saunders is fussy abut this. If navy is unsuitable, would you pass them on to someone else?

The 'Sunday' and party clothes should not present any such problems!

PPS

How thoughtless of me! Of course your children must not miss the pantomime. So I am enclosing the ticket for one box and I shall return the other to the theatre.

Visit to the Pantomime — January 1915

Every year from 1912 to 1917, Aunt Annie Danby arranged the perfect Christmas treat for her family and ours: the Pantomime. She booked two boxes in either the sumptuous Theatre Royal or Grand Theatre in Leeds, and for weeks before the visit we literally counted the days, ticking them off on a chart on the wall.

The Danbys would drive in their brougham from Snainton to Scarborough, travel by train to Leeds and take a cab to the theatre where we all met.

Long before 'the day' our tucked and embroidered white dresses, originally inherited from the Danbys, were laundered, 'blued' and crisply ironed, then spread out on the bed in the spare room each with its new Christmas sash. Petticoats and knickers were just as elaborately cut and sewn as the dresses and they too were brought out and spread-eagled on the white counterpane.

Although it was sad that the Danbys could not be with us for *Cinderella,* it was this Pantomime which I most vividly remember. Perhaps it was because there was no need to suspend disbelief, for at five-and-a-bit there is no disbelief to suspend.

On that January Saturday morning a fire was lit in the little black grate of our parents' bedroom and a high fender put round on which to air our rarely worn

velvet cloaks. 'Getting ready' was a performance in itself and the dialogue predictable. 'Show me your nails, my dear ... Have you washed behind your ears? Stay in your petticoats until you've eaten your sandwiches and drunk your milk Poor Babs, we must all write to her when we get back, and tell her all about it' ...

We had a four-wheeler 'growler' to take us to the station, the driver sitting outside aloft wearing his top hat and wielding a long, thin whip. Our black patent leather single-strapped shoes had been given a mirror polish, our hair brushed and then burnished with a silk handkerchief, our faces lightened and brightened with Pears' soap. Everything had to shine on such a day.

The smell of the cab, disliked by adults, was Yardley to us. Stained old leather, stale tobacco, stubbed-out cigars — lingering and mingling with the faded violet scent of ladies and the droppings from horses — combined to be a once-a-year fragrance of enchantment; I can recall it now.

We arrived luxuriously early for the doors' opening at one o'clock. There was lots of time to gasp at the gold and cream of the high-domed ceiling, the red velvet curtains, crimson carpet and sparkling chandeliers, to manoeuvre our little gilt chairs in the box so that we could all lean on the velvet rim. We were ready ages before the curtain went up to be on speaking terms with the characters in the Cinderella story whom we knew so well.

Getting ready for the pantomime was a performance in itself.

If there had been no performance we should still have had our moneysworth — or so it seems with hindsight — for the Royal Box holding six people cost only twenty-seven shillings and sixpence and before it all started the Manager came to see us and handed round the biggest box of Rowntree's chocolates we had ever seen or ever would see.

And then down came the huge solid safety curtain, a fireguard and display board for scores of advertisements: anything from Beecham's Pills to Borwicks' Baking Powder or Madame Millicent the Milliner to Bostock and Wombwell's Circus — all became splendid subjects for twenty minutes' playing of 'I Spy'. Then the breath-holding moment when its huge weight was lifted out of sight. 'Where did it go?'

The giant velvet curtains and gold cords swung down and closed tantalisingly but after two long minutes they swung up and out and parted to dazzle us with a whole new world lighter and brighter than all the chandeliers which now dimmed down to put the audience darkly into place. We had heard the adults talk of Principal Boy and Principal Girl but to us Clarice Mayne was never a girl but our Prince Charming, handsome and manly enough to claim our Cinderella. Although we sat wrapt in rapture as the scuttling mice changed to prancing ponies and the pumpkin was suddenly wrought into a gold chrysalis of a carriage and Cinderella's raggy clothes blossomed into endless petals of silk, we never doubted that it could happen. After all *there* was the Fairy Godmother with her magic wand. Everything was possible ... until the curtains swung down for the last time and we had to leave our little gilt chairs behind in their glistening world and adjust our eyes and minds to the dark and cold of the Leeds street.

We climbed into the smelly cab, now dimly lit with a little paraffin lamp, far too entranced and bemused to speak. It was our gentle sensitive nine-year-old sister Nancy who whispered against the clackety wheels and the cloppity hooves: 'Weren't we lucky to be there when it all happened?'.

Two years later: April 1917

The War Office telegram came at the end of the Easter holiday when the Danby sisters were all at home. Doris and Mary, having finished school for ever, were inevitably learning how to become little women and good wives. Babs, now fifteen, was preparing for her return to boarding school the following day. Exciting plans were in the air for Henry's home-coming and twenty-first birthday when, with his coming of age, he would take over Foulbridge farm.

Grief strangled speech. The whole future crumpled in front of their eyes to the size and shape of the blunt but piercing scrap of paper. Outside the spring wheat and the loose-limbed lambs and calves, all burgeoning with hope and promise, suddenly seemed alien and out of place. Poppies waited in the hedgerows green-masked, dallying behind those in the quickened Spring of Flanders.

Babs crept upstairs and knelt down at her half-packed trunk and wept into her summer clothes. Her mother followed her a few minutes later, walking up the stairs with her usual stoic spine, and knelt down beside her youngest child. 'We all need one another now, Babs. I'll let Mrs Saunders know that you're going to be at home for another fortnight ... You'll be back in time for your confirmation ... Mrs Saunders will understand ... Leave your trunk, love, and come downstairs and we'll have some tea and toast ...'

Two weeks later, Babs returned to Ravensworth School, safely evacuated since January 1915 from Scarborough to a lovely dale in the North Yorkshire moors. The sea-smell of Scarborough had been exchanged for huge cool gulps of hilly air alive with the smell of peat, heather and honey. Entering the form room of chattering girls — they in school uniform, she in a black dress — Babs blushed self-consciously . Sympathy stunned her friends into silence. Her form-mistress, silent too, relaxed her usual stiff upper lip to kiss Babs on the forehead, then gently led her to the waiting desk. It was a long, long morning which could only be relieved with the harsh school bell for lunch. The noise of eighteen scratching map pens suddenly stopped as the head girl entered and announced: 'Will Babs Danby please go at once to Mrs Saunders' study'. (Thoughts pierced the polished corridor as she hurried on. 'Now what have I done?')

Mrs Saunders, dressed from neck to toe in black alpaca, softened her headmistress mask: 'Babs, my dear, go down to the cloakroom and bring your summer hat!' Panic thoughts again in the breathless rush down the cellar stairs and up again: 'Is my badge the wrong way up? Has my name-tape come off? Is the lining torn? ... ' There were so many delinquencies that could arise from those stiff-brimmed, flat-crowned, hard-headed boaters.

But Mrs Saunders received the hat almost reverently and, taking a pair of tiny silver scissors from her recticule of silver chain, she snipped the stitches anchoring the red and navy-blue striped hatband and released it from the crown. Then, unfolding black tissue paper, she took out a band of black corded ribbon and deftly encircled the straw hat, adjusting the hooks and eyes so that they were hidden by the stiff bow. 'Now, my dear, you are privileged, in honour of your brother, to wear this mark of respect for the whole term.' She then, ceremoniously, as if it were a crown, lowered the hat on Babs' forehead at the regulation angle — parallel to the floor and ceiling — the edge of the crown and brim cutting her forehead in two. Her whole face was now appropriately in the shade.

'Ooh, I was proud of that hatband,' Babs was to say for years. 'All that long crocodile of red and navy and me with the only black one — Eeh I was proud.'

The confirmation ceremony was the one special occasion when the hat was not flaunted. It was a short walk down the drive to the little church of Appleton-le-Moors where the white-frocked girls were to be confirmed. Hair that had been brushed and polished freely by mothers and matrons was now clamped demurely into plaits and covered with white veils. As the girls knelt down at the altar rail, the virgin soles of their first-time-on shoes caught the sunset light from the west window. So small was the nave and so near were the pews that one sharp-eyed mamma spotted a Start-Rite price label 12/11d and righteously noted that it was not her daughter who was so careless and badly brought up.

The girls peered through their veils at the Bishop, who, mitred into magnificence, towered above them ready to receive their virgin souls and pass them on to God. His ringed hand paused on each head as he intoned the blessing. Did he realise, thought Babs, that she'd changed her black dress for white? Did he know that, this very evening, all the rest of the family and a hundred others were at Snainton church for Henry's memorial service? Did they all understand why her mother was not here? Mercifully the veil hid her tears.

Perhaps his hand really did rest longer on her burdened head as he repeated once more: 'Defend, O Lord, this thy child with thy heavenly grace, that she may continue thine for ever'. Somehow, it seemed to Babs that the black band, the white frock and the Bishop made grief less raw, more — she searched for the right words and found those her mother often used — somehow, more 'shapely', more 'comely'.

(The Hyde girls, confused by a miscellany of intellectual doctrines, were never confirmed to one. Secretly we rather envied the Danby girls their life of custom, ceremonies and celebrations. We five, too young to profit from freedom of choice, had to grow up before we appreciated the ecumenical patchwork quilt which my mother laid over us and her utterly unprejudiced view of every race under the sun.)

For fifteen years Aunt Annie Danby had stayed on in the well-ordered home-farm house in Snainton to supervise the farms and keep them in good fettle for her two sons. Now she stoically dismantled the home-farm house. There would be no nursery in the compact town house in Bridlington in which she was to settle with her three daughters, and there would be no need for one, as her youngest child, Babs, was now fifteen. She glanced at the family rocking horse as if she almost expected him to show reproach. 'It'll have to go, love, but never mind, it'll still be in the family with the Hydes. Foulbridge will be alright with Allan. He'll farm the way your father did.'

Farming changed dramatically in the years between and after the wars. Mechanisation, food preservation, over-production, speedy transport, urban encroachment, foreign competition, government controls, and the new horizons and ambitions of the land workers all contributed to the dissolution of patronage and paternalism, the orbit in which farming had traditionally thrived.

Allan Danby, as pragmatic as he was personable, changed with the changing times made possible by his inheritance, not merely of goods and capital, but of knowledge, expertise, kindliness and courtesy. Even when in 1953 he was the victim of a violent motor accident — disabled as he was for over twenty years — he managed with great fortitude and a devoted wife to bring out the best in his land and his men.

He died in 1974 and, with no son to follow him, the last of the Danby farms went out of the family.

So ended over a hundred years of demanding response to the rhythms of the seasons, the 'sheer plod' and proud custody of one fragment of the great Yorkshire wolds.

Diagram of the Danby farms near Troutsdale; Cockmoor Hall; Snainton; Welldale and Foulbridge.

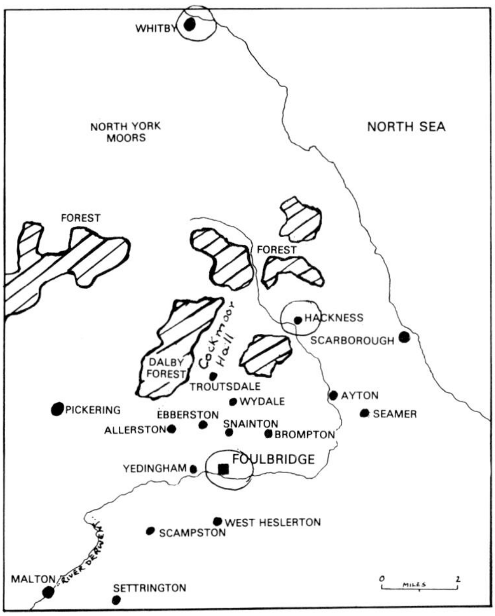

During the excavation of the Knights Templars Hall at Foulbridge.

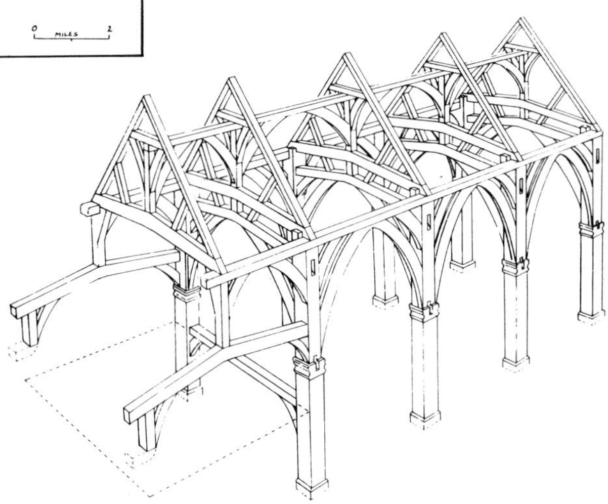

The structure of the timber framed Hall at Foulbridge

Postscript

Foulbridge has a long and distinguished history going back to the 11th Century but when we were young we only knew it as a farm where our cousins Allan and Rhoda Danby welcomed us warmly on our visit to Snainton to Allan's mother, Aunt Annie Danby. I remember the farm as looking as if it had grown there — old and remote but cosy inside apart from its ancient lack of plumbing.

We knew nothing of its history; that was to wait until the year of 'Foulbridge Revisited', a great occasion in 1993, and two years after the first *Life in a Liberty Bodice* was published.

For many years Jill and Pat Nutt (the present owners of the two connected farms, one medieval and one Georgian) had been researching the history of Foulbridge, following every clue and scrutinising a multiplicity of archives to prove what they had known only through hearsay, that the medieval wing of their dual farm had once been part of a vast and prosperous domain of the Order of the Knights Templars, built, as far as could be judged, between 1288 and 1290 at an important point of the one-time highway linking the monasteries of Whitby, Hackness and York where Foulbridge crosses the River Derwent.

Jill literally took courage and action into her own hands and, chipping away at the plaster, discovered ancient beams behind the walls. There followed a long and systematic removal of all the interior walls, floors and ceilings of the three storeys. Bedrooms and attics disappeared to reveal a high splendidly timbered vaulted roof which now is exposed in all its glory.

So in 1991, with its original stone fireplaces, deeply set windows, restored balustraded galleries, the Knights Templars Hall exudes a convincing resonance. The Nutts, supported by professional historians, collated all the documentary evidence of the evolution of Foulbridge and produced a fascinating account dating from the Norman Conquest to their own conquest: 'The Story of Foulbridge'. I am indebted to them not only for the story but for their courtesy and generosity in hosting signing sessions of *Life in a Liberty Bodice* in this magnificent hall. An extra bonus to these two sessions was hearing Pat Nutt show and tell the sequence of the discoveries and to share the conversational delights and hospitality of Jill who had been the prime mover in this imaginative project.

Another bonus for me during my talk was to catch the eyes of the two 90-year-old Danby cousins, Rhoda and Babs, who knew every inch of the ground on which we stood, recalling living there in another world, another age.

Babs' grandfather (my great Uncle Henry) bought 'Fowbridge' (the medieval half of Foulbridge) in 1874 and her father (my Uncle Richard) inherited it in 1887. Sadly, when Richard died at the cruelly early age of 39, his two sons, Alan and Henry, were too young to succeed him. Happily in 1923 Allan bought 'Fowbridge' back into the family and, with his lovely wife, Rhoda, lived there from 1930 to 1947 but farmed 'Foulbridge' until he died in 1976.

Everyone rejoiced when that year the good neighbours, the Nutts, bought the Danby farm and thus linked the two farms again after a separation of 300 years.

CHAPTER TEN
TWO SCHOOLS

Halton Village School

Long before I started school at the age of five I could read. There were no concessions for infancy for I shadowed and chorused all the stories and rhymes which my sisters knew. Print of all shapes and sizes fascinated me, from cereal packets *(High in the air leaps Sonny Jim; Force is the food that raises him!)* to loftier inscriptions.

A vivid picture emerges when the letters and words were well beyond me both physically and mentally. On our Sunday walk, with Temple Newsam House as the target, we not only read in chorus the rhyme on the Whitkirk tombstone but the heaven-hung words of the stone parapet edging the 'E'-shaped roof of Temple Newsam house. My father stood us in a row in age order: Kathleen 14, Nancy 10, Betsy 8 and me 6, and pointed with his stick while we, with necks bent back to breaking point, bluntly declaimed:

ALL GLORY AND PRAISE BE GIVEN TO GOD THE FATHER,
THE SON AND HOLY GHOST ON HIGH
PEACE ON EARTH GOOD WILL TOWARDS MEN
HONOUR AND TRUE ALLEGIANCE TO OUR GRACIOUS KING
LOVING AFFECTION AMONGST HIS SUBJECTS
HEALTH AND PLENTY BE WITHIN THIS HOUSE

There were a few words like *God, King,* and *House* which were easy but my 'sounding out' of *Allegiance* produced 'All EGG I ANC' which made as much sense to me as 'aleejenss' which my father tried to explain. Betsy, who had all the answers, said, 'I don't see how we can 'aleej' to the King when we never even see him'.

I suppose that people who designed elementary schools at the end of the 19th century never intended them to be places of joy but rather to be structures within which there were only two objectives: to teach and to learn.

The village school in Halton ran true to type. There were long hard narrow desk-benches where four children sat in sweaty proximity. Thin high windows well above eye-level ensured that the grimy sunlight of Leeds did not trespass into the building. Near the teacher's high lectern was a black 'tortoise' coke stove with a bald black pipe set against the institutional green walls. Years of defiance had left a column of grime at both sides; on one side of the pipe was a large map of the world boasting through its red patches the dominance of the British Empire. We were conditioned to believe that all those parts of the world shown in red were permanent and inviolate. On the other side of the stove was a blotched photograph of King George V and, staring us in the face further along the wall, was a poster of Kitchener pointing menacingly at the young innocents to say: 'Your King and Country need you!'

There was something about the smell of the whole building which suggested unwilling cleanliness: a strange mixture of dead coke and Sunlight soap.

The blackboard, which more than earned its keep, was plain on the one side with red squares on the other, with enough squares to take the longest of long division sums. The mean grey-covered exercise books had narrow blue lines to encase the bodies of the written letters and red lines above and below for the tops and tails. Individuality in writing was not encouraged. A can, with a thin spout, filled with ink made on the spot from navy-blue powder which never seemed to dissolve, was carried round by the ink monitor (this was a much envied job) who filled up the little white pots by pouring ink on to solid sediment below. If your dip-pen — with its ungiving nib — went beneath the surface, a blob of navy-blue mud landed on your page and you made a blot for which you might be caned.

Exercise books were for fair copies; the transient exercises were squeaked on to indestructible slates and wiped off after correction. The thought of slate pencils scraping and squeaking in unison even now sets my teeth on edge and my ears rebelling. There was no such thing as 'art' on the timetable; the subject was 'drawing' which never seemed to go beyond 'still-life' or 'memory' with H or HB pencils. The total music department was a hit-and-miss piano and a margarine-coloured linoleum banner with the Sol-Fah scale (doh ray me fah soh lah te doh) in vertical file. This and the pointer switched by our Welsh headmaster, who had a true sense of pitch and rhythm, were all we had to 'make music'.

But we could, and did, SING!

For the singing sessions, the two partitions, making three rooms, were pushed back and all three classes stood on their bench seats, and there — all of us two feet taller — we had a better chance of seeing the sun and the sky. It was the one lesson in the day, and it happened every day, our cramped little souls soared.

'And you hear the fond tale
Of the sweet nightingale
As she sings in the valley below,
Oh oh oh … oh …
As she sings in the valley below'

and our expanded horizons made it possible to bid:

'Nymphs and Shepherds come away …
Come, come, come, come away'

The top classes' triple room, made into one, was hardly a grove for nymphs and nightingales and was never intended for sport and play but singing opened our mouths, hearts and lungs. Even Miss Porter, usually so waspish, became more like a humming bee as she strummed the piano.

You would have thought from his appearance and manner that Mr Thomas was conducting the Port Talbot choir at a Welsh Eisteddfod so sleek was his black hair, so stiffened was his black moustache, so brushed his navy-blue suit, so starched his white collar. He dressed for his professional role as a head master. He was rigid, disciplined and frightening, but even so, I remember, if we passed his way when we were outside the school, he raised his bowler hat even to the five-year-olds.

He was determined that all children — even those from illiterate impoverished homes — left his school with more arithmetic than could be produced from a present day calculator, that they could spell every word they were likely to meet in their after-school lives, that they had a reasonable understanding of appropriate punctuation and enough grammar to write and speak standard English. He made sure that his pupils would be able to cross the frontiers of the West Riding without feeling that they were in a foreign country.

And, somehow, all the five teachers in that grim overcrowded little school managed, progressively, to hear us read aloud, recite poetry and repeat lines from the Authorised Version of the Bible. True it was often in unison and may have sounded dreary but at least even now those quotations can cheer and comfort me.

Hymns and prayers had, of course, to be known by heart; we never saw the print because there were no hymn or prayer-books — hence the 'cross-eyed bear' (for 'the cross I'd bear') and 'pity mice and pity me' — ('pity my simplicity') and the more puzzling 'gooseberries and raspberries' which I later saw in print as 'good spirits and bad spirits'. 'Keep us from unkind words and unkind silences' I heard as 'unkind birds and pineapple slices'.

'Dictation' was almost a daily occurrence, and having come from a bookish home it was for me an easy option. Formal as it may seem to children of today — who are spilling out rapturous lines of mis-spelt original creative writing — it did ensure that writing was legible, that punctuation was appropriately used, and that spellings were correct or corrected. The added bonus was that poems, hymns and prose were recorded on paper and became our personal scripts. Those of us with well-exercised memories and quick hands almost knew the stuff by heart when the scratchy pens were put down. Death of a poem by dictation one would think, but no; when we 'recited' we were urged to 'put expression in', a revolting phrase but not as deadly as using poems for comprehension exercises in English Language and English Literature.

The few books we had for class work and in the school library (four small shelves) were read over and over again, which at least ensured that even children from bookless homes were on speaking terms with David Copperfield, Oliver Twist, Jane Eyre and the sisters in Little Women and had read a few moral tear-jerkers like Jessica's First Prayer, The Wide Wide World, Eric or Little by Little and A Peep Behind the Scenes.

But to begin at the beginning. I started my school life in 1914 just before my fifth birthday and went, hand-in-hand with my two sisters, Nancy aged nine and Betsy aged seven, to what seemed to me a giant-sized building. My tightly-gripping hands had to be pulled apart to steer me through the heavy doorway under the arch where cut deep in the stone was the inscription: 'Mixed Infants'. I could read at home but the meaning of these words baffled me. I had never been called 'mixed' before, nor had I ever had a mixed infant for a friend. It was all very puzzling.

All my family and most of my peers could read fairly fluently long before we started school. Reading aloud was a shared social accomplishment and a pleasure. So it was rather daunting when I was handed a Nisbet Reader with all the consonants in blue and the vowels in red for the stunted vocabulary of three-letter words. These tired little red books with their frayed edges and grubby pages took us haltingly through such stirring phrases as 'Nan has a hat' or 'Jill is ill' or 'The fox in the box sees the ox'. Not a single story anywhere. In order to be 'like the others' (very important when you are at school), I kept for home use the delicious cadences of Beatrix Potter and The Golden Staircase of poetry and muttered and jerked each separate syllable with the rest of the class. Analysis led to paralysis. I was almost a case for speech therapy. Most of the reading aloud was in unison so it was the dullest and slowest mixed infant who determined the tempo.

But everyone eventually could read, and with hindsight I can appreciate Mrs Oates' battle every day, without help, to make 40 little five-year-olds read.

Most teachers seem old to the young, but Mrs Oates, a widow (no woman with a husband was ever appointed), I think really was old, for before I was six, she died.

A chill runs down my spine, even now, when I remember that gruesome day when she was buried. Everyone in the school, even her class of infants, walked in procession on a cold winter's day to her funeral. All I knew of death was that rabbits and kittens died, and soldiers 'at the Front' in France. It didn't happen to anyone you knew.

We must have been told, though the memory of it is all blurred grey, that we should wear something black. The easy and economical option was a black arm-band, which most of the children produced, but my mother — though utterly unorthodox about religion — had a sense of the dramatic so I was kitted out in a family hand-down: black fur fabric coat, which reached to my ankles, and a black cap to match completely covering my ears and almost blacking out my eyes. The horror of watching the coffin lowered into that dark grave, the rattle of stony soil, and the boy standing next to me pointing and hissing: 'She's in there!' still flare up in my memory. And standing round the grave with eyes and noses running and our breath steaming out over the cold damp clay of Whitkirk Churchyard, we sang:

'Sun of my soul, Thou Saviour dear,
It is not night if Thou be near...'

That hymn, which I hoped I should never hear again, brings it all back to me: the deadness of the dead, the blackness of the black, the coldness of the cold and the bewildered children trudging back to the school where Mrs Oates' writing was still on the board.

I had five more years at that school; geography was names of places, history was dates and kings, mathematics was long division sums and 'problems', English was nouns and verbs and adjectives, needlework was setting gathers into an unattached band as a 'sample'; Monday morning was the ten commandments repeated in unison, followed by scaring mental arithmetic; games were relay races on hard asphalt and botany — or nature study — was 'naming of parts'.

It cannot all have been bad, for we survived without complaint and even became used to 'going down the yard' and seeing in the winter the watered down urine frozen in the open drain-pipe which linked all the squat deal-seated loos. The squares of Yorkshire Post strung on to a nail were unhealthily scratchy and not a very good way to introduce us to the prestigious Conservative Press! It was wartime for almost the whole of my life at that school so 'shortages' were not referred to — they were the norm.

Of course I must admit that our education at home gave us the edge on most of the other children, but I owe something to this school — a Dickensian slum by contemporary standards — that when I went for the scholarship viva voce I could answer the questions levelled at me by the three up-market ladies. Yes, I was able to tell them that the hedge lining the drive was copper beech, and when one of the three took me to the window to look out on the garden, I could tell her the names of all the trees. I could enthuse about Jo in Little Women, describe the fire in Mr Rochester's house, and recite 'If' with a suitable degree of sanctimony. I had learned the poem on my own and made the unfamiliar word 'imposter' rhyme with 'toaster' and could not tell them the meaning of the word. I was evidently not penalised for that for they gave me the scholarship, and so in 1920, with the war over and armistice signed, I said 'goodbye' to my teachers, who became more friendly now I was leaving.

My mother then set about preparing new clothes, new pens and pencils, new pencil-box and new leather satchel.

But no one could have prepared me for the culture shock of my new school.

Chapel Allerton High School

I suppose that language and lavatories were the biggest two contrasts in the two schools.

In my village school, conversation never got much further than: 'Yes Sir,' 'No Sir;' 'Yes Miss;' 'No Miss' or 'Who's that speaking? Come out to the front!' And then, '**Do not talk**' could be lashed out with three strokes of the cane.

The measure of a 'good' teacher was the dumbness and the silence of the pupils. Miss Porter's one-up-manship with other teachers was: 'No one talks in **my** lesson!'

'Hello, are you Christabel? My aunt is a friend of your mother's in the Theosphical Society. She asked me to look out for you and show you the ropes.'

If it had been Helen of Troy I could not have been more impressed.

'I'm Kathleen James.' Her hand clasped mine in friendship. She was tall; I was small; she was beautiful; I was plain. She had a halo of dark chestnut hair with a mane tied at the back with a large black bow; I had straight short cut beige hair pulled to one side with a plain tortoiseshell slide. She was poised and elegant; I was awkward, nervous and flat-chested. She had medals and badges on the yoke of her gym-tunic crowning a shapely bust. Her arms were in an open gesture of confidence and warmth; mine were clinging to my sides until her handshake comforted me. 'I've checked the lists on the board,' she went on, 'and you are in Form IIIa. Lucky you, Miss Butterworth's form; you'll love her! I'll take you along to meet her.' We walked down the corridor, I noticed, in silence.

'Good morning, Miss Butterworth! May I introduce you to Christabel? Christabel, this is Miss Butterworth.'

I write this conversation in detail because never before had I encountered anyone with such attractive savoir-faire. People didn't talk like that in my village school. Not a trace of a West Riding accent but with a voice — I now realise — enriched by years of happiness and success. Something inside me made me realise that I should be expected to use that speech and that voice from now on — the kind my mother used and advocated — and here, at this school, I should not be accused of 'putting it on' as I would have been just a few weeks ago.

We all looked very new and very self-conscious in our first-time-on tunics and blouses. Eighteen of us only (such a change from the forty-learning-like one of the elementary school) and we each had a proper desk with a proper chair. Everyone looked newly laundered, and the sun shone approvingly through the tall sash windows on to the reflecting Ronuk-polished floor. And there were central heating radiators — a great luxury in those days — not of course on in September — but promising warmth in the months to come. The air was fresh and flowery; I thought this fragrance was from the vase of flowers on the Victorian mantel-piece, but I later saw the early morning ritual of the freshener pump which ensured that Chapel Allerton High never smelt of 'school'. At break (called 'play-time' for down-the-yard performances at my old school), I discovered one of the Edwardian lavatories, invitingly clean with a generous mahogany seat, a gleaming white pan with blue flowers (like the one at home), and a chain that gave an opulent flush when one pulled the hourglass-shaped wooden handle; the Izal lavatory paper had a response which the Yorkshire Post and Leeds Mercury obviously lacked.

When we were young, before the dons of linguistics created their useful but somewhat dehydrated language analysis, we had our own rough and ready measures of social speech. We had never heard the word 'register' — except as the thing you called out 'Present' to first thing in the morning — but gradually by a sort of aural/oral osmosis we shifted our vowels and our vocabulary in line with the majority and unconsciously got into the right registers. The aim of all was never to sound 'Broad Yorkshire'.

So, in my new school, one took a bāth, perhaps more frequently than one did when it was a băth!; one learned how to 'dānce' and one was on equal social terms with the stāff. The predominant speech-patterns and vocabulary of the Kathleen Jameses gradually ousted those of the Bessie Broadbottoms.

The BB midday 'dinner' refined itself into 'lunch' (or 'luncheon' if the Head were near); the BBs learned the K J versions and said 'mistress' instead of 'teacher'; 'form' instead of 'standard'; changed 'Mum and Dad' to 'parents' or 'people', 'sums' into 'mathematics'; 'front room' into 'drawing room'; 'composition' into 'essay' and 'WC' into the more euphemistic 'lavatory'. Gradually the BBs came to know that if: 'one put some sugar in the pulpit' three of the vowels would have the sound which was considered 'Broad Yorkshire' if one used this same oŏ when one said that 'one loved one's cousin more than one's mother.' It was a linguistic shift which was neither discussed nor analysed. Like Topsy it just growed.

The genuine Kathleen Jameses were as comfortable and at ease with this speech as they were in their supple calf-leather shoes from Daniel Neals. The upstarts — the nouveaux riches — had assertive edges on their vowels and elocuted their consonants. Thus Ermyntrude Ellison-Smith (as we will call her) spoke in her muscle-tightened voice:

> 'Ectually I was **appalled** and could hardly believe my **eahs** when I first heard Bessie Broadbottom **speak.** After all, one's parents are **paying** for one to be with girls who speak the **King's English**.'

Miss Jeyes' sharp but low-pitched comment to Ermyntrude on another occasion was: 'Do you have to talk like a pair of scissors, Ermyntrude?'

Hindsight gives one the advantage of adult analysis, and looking back I realise how differently and significantly *hands* were used in the two schools.

At the village school in Standard II we had laboriously copied out the phrase: 'Cleanliness is next to godliness' six times in our copper-plate writing copy books but at that school we were never able to put it into practice. It was salutary to see that wash-bowls (lavatory basins), nail brushes and proper linen towels were near the lavatories at our new school and that all of us 'washed our hands'. This injunction from home was an impossible feat at the village school as there was, as far as I remember, just one stone slab sink nowhere near the down-the-yard horrors.

Hands, at the village school, had to be kept out of sight by folding the arms. This was disapproved of at Chapel Allerton because it disfigured our deportment, and if the Board School teacher found any fault in the class we had to sit for minutes on end with hands-on-our-heads. Both these imprisoning gestures made relaxation and response an impossibility.

Here, at Chapel Allerton, as in my home, gesture freely reinforced thought and speech, and hands were given an 'airing'; that is except in the corridors where one had to walk with hands clasped behind one's back and freeze against the wall if staff wished to pass. There was some sense in this as the school, manoeuvred into one building from several houses, was a network of passages each of which only accommodated one line of traffic.

The Staff

There was an unquestioned permanence about the staff; they had all been there for some time when I entered the school, were there for the whole of my school life and looked exactly the same when I left. Most of them were still there when I returned many years later as an 'old girl'. We never speculated about their ages; to us they were all middle-aged ladies, yet when I look back I realise that some of them must have been in their twenties and thirties when I first met them.

Miss Butterworth: Botany Mistress

Kathleen James — our head girl — was right about Sarah Butterworth, our form and botany mistress; she was rounded, relaxed and fun.

She knew all the wild flowers, trees and grasses which grew prolifically in lanes and fields within walking distance of the school, and she made no bones about being glad to escape from the school buildings. And walk we did down all the lanes and winding footpaths through the fields and woods which now have been slaughtered and 'developed' into an endless conurbation of red brick villas, concrete roads and television aerials.

Miss Butterworth made us, not just look, but *see* the minute herbs holding their own in tangled hedgerows and green pastures. To her not one of the plants was a weed; she had as much respect for the dead-nettle as she had for wild orchids and roses, and this, I think, was her attitude to all of us. She didn't patronise us with artificial smiles but talked as if we had a right to be there and that life was for the taking if we had eyes to see and ears to hear. No one felt weedy or stunted in her presence; she respected our varied roots and encouraged us to branch out into the air and the light.

Of course we could all recognise the Oak and Ash and Thorn — the three trees which were the names of our school houses — but she made our eyes skim round the silhouettes of all distant trees and recognise their individual shapes, then she would lead us on to examine at close quarters whether it was the wind, birds or explosion which scattered the seeds. She showed us how to trace the evolution of unfamiliar plants through a Flora so that the task was not a chore but a treasure hunt. We understood how sap reached the tips of leaves, how some flowers had bee-markings and why others drooped their heads in lonely self-pollination. Why green was green. She taught us the Latin family names and the everyday ones, and the homely ones like: 'Go-to-bed-at-noon' for goat's beard, 'Piss-a-beds' for dandelion, 'Devil's bit' for scabious, and 'Jack-by-the-hedge' for wild garlic.

We stood in meadows of tall grass while we examined the differences between the Timothy, Trembling Couch, Rye, Rattle, Scurvy, Fox's Tail, Mare's Tail and Willow. It had all just been 'grass' before.

Today when I stroll in unspoiled lanes of Yorkshire or Gloucestershire I feel I am letting Miss Butterworth down when I can't tell St John's Wort from Saxifrage and when words like umbelliferae will not surface.

Miss Butterworth, like all lovable people, was not entirely virtuous — and I remember, with a shameless lack of guilt, how she nudged us into success for our botany examination for what was then the School Certificate.

One hot day in June, when it was better for our lesson to be outside than in, she said with a chatty 'throw-away': 'By the way, I've noticed that in the University experimental grounds they are actually *growing* rose-bay-willow-herb.' Nothing was added to this non-sequitor but the brightest and most devious of us later 'swotted up' all the minutiae of the willow-herb from our *Floras.* Sure enough, on examination day, there were the specimens on our desks with the botanical flora through which we had to trace and record the plant's origins. From seed to dicotyledons and eventually back to seed we already knew it all without reference to the books and were able, therefore, to deal with that first question in a matter of minutes. Thus we had the remainder of the statutory half-hour, when the books would be collected, to run through the rest of the questions and filch from the *Flora* anything which would fill the gaps. I think no girl was less than Credit that year.

Miss Butterworth had, too, her moments of delightful and understandable rage (for I can imagine that teaching in a strict, Head-dominated school must have been frustrating); I remember with a frisson of fear and elation how, one day, she threw the chalk and the board-rubber across the room and roared: 'I'm not here because I love children; I can't stand teaching; I only do it to earn a living and you lot make me realise I'm grossly underpaid!'

Were we, I wondered, the safety valve for a broken love affair?

Above my desk, as I write, there is an authentically framed faithful reproduction of the 15th-century artist Antonio del Pollaiuolo's *Profile of a Woman with a Muslin Headdress.* Over 60 years ago this was given to me by Sarah Butterworth on her return from a holiday in Florence. This picture has little monetary value but it has been on my bedroom wall through seven removals. Charming as it is in its own right, it is far more than a beautiful face; it is a reminder of that small band of teachers — epitomised by Sarah Butterworth — who give generously of their warmth, wit and wisdom.

Though their price may be 'far above rubies' they are well down the list of those who receive them.

Miss Glees: History Mistress

How very different was the teaching of Miss Glees our history mistress. There was no doubt about it, Miss Glees was steeped in history, but the liquid she squeezed out for our lessons was neither juicy nor colourful.

The phrase 'typical teacher' must evoke some sort of caricature; certainly even in that period there would never have been any doubt about Miss Glees' profession. But typical she was not. She was herself.

She was thin rather than slim; compressed rather than compact; informed rather than brilliant; efficient rather than capable and reliable rather than resourceful. The general impression was *fawn.* I could not possibly remember what she wore but the total effect of the beige to brown garments was fawn. Her *fawn* hair was scraped back into a caged little bun; the pale fawn skin was tightly stretched over the small bones of her face, leaving nothing to spare for smiles or laughter. Her tidy little nose was used as a prop for her pince-nez spectacles; it could never have sniffed Chanel.

Walking backwards and forwards across the width of the class room — without reference to notes or text books — she poured out dates, facts, names of modern European history, a spoken paraphrasing of every revolution, war, battle, statesman, king or treaty. Neither the pitch nor the pace of her profiled monologue ever changed. Nothing altered vocally or visually whatever the crisis. The storming of the Bastille made no more sound than a falling pen-nib; the guillotine was as blunt as a school ruler; Danton as dead as a dodo. Never once did Miss Glees look our way; her eyes concentrated on the floor two yards ahead of her. But as we had our eyes on our rough note books and pencils desperately trying to get down the facts, it was of little consequence that there was no eye contact. Some of us opted out and quietly read Ethel M Dell (the Barbara Cartland of the day) or neatly lined our rough note books with a copy of Magnet or Gem.

Before the merciful bell rang she announced the subject for our home-work history essay in which we were supposed to keep as near to her dehydrated dictation as memory and rough note-books could determine. These essays were marked neatly in red ink with every fault in spelling, punctuation, grammar or historical fact underlined and commented on. One such essay of mine, The Cause of the French Revolution included the evasive phrase: 'the King of France at that time'. This was returned with the red comment: 'Do you think you could hoodwink an examiner into thinking that if you knew that it was Louis XVI, you would put such a fact-less phrase?'

My end of term report was a masterpiece of perspicacity: 'When Christabel realises that precise facts are essential to historic truth, her attempts at historical fiction might have more credibility.'

Miss Jeyes: Form Mistress

In my second year my form mistress was Miss Jeyes: this is a somewhat antiseptic version of her real name but her effect on children was as 'Jeyes' is to germs.

An Anglican upper class upbringing, far away I should imagine from Yorkshire, perhaps contributed to her confident disdain of those she considered beneath her. She could look down her acquiline nose longer and more dismissively than anyone I have ever met and the sneer continued to the downturned corners of her thin-lipped mouth.

The triple impact of her role: French, scripture and form mistress meant that no day passed without her sarcasm: 'Did your mother buy those stockings for your elder sister?' she said, sweeping her eyes over the woollen wrinkles covering my matchstick legs. I shrivelled.

Miss Jeyes taught French from a jaundiced hard-backed little grammar book which had few white spaces round the solid block of grey print. Of course, no pictures. Every tense of 'aimer' was memorised and parroted with no sign of love in either the present or the uncertain future perfect.

A whole year of scripture was doggedly devoted to the Acts of the Apostles. It created an allergy to St Paul from which I have never quite recovered. However it did drive me to prayer. Every Sunday I prayed that Miss Jeyes would die. All confidence in the power of prayer was shattered when she sailed into the room every Monday morning, more omnipotent and more ruthless than the week before.

Her versatility and energy cannot be denied for she also took us for netball and tennis. This was even more frightening than lessons. Wrapped in layers of sloppy woollen sports coats, while we shivered in our gym tunics, she bawled out the length of the court: 'You stupid idiot, Christabel. Keep your eye on the ball. Run, you little fool, run!'

Her voice, without any amplification, could have filled St Peters or the Coliseum in Rome. But even her games' voice sounded pontifical: 'Don't stand there useless, Edie, run for the ball!' with which she gave Edie a mighty shove into the netball post. A gashed head did not bring an apology from Miss Jeyes. Edie's parents, like mine, never complained against staff. It was an unwritten law that they were always right.

I think Miss Jeyes quite enjoyed seeing how much caustic acid she could squirt into the confines of the termly report. One cannot help but admire her trenchant dismissal of my French: 'Christabel's purported intelligence is mainly used for evasion of work.'

One had only to look at Miss Jeyes to know that she would be a well-to-the-right Conservative, whereas my parents and many of their associates were — if not members of the Socialist Party — sympathetic towards its crucial objectives. It was more in my father's nature to be a Liberal but my mother's reforming spirit pulled him to the left of the Liberal Party while still steering a moderate course to the right of the Socialists. It was difficult, therefore, for me to join in the cheers in Miss Jeyes' lesson when Miss Scotson-Clark, our head-mistress, blew into our classroom like a galleon in full sail and proclaimed: 'Dorothy, your grandfather, Sir Charles, has got in by the splendid majority of over four thousand. Conservatives are sweeping through the country!' It was one of the few times I saw Miss Jeyes' thin lips bend upwards into an approving smile to include Dorothy, Miss Scotson-Clark and, of course, very much at home in her world, Sir Charles Wilson MP.

Yet if I were to meet her socially today, as she was then and I am now, I think I should be impressed with her patrician good looks, her unshakable confidence and her style. Perhaps I should find that her intellectual arrogance and sarcasm were modified in the presence of adults to whom she no doubt would seem to be witty and urbane.

But with the eye and ear for theatre, I think I should want to cast her in Henry

Forms IV A & B at Chapel Allerton. Author front row 2nd from left — the plain one!
Notice that there are two form-mistresses for twenty-four girls.

VI, Part III as the outrageous Queen Margaret.

Miss Coutts: French Mistress

After three or four years of paper-weighted French with Miss Jenkins and Miss Jeyes, we moved up to the next form and were taught French by Miss Coutts. Shades of the prison-house lifted. French was no longer a penance but a delight.

Speaking English, Miss Coutts was mellifluous; speaking French she scintillated.

So we had: French for speaking, eating, drinking; French for shopping, singing, thinking; French for loving, playing, giving; French no longer dead — but living.

I regretted that this change of teaching from formal written exercises to oral competence had come to me so late. I was 15, and by that time speech muscles (unless used otherwise) have settled into the habitual pattern of the native language. Would that we had been taught the Coutts' way from early childhood!

But we did our best. And joyfully. It was a revelation to hear lyrics and epic poems spoken with the heartbeat of the poets themselves and to gather the sounds into our own ears so that we too could speak and keep for ever such poems as the sonorous L'Expiation ofVictor Hugo: Napoleon's retreat from Moscow —

> 'Il neigait. On etait vaincu par sa conquête
> Pour la première fois, l'aigle baissait la tete.
> Sombres jours! L'empereur revenait lentement
> Laissant derrière lui bruler Moscou fumant.
> Il neigait. L'apre hiver fondait en avalanche
> Après la plaine blanche, une autre plaine blanche.'

So I keep for my remembering the tolling bell weight of her voice on 'L'empereur revenait lentement' and the long slow vowels of'sombres jours' and 'Moscou fumant'

In lighter vein, we learned by heart the fables of La Fontaine and brought the pert and wise characters' dialogue to life: la cigale, le corbeau, le rat de ville. . . and all the rest.

Miss Coutts was fond of us all but she had, understandably, a special affinity with a French/Belgian girl in our form called Simone with whom she could escape from our laboured pace and enjoy sparkling conversation and reciprocal repartee. Because of this we all thought that Simone was brilliant — a genius; it never occurred to us that we too could speak our mother tongue, not perhaps with such grace and charm, but at least with reasonable fluency.

Perhaps Miss Coutts' bubbling joie de vivre was heightened that year because she was in love. She married and returned to the school with a somewhat Anglo-Saxon name: Monkhouse. It was the first time there had been a 'Mrs' on the staff, apart from Mrs Barford who was widowed, so it must have been a shot in the arm for the spinster staff room.

We girls rather resented the disappearance of the debonair name 'Coutts' from a favourite mistress, but in fairness to Mr M, judging by his wife's starry radiance, I think the syllables 'Monk house' were very far from the name of the marital game.

Miss Taylor: Latin Mistress

Miss Taylor, our Latin mistress, looked incongruous amongst our genteel, under-stated staff for she was MADE-UP. What she was made-up to or for (the dative case we assiduously learned) it was difficult to know but my memory of her is in *colour*.

Imagine, if you can, a 1920s edition of a Rossetti Pre-Raphaelite. Her hair, cut into a page-boy bob and fringe, was evenly and shinily hennaed, her skin a rich rachel, her eyes an arresting greenish turquoise, her lips invitingly coral and her deep orange or veridian dresses at least 18 inches shorter than those of her colleagues. Wafting from her neck — and worn with the same éclat as Isadora Duncan — were chiffon scarves which trailed out behind her as she winged her way in and out of the room. She brought with her and left behind an alluring cloud of Worth's crepe-de-chine perfume which somehow was at odds with the aggressive 'Bellum, bellum, bellum' declension which we had to chant in chorus.

She became more animated when she introduced us to Latin lyrics and we could parrot away about Lesbia and her sparrow but she closed her long-lashed eyes in despair as we floundered our way through Caesar's Gallic Wars.

Of course we speculated how and with whom she spent her evenings, weekends and holidays but we were never given a clue. The ablative 'by, with or from' eluded us.

Most of us failed in Latin for School Certificate, an essential subject for Matriculation and entrance to University, but, on hearing this, Miss Taylor swept her rachel eyelids and darkened lashes into closure signifying that she took not the slightest responsibility for the 'ignoratio' of her philistine pupils.

With the salutary vision of hindsight how I wish I had worked harder in my four years of Latin but how I also wish *much more time* had been spent on the semantic glory and gift of Latin to our own big lucky-bran-tub-of-a-language: English. To know the roots of a word leads to a whole world of discovery and perhaps the discipline of Latin gives us an understanding of the right word in the right order and helps us to avoid the slovenliness of language which George Orwell deplored: 'English made it easier for us to have foolish thoughts!'

Certainly it would be salutary for long-winded bureaucrats to know how to use ten words that 'tell' rather than a hundred that bore or bewilder.

Apologies, please, Miss Taylor from an errant schoolgirl.

Miss Williams: Music Mistress

A Victorian statue of a Greek goddess comes to mind when I think of Miss Williams. She was draped rather than dressed and crowned with a cornucopia of cream marble hair which defied gravity. We all marvelled how this lofty coiffure stayed vertical when she was conducting but, as none of her movements ever got out of hand, the head and the hair remained unified.

It was odd that the nymphs, shepherds and nightingales which had capered with us at the village school still warbled in the more genteel surroundings of Chapel Allerton. Mr Thomas, the Welsh headmaster, had put some blood and fire into their veins but Miss Williams' nymphs, shepherds and nightingales languished with anaemia.

Diction was considered of primary importance at Chapel Allerton so a considerable part of the singing lessons was taken up with 'rounds' — to perfect our consonants: 'Around the rugged rocks the ragged rascal ran' we sang with self-conscious tartaning of the Rs, 'Dear Dora dances delightfully' with puckered lips and biting teeth, 'Pearls please pretty Polly' we simpered — all of them with tunes as banal as the words.

I don't know what John Wesley would have made of Miss Williams for he exhorted all the Methodist church choirs 'to sing lustily'. The very word 'lust' would have shocked Miss Williams so we 'clanged on the anvil' 'fought the good fight' and dealt with 'the drunken sailor' with clean hands, pure hearts and faultless diction.

The singing classes were held in Ash Hall where we were arranged to sit on — or stand in front of — six-seater benches. But for the 'rounds' or 'cantons' it was necessary to divide the sixes into three columns of twos. With arm movements more suitable for ballet than for London's Burning Miss Williams lifted us to our feet with 'All stand' then 'Two to the right, two to the left, girls, please.'

It happened that one afternoon the six girls sitting in front of my friend Mary and me all had long plaits with bows at the tail ends. With the sleight of hand of pickpockets we quickly fastened the six bows one to another in a horizontal line. On the sylph-like gesture to divide right and left, the plaits were pulled both ways

Expedition to London, 1924.

like a tug of war and the singing lesson ended with piercing screams more like a pig-killing yard than a ladies' seminary. For such a crime we were given 'Name Entry' punishment which meant that our badges were removed from our hats and blazers and we were banished from all outings and treats.

This is why neither Mary nor I are in the photograph taken of the school visit to the Houses of Parliament and the Wembley Exhibition.

It was also not surprising that two of the girls with vandalised plaits decided to have their hair bobbed and shingled.

All the same I am a great advocate of class-singing for even with Miss Williams it was a bonding, liberating exercise and I am glad to have the huge repertoire of song soaked into me at school, home, guide-camp, church and chapel. Singing, even if slightly off pitch, gives us a great sense of one-ness. Deep down in all of us, from the organised chanting of native workers in Africa hoisting electric cables to more inhibited Western folk at a wedding or funeral, there is an innate yearning to sing.

Sadly class-singing seems, like hymn-singing, to be a casualty of the 'politically correct', and overlarge-for-assembly schools. The computer-minded see no 'relevance' (the blessed word!) in a subject where only heart and voice are involved.

Do miners, with little to sing about, still sing? I do hope so.

Adolescents show no mercy in their quick sketches of their teachers but with mellowed hindsight I must add that our teachers had unquestioned authority, cultivated voices that ensured attention, precise but well-formed speech, decorous good manners, scrupulous and demanding marking of our written work, dedicated use of time, calm acceptance of the Burnham scale of pay, and were highly respected by parents and the public. Moreover they *stayed*.

Miss Prismall: English Mistress

Miss Prismall, Head of English, was a teacher in the truest, noblest meaning of that word. She made it her professional business to give us the discipline and delight of the English language in all its complexity, glory and variability. She neither generated nor wanted sycophants but earned our respect. There was no question of her imposing discipline, for she had only to walk into a room for attention to be drawn her way.

In that period there were no 'sops' in the set books as there are now and no concessions to contemporary teenage taste. I think in the long run we profited from adults who did not bend over backwards to be one of us, though I do admire the best of our teachers today who are at one with the children they teach and together can discover and discuss — a climate which my generation rarely experienced.

We profited on the whole, I think, from the stability and the permanence of the staff; I had an unbroken six years with Miss Prismall as my English mistress. (Disastrous, of course, if one had six years of an inadequate teacher!) She never wasted one minute of it.

Miss Prismall had a built-in time and motion mechanism. On opening the classroom door she took for granted that the girl at the nearest desk jumped up, held the door, closed it while Miss Prismall announced — synchronising walk and talk — 'Good morning, girls; you need out your rough note-books, your vocabulary books, your little blue Miltons — thank you; sit down.' We, in turn, synchronised our sitting down with the opening of desk lids and retrieval of books, and within seconds we had contributed the silence in which Miss Prismall need never raise her voice. 'We will start today by saying the extract from 'Paradise Lost,' which you memorised for your preparation. Barbara, will you begin with: 'Is this the region, this the clime? ... 'and then each of you be ready to continue when I say your name.' Miss Prismall thus made it impossible to count the lines in advance to work out when it would be one's turn. 'Then when you have all spoken, we will say it in unison.'

And from there she skilfully allotted not an equal number of lines — for that would have broken the sense-rhythm — but sensible 'thinking-chunks' so that no rendering could be mechanical. On this occasion, I remember, I was the third speaker and had the never-to-be-forgotten:

> 'The mind is its own place and in itself
> Can make a Heaven of Hell, a Hell of Heaven.
> What matter where, if I be still the same,
> And what I should be, all but less than he
> Whom thunder hath made greater? Here at last
> We shall be free; ...'

To present day teachers this would seem to be a tough way to teach Milton — though I doubt if anyone even attempts Paradise Lost nowadays.

But strangely enough most of us enjoyed it because, in the lesson prior to the memorising, Miss Prismall had read it aloud searchingly and well, and then explained the allusions, metaphors and similes. So we did, in fact, learn with our minds and not just our memories. Miss Prismall was equally exacting in the demands on our written work. Lower down the school I wrote a melodramatic essay on 'The Highwayman', probably plagiarised from some out-of-school reading, which began:

> 'It was a brilliant moonlight night; fleecy white clouds scudded across the clear starry sky, the stage coach Exeter Fly, was uncomfortably crowded but the four young spirited bays pulled it quickly along in splendid style.'

(How awful that one remembers such juvenilia!)

The essay was returned with the salutary red ink comment:
'Your essay has a certain mobility and atmosphere but there are too many purple passages. Go through it, getting rid of at least twenty adjectives and several adverbs, then re-write the condensed version.'

I took out the scalpel and returned the essay now shorter and sharper than the original. The red ink comment was:

'Good! You have reduced the purple passages but it is still faintly mauve.'

Sensible, Miss Prismall! Hindsight enlarges my gratitude.

There was very little drama in the school, just painfully self-conscious productions for celebrated occasions; however Miss Prismall did do her best to bring words to life. In the narrow space in front of the density of desks in the small form-room she made a commendable effort to match dialogue with characters.

The memorising of all the major speeches in any play we were studying was taken for granted by Miss Prismall and was evidently common practice in all senior schools. I have good reason to remember the School Certificate year of Macbeth. A special matinee was put on at the Grand Theatre — a building of great opulence — for the Grammar and High Schools of Leeds. I don't think the actors had the slightest idea what they would be up against. Throughout the play there was a murmured undercurrent of joining-in. When it came to Act II Scene I, where Macbeth is realising that Banquo is his final obstacle to his ambitions, the actor playing Macbeth stumbled and 'dried' on the key lines:

> ... 'Our fears in Banquo
> Stick deep and in his royalty of nature
> Reigns that which would be feared ...

And all the audience of schoolboys and schoolgirls prompted and said the whole speech aloud. I noticed a faint smile of inward satisfaction on Miss Prismall's well-behaved face.

One important episode in my life epitomises her sense of duty and generosity.

In February 1924 my brother, Sonny, contracted whooping cough, making a six-weeks' quarantine obligatory for his family. My two eldest sisters were away at college but Betsy and I whooped with joy at the idea of an unexpected holiday. We reckoned without my headmistress and my mother who quickly got into collusion to plan how work could be kept going. By arrangement with Miss Prismall, now my form mistress, it was agreed that twice a week I should take and return work which would be set and marked by five of the staff.

The school was eight awkward miles from my home but even so my mother, with an exaggerated social conscience, made it clear that on no account could I spread the germs in local transport. So it was arranged that I walked.

My usual route to school was: three-quarters of a mile walk to Crossgates Station, about four miles in the train to Leeds, half a mile across the city to the tram stop and three miles by tram to the school. A daunting journey in any case — but to walk! My father, who considered walking as important as learning, worked it out that I could, by making a bee-line of minor roads and bridle paths, cut it down to about six. This he plotted out for me on an ordnance map. So, armed with a heavy leather satchel on my shoulder, and the ordnance map in my hand for the first journey, I worked my way through the unfamiliar circuit of Killingbeck, Seacroft, Potternewton to Chapel Allerton.

The six weeks covered the whole of February and two weeks in March. Every kind of weather known to the north of England happened in those six weeks: cold, fog, snow, hail, rain, wind, and gale. An occasional meagre ration of sun, filtered out by pale grey Leeds smoke hardly reached this underweight, undersized 15 year old. There was no let-up; it would never have occurred to my parents or Miss Scotson-Clark that one could be defeated by such an everyday thing as weather. For Miss Prismall my first task was to learn by heart Part I of the Ancient Mariner, so in the first weeks' walks, with Lyrical Ballads in my hand I spouted out loud, until they were firmly in my memory, lines which have remained with me ever since. Much of it fitted the weather:

> 'And now there came both mist and snow
> And it grew wondrous cold.'

It was not difficult to fit that into the picture for, in fact, it was snowing and with a heavy satchel full of the Bible, North & Hillard; Kennedy Latin books and Hall & Knight's algebra and all the accompanying exercise books I certainly had an albatross round my neck:

> 'At length did cross an Albatross;
> Thorough the fog it came ...'

And so I arrived at the school, timing each arrival to coincide with the bell which signalled Miss Prismall's free period. For half an hour we stood on the outside steps, front door closed against the germs, she with the black velvet band round her hair, I with my sodden school hat, both of us with red noses and watering eyes. Generously, she also heard my Corinthians for Miss Jeyes: 'Charity suffereth long and is kind...' (did Miss Jeyes really practise this?), took in my maths and physics for Miss Umpleby, history for Miss Glees and finished with the ten stanzas of the Ancient Mariner. Then I set off for home, reading the first stanza of the next instalment due in three days' time:

> 'And now the storm-blast came and he
> Was tyrannous and strong.
> He struck with his o'ertaking wings
> And chased us south along.'

So I turned south, reversing the six miles for the trek home. So strict were the rules of 'No eating' that there was no suggestion of 'iron rations' for the journey. Not even a cough-drop.

'How *kind* of Miss Prismall!' my mother enthused when I arrived home with hurting feet. It never occurred to her to praise her daughter. In Yorkshire you didn't praise your own. They might become vain.

I think I enjoyed the words of the Ancient Mariner Part II more than any other.

With the yellow-grey of Leeds smog up my nose and in my throat I identified with the slimy things:

> 'The very deep did rot: O Christ!
> That ever this should be!
> Yea, slimy things did crawl with legs
> Upon the slimy sea.'

And in the sixth week — now on Part IV — I rose to Thespian heights as I passed the Killingbeck cemetery:

> 'The many men so beautiful,
> And they all dead did lie,
> And a thousand, thousand slimy things
> Lived on: and so did I!'

But only just. Only those who have lived through the smog of Leeds in the twenties and thirties can know that something called 'air' could be yellow and black slime.

Having got hooked on the Lyrical Ballads of Wordsworth and Coleridge, I gave myself an ego trip learning bits of Christabel. There was a week of crisp clear March sunshine so I could indulge myself:

> 'The lovely lady Christabel
> Whom her father loves so well'

and

> 'Hush, beating heart of Christabel;
> Jesu, Maria, shield her well!'

Incongruously — since I was heavily encased in school tunic, hat and coat, with thick woollen stockings hitched to my Liberty bodice — I recited:

> 'Her gentle limbs did she undress
> And lay down in her loveliness'

and revelled in:

> 'A sight to dream of, not to tell!
> And she is to sleep by Christabel'

I was rather proud of myself having learned it off my own bat, but Miss Prismall would have none of it. Perhaps she fought shy of the Lesbian implications for immediately she made me turn to Kubla Khan and there, standing on the top step, she told me of Coleridge's drugged dream and how the wonder of it all was shattered by the man from Porlock calling on business.

The poem sang its way into my heart, like the damsel with the dulcimer, and has been there ever since.

With the whooping cough phase over, I returned in time for Wordsworth's Ode. How grateful I am that we learned that supreme poem.

Sybil Marshall, a great friend and a wise educationalist, talking to me in the Sixties about children never knowing anything by heart, said, 'What will they have to comfort them?' I have Miss Prismall to thank that in times of grief or stress I can take heart from:

To me alone there came a thought of grief;
A timely utterance gave that thought relief,
And I again am strong.
The cataracts blow their trumpets from the steep;
No more shall grief of mine the season wrong.
I hear the echoes through the mountains throng;
The winds come to me from the fields of sleep.

and banish self-pity with:

Though nothing can bring back the hour
Of splendour in the grass, of glory in the flower,
We will grieve not, rather find
Strength in what remains behind.

And now that I am well into my eighties —

In the soothing thoughts that spring
Out of human suffering,
In the faith that looks through death,
In years that bring the philosophic mind.

Thank you, Miss Prismall — and of course, Wordsworth.

Miss Kathleen Scotson-Clark: Headmistress

Miss Kathleen Scotson-Clark, our headmistress, was a force to be reckoned with. She had built up Chapel Allerton High School from a small private academy to a direct grant Grammar School without forfeiting any personal omnipotence. True, she now had to take a few scholarship girls but she managed by conducting awe-inspiring interviews to make those she did not want be the ones who did not want her. 'Her' scholarship girls she would boast were *la crême de la crême.*

As far as we knew she had no professional qualifications but she had an uncanny gift for choosing staff, not only of academic distinction, but who could cope with all the demands made on them and willingly subscribe to the idea that all who worked under her, staff and girls alike, were privileged. She was not merely dressed, she was upholstered. The whale-boned antique lace propping up her lengthening and stiffening throat stood at the peak of a mountain of heavy black gaberdine which outlined her formidable frame. A vertical line of black buttons measured out her huge height and her protruding eyes, as black as her buttons, swivelled well in front of her eyelids and missed nothing.

Donald Boyd, who spoke on BBC radio on the occasion of her retirement in 1935, said: 'In 1904, when I was five, I went to a new school. Miss Scotson-Clark, the headmistress, was seven or eight feet high, dressed from neck frill to toe in black, ornamented with a frontal fin of agate buttons like very black glossy currants. She was as a dolphin. We had lunch together, the majestic headmistress and the little boy in the holland smock, and she taught me some table manners, and discovered at a glance my delinquencies. I had 'found' a ruler and a rubber. I think ever since then I have been unable to tell lies with the necessary confidence, and I do not think that I have ever again been tempted to blow on my soup. She was destined from the beginning to assert an influence of late Victorian uprightness on thousands of children under her care.'

Kenneth Thomas added his recollections of his school days in the Kindergartan at Chapel Allerton:

'I went to the school in 1904, a week before my fifth birthday, and that is my first memory of Miss Scotson-Clark in her little study. She was about seven to eight feet high as Donald Boyd had suggested. She asked me if I could read, and I said I could read **anything.** She exclaimed: 'I don't believe you.' She then gave me that day's edition of the Yorkshire Post and told me to read the leader. This I did to her utter astonishment, and that was my entrance examination.'

School started with prayers at 8.45, when we solemnly marched, hands clasped behind our backs, from our various form-rooms into the tight-standing rows in the far-too-small hall. After the march to the stirring musical doggerel composed by her brother, Scotson-Clark, we subsided into a somewhat spine-chilling silence and waited for the presence.

Her entrance was magnificent. If Thor had stormed into the room we could not have been more electrified. Standing high above the lectern, not a second lost, she announced the hymn number, and rivetting her eyes on the pianist and thumping her left hand impatiently on the pianist's shoulder, she beat out the bar-lines with her right foot. There was never any legato in the hymn singing; Christian Soldiers have never marched so relentlessly and speedily as we did. We were urged on to Fight the Good Fight with battering-ram persistence, and must have broken the speed record in reaching the finale of 'Christ is all in all to thee'. If in the hymn announcement she asked for verse omissions, then we knew that those precious moments saved were to be thriftily used for some terrifying tirade to follow. She didn't need much ammunition for her attacks: without school hat – not wearing gloves – eating a sweet in the street – riding on the top of a tram-car – unladylike speech – not changing into house-shoes – a poor weekly report – running in the corridor; any of these produced a verbal and visual withering of the culprit in front of the whole school. A school friend of mine recalls the day when Miss Scotson-Clark, riding to Leeds in the tram-car, spotted two of her girls walking on top of a wall. Promptly she took control. 'Tramway car driver', she ordered, 'stop the tram-car!' Of course he stopped: no one disobeyed that voice. Towering over the girls, even though they were on top of a wall, she gestured them down. 'Home!' was her only command. She then withdrew to the waiting tram and ordered the driver to start. Sadism reached a peak when the next morning at prayers, using a cunning strategy of elimination of those not likely to be culprits: 'All those who live in Moortown... Alwoodley... Roundhay... sit down', the two sinners were the only ones left standing out of the three hundred apprehensive girls. They were not expelled but their school hats and blazers were confiscated for a month thus denying them any school outings to theatres or concerts. 'I let everyone on that tram-way car see that I didn't allow my girls to walk on walls.' Thus another 'shall not' was added to the school commandments.

Miss Scotson Clark, Headmistress 1901-31.

But my own transgressions were far more unspeakable.

I arrived, as I have already said, as a very diffident 11-year-old, under–weight and in rather mother–makeshift school uniform. The building was also perfected makeshift: a whole terrace of large Victorian houses knocked into one; thus five or six staircases and five or six hall passage-ways created a toast rack structure. At the end of each passage was a lavatory with, though I did not realise it, an unwritten code of possession. Desperately needing to 'go,' I made for the loo (not a word we used then) at the end of the corridor near the Assembly Hall. After my quick nervous visit the door rattled and there was Miss Scotson-Clark towering to the ceiling of her corridor. With lips pulled in and out in speechless rage and eyes bulging, she flung her right arm in the opposite direction of the lavatory and in silence withered me into a shameful scuttle. All I wanted to do was to die. how could I return to school the next day? How could I ever look up to her or she down to me?

The phrase 'turned on' was unknown to Miss Scotson-Clark except in relation to taps, but she was frenetically concerned how we were 'turned out'.

Mercifully, after a year of deadly navy blue tunics, navy blue blouses with pin dots of white, and thick black stockings, the school was revolutionised by the new gym mistress, Miss Harris — a formidable redhead of enormous power and personality. She designed a rather fetching gym tunic of soft sage green gaberdine, with three-curved bands for the box pleats, worn over the best tussore blouses with square necks edged with two rows of green stitching and cuffs to match. The stockings were now fully-fashioned brown botany wool of enormous length to reach the buttons of our Liberty bodices. All top quality Marshall & Snelgrove. Nothing less would do.

Miss Scotson-Clark, who always referred to 'my girls in my uniform' now gave new meaning to the phrase by having a total outfit made in the same sage green gaberdine — in no sense a gym tunic — but a faithful duplicate of the black monumental robe. To complete the ensemble, she had a green velour hat, exactly the school material, but fashioned into a Queen Mary toque with a vertical rust-coloured osprey feather nodding still more inches to her Olympian height. It was an impressive General who led us to the Grand Theatre in Leeds and who checked the precision of our girdles and stocking seams before we boarded the char-a-banc. Miss Scotson-Clark's pronunciation of this coach lifted it out of the hoi-polloi class. With the flourish of a General giving orders to advance, she declared:

'Lead on, without speaking, into the Share-a-Bong.'

No wonder I had the idea that the 'bong' was a sort of bench which you 'shared' with a partner!

Perhaps the 'share-a-bong' deserves a little closer observation, for a more hybrid vehicle has never been seen before or since. It looked, at first glance, as if the horses were missing for it still had a high wagonette look about it with its open top and seats stretched across its width. Although one climbed steps to get into it, these were allowed by Miss Scotson-Clark because — unlike the tram — it would be impossible for a man to climb the few steps at the same time and thus have an indelicate view of our thighs and our green elastic-closed knickers. As with all motors of the period, starting involved the thrust and pull of the L-shaped iron starting handle; in the case of the 'share-a-bong' this was enormously heavy, and therefore it was imperative that the driver never let his engine stall — so a huge roar growled from the unwieldy body.

Hats were clutched, skirts were held down, conversation lip-read over the noise until with quick re-adjustment of our clothes we stood in prim crocodile outside the Grand Theatre. Suppressing bubbling excitement, we followed Miss Scotson-Clark into the centre seats of the front rows of the dress circle. Other schools in the auditorium — in cheaper seats — had no 'sweet' restrictions; the only rustle from our seats was the passing and reading of programmes and the very discreet removal of our hats. Even Miss Scotson-Clark's triumph of the modiste's art had to be removed — more than necessary for anyone unfortunate enough to be seated behind her.

After the show, I remember the horror on the face of our headmistress when one

"Lead on without speaking into the Share-a-Bong"

of 'her' girls shouted to a friend: 'Ethel, coom on, we're getting inter t'sharrer': the kind of speech which her born-in-the-market parents were conscientiously paying for her to lose. A firm hand closed in on her, and she was scooped into the 'share-a-bong' and put in the charge of an elocutionary exemplary prefect. I do not know, but I should guess that a visit to the 'study' was a dark spot in the culprit's next day's time-table.

The school was divided vertically into three houses: Oak and Ash and Thorn, a theme derived from Rudyard Kipling's book, Rewards and Fairies. The point of the book was that it provided an incredible school song for Chapel Allerton High School. Imagine 300 girls: 100 Oaks, 100 Ashes, and 100 Thorns, with badges of the trees on their bosoms and hair ribbons to match, singing:

'Of all the trees that grow so fair
Old England to adorn
Greater are none, beneath the sun,
Than Oak and Ash and Thorn.
Sing Oak and Ash and Thorn, good sirs,
All on a midsummer morn,
Surely we sing, no little thing in
*Oak and Ash and Thorn

(Oak only) Oak of the clay lived many a day
Or ever Aeneas began.
(Ash only) Ash of the loam was a lady at home
When Brut was an outlaw man.
(Thorn only) Thorn, of the Down, saw new Troy town
Or ere was London born,
(All) Witness hereby, the ancientry
*Of Oak and Ash and Thorn.

Oh do not tell the priest our plight
Or he would call it a sin,
But we have been out in the woods all night
A-conjuring summer in.
And we bring you news by word of mouth
Good news for cattle and corn,
Now is the sun come up from the south
*With Oak and Ash and Thorn.

Sing Oak and Ash and Thorn, good sirs,
All on a midsummer morn.
England shall bide, till judgment tide,
*With Oak and Ash and Thorn.'

(*Each house said its own name synchronised with a 'bob curtsey'.

Of course we changed 'summer' to 'someone' to 'conjure in', which was very daring. The idea of girls being out in the woods all night. We weren't even allowed to ride on the top of a tram!

No one ever told us who Brut was (though I think I was the only woman in a much later period who nodded familiarly when the after-shave of that name appeared) nor were we even enlightened about when and where 'Aeneas began' or what connection Troy had with London.

The school motto, worked into the coat of arms and embroidered in pink on our green hat-bands, summed up the school's priorities and Miss Scotson-Clark's sledge-hammering attack on minutiae:

'In minimus fidelis'

We certainly were made to be *'fidele'* about such minima as: wearing a strap purse over the left shoulder; using a long *'ah'* instead of the flat West Riding ă; flattening ourselves against a wall for a member of staff to pass; tilting our soup plates away from us; addressing staff with full name; answering invitations correctly in the third person; never putting 'Mr' but 'Esquire'; saying 'I beg your pardon' not 'Pardon', and writing 'thank-you' letters the morning after the night before which we put in an *ahnvelope.*

No wonder this compact Latin motto was translated for us into lengthy English:

'He that is faithful in that which is least is faithful also in much.'

This school-spun philosophy was securely monitored from Miss Scotson-Clark's three reception rooms (the rooms themselves came into the mini category): an office, a study and a drawing room. If we were summoned about trivia, though no misdemeanour was trivial in her eyes — perhaps a lost book or failure to bring a clean linen table napkin on a Monday — the venue was the **office.** If the lapse were more serious: disorderly behaviour, slovenly work, or unpunctuality, it was the **study,** but if the crisis were death, delinquency or deception, then it was the **drawing room!**

Visits to the office and study punctuated my school years. The queue on Monday morning to the office was for new exercise books. Not one blot, spelling mistake, torn-out page escaped her eagle eye. But no new book was given until she had scrutinised the old one. She knew everything and everybody. All the three hundred. But when I was 15 I had one memorable summons to the DRAWING ROOM!

As you have read earlier, part of my journey to school was the train drive from Crossgates to Leeds. My three sisters and my brother and I all had railway contracts, quite an expensive item out of my father's modest salary. One day, my sister Betsy, by this time a student at Leeds University, lost her contract, and eventually we contrived to split the green two-sided cardboard pass and have half each. The contracts had the owner's name on one side and the expiry date on the other.

For some reason, since it was I who should have been earlier, my sister caught the earlier train. She was on the 8.14. I caught the 8.24, which meant not getting to school until about 9.15.

Halfway along the line, an inspector — not the usual ticket collector — came along examining both sides of every ticket. I showed mine, clamped down in its cellophane case, green side and date side up. He pulled it out, turned it over, saw the white blank reverse side, took out a pad and pencil, and asked my name. The name and address and all the rest of the evidence were solemnly recorded and the contract confiscated. All I saw after he had gone was my red reflection in the window; I daren't face the other passengers. By the time the train steamed into Leeds station, I saw prison as my only future. What to do?

The only answer was to play truant from school, and go and find my sister in the University — quite the opposite direction and four miles to walk from my own school. I vaguely recall doors, corridors, stairs, and gowns. At last I found my sister, who flashed out: 'You've no right to come here!' I made her listen. She then confessed that she had given my name to the detective. So not only fraud, but lies complicated the whole frightening business. Of course it was my name on her borrowed sliver of railway contract, but I had given my name too. A tangled web indeed.

For the next three weeks we begged, borrowed, stole money to buy our railway tickets, for we daren't tell them at home. The day of reckoning came. Sports Day at Chapel Allerton was more like Ascot than an athletic arena. How we and our parents were turned out, the eating of strawberries and cream, and the general air of 'Jolly Good', 'Top Hole', 'Ripping', 'Topping', 'First Class', 'Oh, Well Run!' mattered much more than if we broke the high or long jump record. On these occasions, Miss Scotson-Clark, in full sail, wore a replica of her 'school uniform', but in cream, with a wedding cake Queen Mary toque and a long cream parasol.

It was the end of the morning of the Sports Day. We could have been being groomed for Crufts, so thorough was our form mistresses' inspection. As we all stood in line, the door was flung open by the secretary, who tersely demanded 'Would Christabel Hyde go at once to the DRAWING ROOM?' The whole class was stunned, whispering sotto voce: 'the **drawing** room.'

When I arrived, a stocky little man holding his bowler hat and a pencil and pad was standing several storeys below the high-rise cream-coutured Scotson-Clark. Her lips were rolling in and out, and on my entrance, the globular eyes on stalks sprang from him to me. He began with the usual warning: 'You don't have to speak, but anything you say will be taken down as evidence against you.

'Of course she will speak, my good man; my girls have courage and elocution,' declaimed Miss Scotson-Clark.

The cross-questioning began. My replies came out haltingly, my 'courage and elocution' seriously deflated. If it had been the Old Bailey, it could not have been more terrifying. My limp story necessarily centred on my sister's borrowing and my trying to help her. His final question: 'Have you told your parents?' drew Miss Scotson-Clark to her full eight feet while she thundered at him: 'She is not the sort of girl to go whimpering to her parents!'

After half-an-hour's grilling, she manoeuvred him into departure, and — closing the door to speed him out — turned on me with sibilant Ss and a cunning pianissimo: 'Christabel, that was collusion .' I hadn't the slightest idea what that meant, but mercifully the secretary came in to hurry my canny headmistress into the waiting car. 'Colonel Bousfield has arrived; you must leave for Sports Day — it's getting late.'

I was too stunned to realise that Scotty's priority was that no disgrace, no publicity, no court case should blacken the name of her school and that her Ascot must have its Royal persona and its Royal punctuality. She had, in her own imperious — albeit devious — way, stuck up for me.

The figure that stepped out to the Daimler, her cream lace parasol poking and speeding the chauffeur, could only have been matched with a composite woman of Boadicea, Queen Mary, Lady Bracknell, Emmeline Pankhurst, Miss Beale and Miss Buss. Like Shakespeare's Cleopatra, she was unparalleled.

The tailpiece to this story is somewhat of an anti-climax. My sister and I screwed up our courage to tell my father. Never was his home-coming so contrived. We lured him with cigarettes, warmed his slippers, put on daughterly smiles, and confessed.

To our utter astonishment he chuckled and said: 'Well, I've been buying LNER contracts for 20 years; they've had enough money out of me.' Of course he was told off by my mother for being 'soft' with us, but it was a mercy for the two delinquents that they lived in an age before juvenile courts!

Delinquency at Chapel Allerton rarely reached 'drawing room' censure; in fact, some of the girls so neatly fitted into the prescribed decorum package that the nearest they ever got to delinquency was in confusing or losing shoe-bags. The four shoe-bags were strictly defined: black for house slippers, blue for gym canvas plimsolls, green for games shoes, and white for ballroom dancing pumps. We had to embroider our names on each bag in large white copperplate letters; the house and gym shoe-bags had two taped hangers, but the games and ballroom bags had 'Dorothy' draw-strings so that they could be transported modestly, the white ballroom bag also contained white gloves. Our walking shoes were housed in wooden pigeon-holes, and were sprayed each day with a hand-pump of floral essence. This was a round-the-school floor-to-ceiling task carried out each morning by a senior prefect. It was the one duty I aspired to and never realised.

Unlike the hundreds of schools I have since been into, the Chapel Allerton 'smell' was one suggesting well-groomed living: rich furniture polish, Pears soap, lavender and Eau de Cologne impregnated air. Not a whiff of feet or armpits anywhere.

School luncheons, never called lunch or dinner, were definitely not for relaxation. This was just as much a teaching session as any other subject on the time-table.

We walked sedately in a prescribed order, picked up our white linen napkin in its labelled ring, and proceeded to a precise position. Not a word was spoken until grace was said and staff were seated. These places were regularly changed so that we had to socialise in a rota system with the long and the short and the tall. This meant that at least twice in a term one sat at the headmistress's table. Here, dominating the long white damasked table, with eyes like searchlights, sat Miss Scotson-Clark flanked by a large bottle of Keystone Burgundy — no doubt a tonic to build her up. Woe betide any girl who used only a spoon for her pudding. 'Spoon and fork sometimes, spoon never, fork ever' was one of her oft-repeated texts.

'Knife with the handle in your *palm*, Tabitha; one does not hold a knife like a *pencil*.'

'Christabel, you have talked only to your right-hand neighbour; kindly direct your conversation now to your left-hand neighbour.' (LHN couldn't have cared less as she was already deep in conversation with *her* LHN)

It was, of course, table service with a mistress at the tureen end of each refectory table. It was the luncheon duty mistress who checked that each girl brought a clean white napkin every Monday morning. For this sin of omission, one went foodless even though parents had paid for the lunch.

It was 'not done' to help oneself or to ask for anything to be passed. We had to wait to be asked. This became a miming, nudging operation in order to receive the salt or bread. No one ate until everyone was served so the 'hot lunches' invitingly described in the school prospectus usually congealed on the plate. However, there was no doubt that Miss Scotson-Clark was what might be described as a 'good trencher woman'. She liked her food and wine, and considered the food, at least, important for her girls. This was proved to me dramatically when I visited her after I had been teaching for a year in an expensive, but suspect, girls' boarding school in Harrogate.

In 1929 jobs were not easy to find, and the unwritten code was that — however disastrous the first job — one stuck it out for at least two years.

At the end of the year, exhausted with a 70 hour a week stint, arctic temperatures, and food poor both in quantity and quality, I gave in my notice. No teacher today would understand the courage that needed. Yorkshire was suffering from a woollen slump, jobs were few and far between. One did not resign but rather became resigned to whatever the gods provided. So, it was with some trepidation that I went to report to my former headmistress. This time, all past sins forgiven, I was ushered into the drawing room.

Apologetically I explained the situation: the staff house heated with a reluctant coke fire which was lit only in the evening, the 7 am run round St John's Well on the Stray with the 50 juniors shivering inside their cloaks, the conflicting headmistresses — one deaf and kindly, one scholarly and severe — a drug addict I learned later.

However, it was the conclusive report on the food which made Miss Scotson-Clark mount her chariot of fire. I described a typical high tea, our last meal of the day: 'one sardine on toast'. With her eyes nearly taking off from their sockets and her lips well massaged with the inward roll of outrage, she tipped her head heavenwards, lifted her clasped hands to bosom height and exploded:

'I'd like to see anyone offering **me a sardine.**'

Print cannot possibly convey the compound inflection, the Bracknell/Evans convoluted vocal swoop on the 'me' and 'sardine.' and the picture this projected. Now in full spate she continued: 'When I was at Cheltenham, we had soup, entree, main course, pudding, cheese and biscuits with perhaps a Claret or a Graves, but then, of course, there were **Bishops** on the Board.'

If I have given a picture of a monster, I hope you will most properly recognise her innate kindliness, shrewd judgment, singleness of purpose, and dedication to her school. She truly believed that all the heroes of the Great War had died for the Empire — to keep all those red patches on the map — so that the world of Kipling, Stanley Baldwin, George V, Baden Powell, Colonel Bousfield and Mrs Beeton should 'bide til judgment tide' — bloody perhaps, but unbowed.

There was no-one more adept at rising to an occasion than Miss Scotson-Clark. The nickname 'Scotty' never did her justice, sounding too much like a pet Aberdeen terrier. If we had thought of 'canining' her, a Great Dane would have been more appropriate.

Ceremony became her for she had a noble and compelling presence. No-one who was at Chapel Allerton will ever forget the awe-inspiring remembrance days when the two minutes silence on 11 November stilled every train and tram, bus and bicycle, and every man, woman and child wherever they might be.

In Ash Hall we were all bonded in anguish for there was no-one in the school who had not lost either a father or uncle, brother or cousin, or women relatives who had not lost a fiancé or husband.

Kathleen Scotson-Clark, standing monumentally on that podium, had no husband, fiancé, lover or children of her own but her stilled tears could have been for the small boys she had guided from kindergarten to prep and public schools — potential leaders — victims of that muddy, bloody war. Her time-beating feet and hands, which came into action for other hymns, were stilled - as ours all were as we sang:

> 'I vow to thee, my country, all earthly things above,
> Entire and whole and perfect, the service of my love;
> The love that asks no questions, the love that stands the test,
> That lays upon the altar the dearest and the best;
> The love that never falters, the love that pays the price,
> The love that makes undaunted the final sacrifice'

and ending with that idealistic, well-intended but never achieved line:

> 'And her ways are ways of gentleness, and all her paths are peace'

When she left this world, as she did on 28 March 1959, I can imagine St Peter polishing up his keys, the angels adjusting their wings, the harps being retuned, and St Cecilia flourishing a fanfare to the angelic choir in preparation for the celestial entrance of Kathleen Scotson-Clark.

I trust that all the trumpets sounded for her on the other side.

Orginal photograph of Morritt Avenue, Halton with the gates open 1903

CHAPTER ELEVEN
NEIGHBOURS

The Avenue

If an architect had been commissioned to design a group of houses with the sole purpose of creating neighbourliness he could not have achieved more than Mr Morritt, who in 1903 built 'Morritt Avenue'. This is the recorded name in Kelly's West Riding Directory but it was given a guarded anonymity when Mr Morritt's architectural panache made him bankrupt. We, throughout childhood and even now, refer to it always as 'The Avenue'.

Mr Morritt had been to Italy and so, inoculated with Mediterranean sunshine and no doubt fired with Prince Albert's architectural enthusiasm, he let himself go on the external decoration.

Although each house was a 'like twin' with its adjoining semi-detached neighbour, each pair had its own idiosyncratic features of gables, turrets, towers, balconies, plasterwork and wrought iron. Purists and classicists of architecture would criticise all the added ornamentation, but I rather think that Osbert Lancaster and John Betjeman would cast amused and approving eyes over Mr Morritt's friendly follies. The thirty two houses formed a wide avenue completely surrounded by fields and isolated from the two nearest villages — Crossgates and Halton.

The walk to Crossgates station was through meadows and cornfields which one crossed through footpaths and over stiles. The only other houses on the way formed a little gabled terrace which we affectionately and patronisingly called 'The Dolly Houses'. My mother told us that when the Avenue was first built there were huge wrought iron gates at the entrance with a gate-keeper solemnly opening them for any horse-driven vehicles of which he approved. Residents and tradesmen with hand-carts could enter through the small side gates but no passers-by would have reason or excuse to go through.

A map of 1908 shows the completely rural quality of the whole area; 30 years later a shapeless smudge of suburban houses all the same pattern changed the face of the map. Now, in the 1990s, it is urbanised out of recognition. New roads, supermarkets and shopping precincts have given Crossgates a new lease of life but who will remember the walk through the fields and the hanging baskets of flowers in the station?

Nothing was skimped in the building of the Avenue (though we were told that it was cosmetic rather than functional) but we had a wide road and wide pavements which became our forum, our pitch, our stage and our personally directed arena.

Furnished as the Avenue was with its own ER letterbox, its wrought iron gas-lamps, its 'Private. No Thoroughfare' notice and its avenue of trees, it had an air of protection and security which it is impossible to find in today's urban high-risers or suburban sprawl.

In such a setting everyone knew everybody else: their triumphs and disasters, their needs, their comings and goings, births, marriages and deaths. No one had to ask for help or have dealings with Social Services. Help was at hand. Night and day.

One night, I remember, when all of us had gone to bed, there was a loud knocking at the door and there were the four Crawley boys from next door standing in their pyjamas and dressing gowns saying 'Our house is on fire. May we come in?' No more was said. My father, armed with pails of water and blankets, got to work with their father. Mrs Crawley came in with a box of Thornton's toffee to calm us all down and put a sticky brake on our chattering teeth and tongues. My mother made hot cocoa and brought it up to our bedrooms which now were three-or-four-in-a bed dormitories.

At that time there were no telephones in either house so I think it must have been the Allgoods who summoned the fire brigade. What a wonderful night for children: the gleaming brass of the bells and the firemens' helmets, the red and gold of the fire engine, the gushing hosepipes, the ladders and the well-trained horses. Even though the acrid smell of burning paint crept into our eyes and noses, it never occurred to us that our semi-detached house was vulnerable.

Neighbours arrived with offers of help and stayed until dawn, and we, for once in our lives, were the heroes and heroines of a great drama although we did nothing more active than chew toffee. The Crawley boys stayed with us for a month until their house was restored. It would never have occurred to my parents to do anything less for our agreeable neighbours and their well brought-up sons.

The Dolly Houses

Traditional games came and went with the seasons.

The Gang

Not all the boys in the Avenue would bear that description but it was the 'toughs' with whom we identified, flattered I suppose that they allowed girls into their gang.

Looking down the years I am amazed that our parents never interfered or tried to protect us from the male-dominated gang. We were never prinked up to be feminine. Throughout the year there were the harmless traditional games which by some strange and rhythmic alchemy kept strictly to the seasons. Without any reference to calendars or dates the whipping tops and marbles seemed to come out with the daffodils, skipping ropes with the bluebells and hoops with the hips and haws. Conkers, of course, were our harvest.

In our part of the world boys seemed to favour the squat 'turnip' whipping tops and leather lashes. Girls preferred the slimmer 'carrot' tops even though they were much more difficult to keep spinning. Year after year the same tops came out but were decorated afresh with paint or crayon so that a new design whirled on the crowning disc. We marvelled as we watched the boys in the gang perform miracles of top-spinning; jerking them into the palm of the non-whipping hand, flinging them into the air while keeping them still revolving, slashing the tops yards away from themselves or pegging at their rival's top until they could bring it to a stop or even split it in two. The movement was as speedy and vicious as ice hockey!

One back breaking game which we simply called the 'Wall Game' — 'Jibby Jibby Knacker' in street terminology — was the most inhuman of all. The first boy stood with his back to the wall as the supporting post for the next one to make a 'back'. In succession every player took a flying leap into the great hump of backs which gradually built up. One after another they came thundering on until the weakest back gave way. When the great hump became too long the latest 'jumpers' tried to knock the others over until the leader commanded 'All fall down!' on which the whole lot dropped down regardless of who was battered or whatever the state of the ground. It was supposed to be a game for boys only but we girls joined in, manfully trying not to show a sign of fear.

Another more feminine game was 'Statues', harmless enough if played with reasonable feminine force but, as we often played it with the Turnbull and Leach boys, the speed whipped up could be lethal. The leader swung each player round and round, and then suddenly released him to become a 'statue'. All were 'frozen' into their suggested shapes until the leader went round passing judgment. The most convincing was picked to be the next 'swinger' ... and so it went on. Such was the force with which we were hurled (and I was the youngest and smallest of the gang) that I don't remember ever being an upright statue. I always ended up — perhaps it should be 'down' — by being a hedgehog, snake, mole, caterpillar or gravestone — indeed anything I could think of without legs. One day Ken's horrific hurl threw me against the corner of the brick pillar at our front gate and cracked my skull. All I can remember now are the bowls of blood on my mother's lap.

Another painfully exhausting game was simply called 'Street Lamp'. Projecting from each gas lamp was an iron bar at right angles to the lamp-post on which the lamp-lighter could lean a ladder. The boys used to jump until they could reach the bar and then hang down with feet well away from the ground. A younger, shorter player was chosen who had to jump and hold on to the hanger's legs — also suspended in air — until one or the other weakened and fell. If the tall one gave way, the smaller one could be mercilessly trampled on.

I remember one day, I think it was in 1917, we were playing a harmless but tense game of 'Grandmother's Footsteps'. In this game the leader stands facing the wall with the rest of the team about 20 feet away. Together they all creep towards the leader's back ready to freeze when he turns round suddenly. If anyone is spotted by the leader, even moving a finger, he is 'out'. The game finishes when one of the survivors 'tigs' the leader's back or when all the players are out. On this particular day Ken was 'Grandmother'; not his usual role, but even so he was capable of making her have eyes like the wolf in Red Riding Hood. Suddenly, out of the creeping silence, a boy's voice shrieked from the top of the Avenue: 'Ken, your brother's been killed!'

The callousness of that boy, whose name I would rather not say, haunts me to this day although I was only eight and understood little of what the war was about.

In our dumb way we were all callous too for we none of us knew what to say or do to comfort him. We simply stood in silence watching that lone figure — our tough and mighty Ken — walk down the Avenue crumpled with grief.

'Calling' — before the First World War

The behaviour of both adults and children who lived in the Avenue was full of contrasts and contradictions: the ladies who had their prescribed calling days were the genteel or childless ones or those who kept their children away from the neighbouring ruffians.

Social calendars were marked with all the various calling days, of their own and their neighbours. The personal visiting cards included their husband's name — for no woman had her own card — and the phrase: 'Every third Tuesday' or 'Every second Thursday' according to the hostess's personal choice of monthly entertaining. Thus almost every day of the month, except Saturdays and Sundays, had a tea engagement which also meant that each individual could have about 20 days of neighbourly gossip. Calling days were the exchange and mart of all the local and family tit-bits.

Visitors knew the rules: the visitor arrived elegantly dressed, hatted and gloved. The gloves, usually white, were sometimes put on at the door while the more utility slightly soiled ones were removed and put away in the handbag. Hats, tethered with long hatpins, were the most important part of the outfit, and of course were never removed during a visit. Three visiting cards were left in the special tray in the hall: two for the visitor's husband and the other for herself. The customary length of the visit was twenty minutes but in the familiar surroundings of the Avenue, where folk might have talked 'over-the-hedge' earlier in the day, the time might spread to half-an-hour. A cup of tea was handed on a small tray, which also held the cream or milk, the sugar basin and tongs for the visitor to help herself. It was *'not done'* to put milk in first; people who did so were *'below the pale'* or *'common'*.

Cakes and bread and butter were arranged on three or four-tiered stands on which plates covered with elaborately crocheted and starched d'oyleys set off the finger-held 'dainties' — a fussy little word which epitomised the hostesses' 'refinement'.

The conversation ploy was to extract and give as much juicy gossip as one could without using any word which might be considered vulgar. Ladies (not women!) were 'expecting' — they were never pregnant; 'rich' and 'poor' were avoided and 'well-off' or 'nicely off' or 'difficult circumstances' took their place; the 'porch' was a 'vestibule'; one did not 'buy jam' but rather 'purchased preserves' and one hinted rather than bluntly voiced one's prejudices. Such snobbish sentences might well be left in the air for the receiver to do a mental enlargement:

'Well she's not exactly top-drawer ...'
or 'As my husband says: 'not Mess trained my dear.' ... '
or 'Not exactly one of us, you understand ... '

No one ever died, they passed on, away or over or simply 'left'.

My mother would have none of it, nor did she need to for we had open house for those who did not mind thicker bread and butter or cut-and-come-again cake.

One Avenue neighbour had a stylish way of cutting down on callers: 'Every fifth Wednesday' her card read, so her own days came round with freakish regularity once or twice a year!

But in 1914 all this formal fuss dissolved away. Maids went to work in the munition factories, women did their own housework, joined the VAD or were enticed back as teachers or office clerks. Middle-aged men joined the Special Constables; the young men went to the Front. Many never returned from the filth and horror of trench warfare.

The Dame's School in the Avenue

My mother, having been well-trained as a teacher at Ripon College, did not respond to the Avenue snobbery of the superiority of a 'private' school, though logistically and socially it would have been convenient for us to attend the Dame's School at the bottom of the Avenue, where Miss Tindale had converted the family dining-room into a school room. This was done by the simple expediency of putting all the leaves in the Victorian family dining table, thus enlarging it into a communal desk for about twelve children. The children, all living in the Avenue, ranged awkwardly from those whose feet didn't touch the floor to the overgrown toughs whose feet and fists could reach anywhere and anybody. Copying seemed to be the major basic skill on the timetable: copying from the board, copying from *The Bible,* copying from rather ageing text books or dictionaries and, of course, copying from one another. The last feat depended on the neighbour not using his hand as a screen.

My mother's disapproval of the school was reinforced by the hair-raising account we heard of Miss Tindale having been chased round the table with a ruler brandished by — but I had better not say his name for by now he must have either left this earth or perhaps be a Chairman of the local education committee or a retired JP solemnly saying, 'We didn't behave like that in our day'.

One day in June the children coaxed the barrel-organ grinder to bring his Tingleairy (for that was the only name we ever heard or used) close up to their school room window, which he obligingly did. Miss Tindale, white with rage, rushed out of the school room and put her hand out to stop the organ grinder, who deftly caught her hand with his and, singing away, kept her hand revolving:

'Come, come, come and make eyes at me
Down at the old Bull and Bush.
Come, come drink some port wine with me
Down at the Old Bull and Bush (Bush, Bush)
Hear the little German Band, (der de de der do do)
Just let me hold your hand, do...'

In the end, like Matilda's aunt, she had to pay to get the man to go away. Never had her pupils been so hugely entertained!

When memory is at the Spring, children make up and remember all sorts of rhymes and jingles — some of them excruciating. So for days on end Miss Tindale's privileged pupils sang up and down the Avenue, to the tune of *Frére Jacques:*

'Daft Miss Tindale, daft Miss Tindale,
Played a tune, played a tune
On a Tingleairy very loud and blarey
All through June, all through June!'

We, at our no-nonsense Board school, though realising we were learning more, felt excluded from the agitated ferment which enlivened their school days.

However, we did join in the political jingles without having the slightest notion for whom or for what we were singing:

'Vote, vote, vote for Mr Asquith,
You can't vote for a better man.
He's the man, he's the man,
And we'll have him if we can
And send old ...'

With my somewhat wintery memory I cannot conjure up the end of the verse because we substituted any local aspirant in politics whose name was a household word. We were far too ill-informed to know the names of Lord Balfour, Joseph

Chamberlain, Lord Grey or Keir Hardy. As we grew older, we simply gave our prejudices an airing by making it clear that the Hydes were for Free Trade and Lloyd George while our friends favoured Tariff Reform and Stanley Baldwin. The Hyde parents sympathised with the workers in the General Strike while our friends' fathers drove trains and buses, delivered letters, anything, to keep the country going!

Our parents agreed with Lloyd George's plans to tax landowners (excluding, of course, our farming friends and relations) while our neighbours fretted that the stately homes of England would be in peril.

For the Hyde children this was all very confusing, brought up as we were with Radical notions of 'These things shall be ...'

As far as I can remember, not one family in the Avenue had a son or daughter at either Oxford or Cambridge. The sons tended to slide into their fathers' businesses; the girls, with little or no career-training, were steered into marriage. Yet Oxford and Cambridge, or rather the Boat Race, became as urgent in the Spring as whipping tops or skipping ropes. Each of us had a fervent loyalty to Oxford or Cambridge; the obsession started in childhood and persisted through adolescence. For no logical reason the Hyde girls were 'Oxford' and chanted to the skipping rope beat:

> 'Oxford, Oxford, rowing on forever,
> Cambridge in a matchbox floating down the river.'

When sung by an aspiring little Cantab., the names were reversed. We also used the rhymes for choosing 'It' as leader for our next game. A pointed forefinger jabbed the chest of each player eliminating them all, one by one, with this rhyme:

> 'Oxford, Oxford, you will show
> Cambridge, Cambridge cannot row.
> We are dark blue, we all shout
> Cambridge, Cambridge, you are out!'

Again a Cambridge fan would reverse the names and substitute 'light' for 'dark'

Looking back from an age of radio and television, when we can know the result as soon as the crew, one would have thought the race would be as remote as the Battle of Waterloo. But the shout of the newspaper vendors selling the *Saturday Evening Late News* must have had just as powerful an impact.

Whether it was my mother's theosophy or her membership of the Anti-Vivisection Society I am not quite clear, but the third, fourth and fifth of her children were not allowed to be vaccinated against small pox. Every child at school and in the Avenue had been 'done' and wore an armband of red ribbon to tell the world to steer clear. Our friends thought we were trying to avoid the pain and discomfort but like all children we were embarrassed by being different from our friends. Then we remembered that Aunt Maggie had left a reel of red ribbon — and one of blue — to decorate our dresses for Empire Day so we secretly made ourselves beautiful scarlet armbands, wider and shinier than our friends, and screwed our faces up in torture if anyone came within touching distance of our 'sore' arms.

As I have said, childhood and the First World War synchronised so exactly that there seemed no question of a beginning — for that I could not remember — nor of an end which could hardly affect our day-to-day routine. But throughout the war we children joined the Avenue bandage-rolling parties and we all tried to knit scarves and balaclava helmets. The scarves went in and out according to how many stitches we dropped or retrieved and the balaclavas either obliterated the eyes completely or caused a lopsided squint. Fortunately, as the youngest, I was let off and only did face-cloths which were simply dish-cloths of thick white cotton re-christened for the troops.

Unlike most of the folk around us, my mother sympathised with the conscientious objectors and deplored the way women handed out white feathers to men who were not wearing khaki but she also joined in and, I think, believed in the war effort.

Near by, in Halton, a collection of army huts had been made into an improvised hospital where disabled soldiers could convalesce after the horrors of shell-shock, trench frostbite or war wounds. My mother, anxious that some of the children in the Avenue should 'do their bit,' arranged for us to go in turn to entertain the troops.

Unfortunately we had had no Marie Lloyd, Florrie Ford or Vesta Tilley leavening in our literary home so all we could offer these brave and bored soldiers were slabs of Shakespeare with a little light relief of the *Inchcape Rock* or *The Highwayman*. One painful recital was my rendering of the 'Quality of mercy' where I, a puny ten-year-old Portia — in Liberty bodice and magyar ratteen dress — strained mercy to breaking point with nervousness and anxiety to please. It was hard to divert the boys in blue from *John Bull, Tit-bits* and their Woodbines, but we persevered.

When we got home, my mother, who must have been peering through the hospital door, said: 'Do you know who the soldier was lying on the bed facing you?' Of course I didn't. 'That,' she said without flinching, 'was Henry Ainley, the greatest Shakespearean actor of the age!' The miracle was that he RECOVERED!

My mother as a neighbour

In most suburban areas people tend to congregate together in the same neighbouring churches. It was not so in the Avenue for the neighbours were agreeably ecumenical. Not that this word was ever used or considered; we took it for granted that every family had its own religious haunts.

The three Freemasons were members of different churches and chapels: High, Low and Methodist respectively. The Bleezes and the Dunns were devout Catholics, the Leaches and the Giddings were, I think, Church of England, Mr Cox was a Quaker, the Hydes and Howcrofts Baptist Chapel — not from any firm belief but rather for convenience.

My father supported the Baptists, Wesleyans and Unitarians with, as I have said earlier, an allegiance to the Reverend Leslie Weatherhead. My mother went off to

Leeds to the Theosophical Society but shared tracts and magazines with the lady who lived opposite who was a Christian Scientist. The rest of the Avenue residents seemed to attend the Wesleyan Chapel.

My mother was not in any way a hypocrite but she was a catholic chameleon. Of course I was not present for the following conversations nor did I see the letter which my mother must have written to Aunt May Hutton. But here is the gist of it gathered from hearsay:

'Thank you, Mr Cox,' I can hear her say, 'thank you very much indeed for the brochure about the courses at Swarthmore settlement. . . Yes, Betsy and Coidy will be going to the Saturday morning classes ... I do think Quakers have such firm and gentle ways of teaching. So good for young people. You'll be pleased that we're thinking of sending Coidy to Ackworth — such a good Quaker school!'

Another day: 'Good morning, Mrs Bleeze, it was so kind of you to lend me the prospectus for Notre Dame Convent ... Yes, it would be splendid if Coidy could go with Dominica. I do think the nuns are such dedicated teachers ... Yes, I agree with you the Catholic services do give children a sense of awe but security. . .'

Letter to Auntie May Hutton (Brer Rabbit)

July 1921

My dearest Brer,

The prospectus for St Christopher's is a great delight; thank you so much for sending it.

Of course the Rudolf Steiner schools are so wonderful and years ahead of their time — the perfect key to total education.

I think Coidy would enjoy being a boarder for, living 'in tune with the infinite' would help her to find her centre.

The main obstacle is the cost; the other is that her father would not appreciate the spiritual and aesthetic qualities which are such an important part of the St Christopher ethos.

I will write fully later, dear Brer, when I have found a way round all this. There is absolutely nowhere I would rather she went.

Always your loving
Swallow.

PS Since writing this letter, we have just heard that Coidy (from now on she really must be Christabel!) has been awarded a major scholarship to Chapel Allerton High School. Although the Head is, I believe, a rather dominant Victorian, I think the discipline and formality may have a steadying influence. St Christopher's, I now realise, was a pipe-dream!

Christabel (!) starts school on her 12th birthday: September 12th; that surely augurs well for a Virgo!

Mrs Golightly: our other next door neighbour

Mrs Golightly, our next door across-the-drive neighbour, had the feminine delicacy of Mrs Gaskell's Miss Matty and the tenacity of Jane Austen's Mrs Bennett. Her main occupation was to find a suitable husband for her beautiful daughter Marion.

It was therefore with her mother's full approval that Marion accepted the proposal of an officer and a gentleman whose substantial family would ensure that the son and daughter-in-law never dropped lower than the 'top drawer'.

'Mrs Hyde,' Mrs Golightly asked gently, 'would you like to bring the girls in to see Marion's trousseau?'

Even though it was 1916 there seemed to be no shortage of silk, satin and crepe-de-chine for the camisoles, cami-knickers, nightdresses, negligees and boudoir caps which were spread out on the large bed. Every garment — even the blue and pink pairs of garters — were all edged in lace with Marion's new initials embroidered on the corners.

'Marion did everything except the sewing,' said Mrs Golightly adoringly, a remark which baffled the seven, nine, eleven and fifteen-year-old viewers wearing their navy blue knickers with the closed elastic bands. There was no question of envy; it was another world into which we were thrilled even to peep.

We never realised that, as we were leaving by the back door — conveniently near to our own — a telegraph boy, in his pill-box hat, was ringing the bell of the Golightly's front door.

A few minutes later Mrs Golightly was standing at our door holding a trembling telegram in her hand. My mother read in silence. The blunt statement from the War Office finished: 'Missing, believed killed'.

For many years after the War the Golightlys were our next door neighbours, always considerate and kindly, but pre-occupied with places way beyond the Avenue: possible hunting grounds for a prospective husband. Marion's sapphire eyes had lost a little of their tranquillity and innocence, and her whole personality had slightly sharpened into the frenzy of the 1920s.

It was the time of Eton crops, short chiffon or romaine satin evening dresses with their dropped hip-lines and flat busts. Short hair was now encircled with a band on the forehead, and between vermillion lips long ivory holders held the Sobranies or brown Turkish cigarettes. On the right upper arm a gold slave bangle remained firmly in place seeming to contradict the new-found freedom of the 'flapper'.

Marion's hopeful trousseau had all these things, including splendid woollen coats with flaring fur hems and hugging fur collars, cloche hats and buckled pointed shoes with Louis heels. Mrs Golightly played every ace card for her daughter, not only at her carefully balanced bridge parties but in investing in golf coaching, membership of the most select golf club and five-star hotel holidays where men would help Marion to get out of bunkers. It all paid off and Marion married a portly businessman and went to live in a detached villa with a garage and a Lagonda.

Mrs Golightly relaxed into retirement, slept in the afternoon and let old age take its unchallenged course. Her husband, always devoted, wheeled his loving lace-and-lavender wife in a Bath chair sprung and upholstered to cushion life's jolts.

There was no hurry. Everyone in the Avenue stopped and chatted and approved of Mrs Golightly's gloved hand patting the baby or the dog. No one enquired about her aches and pains for she never complained. She looked perfectly at home against the linen pillows which every now and then were plumped up by her watchful husband.

To everyone's surprise, gentle, attentive Mr Golightly died first. The day after the funeral, Mrs Golightly quietly abandoned her Bath chair and for the rest of her uneventful life she WALKED!

Mrs Allgood: our across-the-way neighbour

Over the years Mrs Allgood's approval of everything to do with herself, and her disapproval of everyone else, had moulded her face into its definitive form. The skin had shrivelled meanly round the mouth, puffed out shiftily round her eyes, shrivelled disparagingly on her forehead and swollen out sensually on her nose. Her hair, banked into a high oblong, was, one would have thought, a permanent structure suggesting that if one hair were released it would disturb the rigidity which had created her smug self-confidence.

The Allgoods' house and its twin were the only ones in the Avenue with bay windows set at an oblique angle, thus giving them twice the viewing range of any of the other houses. Mrs Allgood should have been grateful to Mr Morritt for this whimsy as, with cream holland blinds which always needed aligning and waterfall curtains which had to be symmetrical, there was constant need for her to be busy at her window.

'I just happened to be putting the curtains straight and I saw the *Co-op* van outside the William's gate. Never thought the Avenue would come down to that but then it's not what it used to be when Father and I first came ...' and so on. Any ungloved hand or unhatted head, any carelessly rolled umbrella or spotted spats were added to her gossip-gleanings. She knew how long the doctor stayed, how short the vicar's call, and she could catch the road-sweeper before he disappeared and order him to remove a few odd leaves from her pavement.

Mr Allgood, a monumental Freemason, gave the impression of being a permanent Worshipful Master. His corpulence was emphasised by a heavy gold chain to which were attached his gold hunter watch, his gold sovereign case and his gold cigar-cutter. Mrs Allgood set him up for the day with a dining-room breakfast served from the various silver chafing dishes on the side-board. Her belief that the way to a man's heart was through his stomach was proved by her overloaded larder which was the terminus for the choicest cuts from the butcher and the plumpest birds from the poulterers.

The dining-room, used twice every weekday and three times on Saturdays and Sundays, was a serious affair with its bulbous legged mahogany table, its ten outsize dining chairs to match and its loaded sideboard. Above the sideboard a massive gilt framed picture of Highland Cattle was no doubt a constant reminder not to forget the Aberdeen Angus sirloin for Sunday's lunch.

Brown leather armchairs, brown velvet curtains and brown-patterned wallpaper, brown linoleum surrounds and the huge table under the green silk fringed central light all helped to shadow the deep red and blue Turkish carpet. So precisely was all of this aligned that all Mr Allgood had to do to summon the maid was to put his foot six inches further forward on the carpet and press the electric bell, and the blue and white Spode tureens would be removed.

On the mantelpiece two bronze horses and riders faced the monstrous black marble clock which chimed in unison with the grandfather clock in the hall. At 7.30, 12.30 and 6.30 the brass gong joined in the chorus.

With a maid and a char, both grossly overworked, Mrs Allgood could find time to make unsolicited calls on her neighbours for the sole purpose of exposing their limited resources and the amplitude of her own. If doubtful of her welcome she armed herself with a broken-into charlotte russe or a cream trifle which she knew would be past its best by the next day.

'I see you're making a shepherd's pie,' she would say as her eyes search-lighted the neighbour's kitchen. 'You wouldn't get away with that in *our* house; our father has to have something he can *carve*. Only this morning he was saying 'I don't know what we pay for at Archie's school; they seem to get nothing but mince and rice pudding.'

Archie, a rather spotty boarder at a minor public school, notched the family up one step on the social ladder by being 'away at school'.

One morning, Mrs Allgood arrived just as Mrs Bleeze — our Roman Catholic neighbour — was putting the last of her ironing on the clothes-horse. 'You've finished your ironing then, have you, Mrs Bleeze? You wouldn't get through our ironing by eleven o'clock, I can tell you! It takes Ethel all day to get up our damask tablecloths, serviettes and d'oyleys and of course our Mollie's underwear. All that lace and crochet — not that I let Ethel do Mollie's ribbons — I see to that — threading the ribbon through her petticoats and knickers. She's very particular, our Mollie is ...'

'I mustn't stay long; I've got a ham and a tongue boiling on the stove. Here, I've brought you this charlotte russe; I know your Dominica always likes it — she says she never gets it at home ... "What I really came to ask you was if you'd take in my order from the fishman. It's Ethel's day off and I'm taking Mollie to the tailor's to be fitted. There's a salmon and a lobster coming — never mind about paying; he knows *our* credit's good ...

'Yes' replied Mrs Bleeze with deliberation, whose idea of 'good living' was very different from Mrs Allgoods. 'Yes, I will take your order in Mrs Allgood, but while you've been talking I've been thinking that if only your *mind* were as well-stocked as your *larder,* what a very wise woman you would be!'

It would be pompous to pretend that we loved all our neighbours; it was the wit and good humour of the likeables which made the least likeable extremely valuable as constant subjects for our neighbourly gossip.

CHAPTER TWELVE
HOLIDAYS AT HOME IN THE FIRST WORLD WAR

The Flood: Summer 1917

More kindly folk than I might gush sentimentally about childrens' innocence, but it was our ignorance which made us incorrigibly selfish. Our one thought during the hideous spring and summer of 1917 was that once again we were to be deprived of our traditional holiday on the east coast. We only knew the heroics, not the horrors, of the war and enjoyed all the cheap jingoism. We dug trenches and stalked a man with an artificial hand, day after day, convinced that he was a spy. Through the popular songs: *Pack up your troubles; It's a long way to Tipperary* and *Long, long trail a-winding* and our misguided war efforts (bandage-rolling and balaclava knitting), we thought we were doing our bit to keep the home fires burning. We basked in reflected glory that our cousin, Henry Danby, had been killed that April in the Battle of Arras, and not to be outdone by our vicarious heroics, the rest of the gang lined up brothers, uncles and friends whose names would later on be carved on the stone memorials.

August, a hot and heavy month, did nothing to sharpen our wits or stimulate our imaginations. 'There's not even anywhere to paddle' the inner circle of the gang sulked collectively. 'Let's make a paddling pool!;' Betsy was always first with bad and brilliant ideas. 'I know, Ken,' she beamed, 'your balcony.' Ken did a quick mental check on his mother's shopping timing and the retainer maid's half-day and then took on his usual role of gaffer. Two days later we were into action. 'You Hydes bring the ground sheets of your tents and I'll get the clothes line to fasten it to the railings. And don't forget kitchen buckets!' I was just tolerated as unskilled labour: a small eight-year-old with a leaking seaside bucket.

(Looking back I marvel how little supervision there was around. We really had infinite scope for 'taking liberties' and rough justice had unlimited opportunities to mend our foolish ways.)

With the ground sheet tied halfway up the railings and more or less covering the concrete floor of the balcony, we became obsessed water carriers, from the bathroom along the landing across the floor of the 'best' bedroom and through the french windows. Shoes and socks were abandoned and frocks were tucked into our knickers. The more we increased our speed the more water we slopped en route. 'Fill it, can't you?' Ken kept up the slave-driving. If we had had even a smattering of basic physics we would have realised that far more water was being put into the pool than was registered up our ankles. We soldiered on for two hours, damp but undefeated.

It was a shock to Ken when the grandfather clock on their upstairs landing struck four. 'Stop ! ' he yelled and lined us up on the bedroom side of the ground sheet: 'Hold it! Heave over!' An avalanche of water cascaded through the railings, crashed on the dining room windows, drenched the front door steps and dwindled slowly away into the grass.

It was a long time before the Turnbull parents spoke to our parents; an awkward silence since their house insurance was in my father's hands. With his typical generosity he made quite sure that the insurance claim paid to the Turnbulls by his company, for the sodden ceilings, the flapping wallpaper and the squelchy carpets, far exceeded the normal damages.

With hindsight it would seem in character that my father quietly topped it up; a clear case of visiting the sins of the children on to the father!

All treats and outings were banned for a month; the worst deprivation was the dazzling fair called 'Crossgates Feast'. Brash and brassy it undoubtedly was but it made every September have a special spangle.

Artists at Work

Our creativity shrivelled in the dry dusty heat of August except for one small work of art.

On the outside wall of our house – part of the Morritt folly – was the high-relief sculpture of a Grecian lady, excessively pale and austere. We had always called her Ariadne, for no special reason except that our stock of Grecian goddesses was rather sparse and we happened to know about Ariadne and the golden thread. Having just had the story of Helen of Troy read to us by Mother, we thought of upgrading Ariadne to the more daring and dashing Helen.

'That pasty face would never launch a thousand ships,' said Betsy, and then with a wicked note of conspiracy: 'Let's *paint* her!' It was always Betsy who had the colourful ideas. We collected our Rowney paint-boxes and brushes, then battled with two of the heavy sash windows in the oblong bay of our parents' bedroom. I went off to the bathroom to borrow Daddy's shaving mug and fill it with water. When I returned Betsy was already swivelling on the windowsill, feet well above the bedroom floor. 'You meanie, you've blued her eyes. I wanted to do that! And how can you paint without water?' 'Spit!' Betsy spat her reply through cobalt blue lips. 'Then we'll *share* her face,' I said. 'You do your side and I'll do mine. ' We were now right and left of centre, each at the central window.

With Ariadne's nose separating us we never quite realised the clash of artistic independence we were showing with our Hellenic effort. The crimson cheek on Betsy's side out-glowed my watery vermillion one and the lopsided scarlet cupid's bow — decidedly higher on my side — gave Helen a leer that would have made Paris bolt and ensure that the dreary drawn-out business of the Trojan War was a non-starter. I decided that my side of the hair should be yellow ochre; Betsy insisted that all Greeks had dark brown hair. Helen's centre parting fixed the frontiers for the piebald wig where our yellow and brown glared at each other across no-man's land. We both agreed not to paint her nose — short as we were on the mathematical skill to divide it — so we left it defiantly pure between the flashy cheeks and the lecherous mouth. By the time we added black semi-circular eyebrows and eyelashes, as bold as a chimney sweep's brush, time was up.

We changed places to adjudicate. Our vocabulary was too limited and our criticism too naïve to know words shocking enough to describe the classical-to-bawdy transformation.

Mother, returning from a next-door-neighbour cup-of-tea, used our ever open back door and never saw our front-of-house masterpiece. But Mrs Allgood — with her look-out bay window and her binocular eyes — did. She came storming to confront our Mamma. 'If our Mollie or our Archie had done that they'd have got a thrashing from our Father that they'd never forget. Come and see for yourself.' She marched my mother to the patch of front lawn.

Peeping behind the curtains, we watched the two women looking like the two masks of the theatre. My mother's head lifted in astonished joy at the freakish goddess and, throwing her head even further back, she laughed and laughed. Mrs Allgood's disgust dragged her mouth down into an inverted U and her hands writhed in time to her words: 'It's no laughing matter, Mrs Hyde; they'll come to a bad end, those two. You mark my words!'

'Oh what a pity: it's starting to rain,' said my mother, blinking back tears of laughter, 'I do hope she's not washed away before Fred comes home. He'd enjoy that.'

But Mrs Allgood had gone home to gloat with her husband on the difference between 'our Mollie' and those 'badly brought up Hyde girls.'

It did rain. Gradually Helen's eyes streamed cobalt blue tears; trickles of blood fell from the leering mouth; the yellow ochre and the burnt sienna hair mingled into faded henna and all gurgled into runnels of mud resting on the draperies on her bust.

The rain, with no regard for history or literature, washed away all signs of Helen and within two days Ariadne coolly came into her own. Was there a faint hint of triumph on that born-again face? There certainly was on Mrs Allgood's.

The Hyde creativity flourished in the playground, the recreation ground, the hayfields, the woods, the streams and the attics and cellars. None of our pursuits cost money. We 'played out' every character we'd read about in our story-books. So sublime was our belief in just 'being' that there was no limit to our heroes and heroines or scenes: Sherwood Forest, Plymouth Hoe, The Wash and the exotic background for the Arabian Nights; all were possible in the curtained-off, six-foot strip of our playroom. When I wept at being considered too small to be Maid Marion, they conjured up a young sister for her: Maid Minnie, a non-speaking part for me, an unwanted 'gooseberry' to the courting Robin and Marion. It saved a lot of nautical energy to keep Sir Francis Drake to his bowls (croquet balls borrowed from the Allgoods) but Betsy had made such a huge paper ruff for herself - she always had the lead -that she couldn't tip her chin down to see the ball, at which setback she improvised:

'The red sun sinketh in the west and darkness stops our play;
Soon the red blood, like yonder sun, from Spaniards will flow.
Come, gentlemen, rig up the sails, for it is time to go!'

When she played King Canute, my friend Margaret and I, hidden behind a curtain, waggled a blue dustsheet across the stage and swished out sea noises to orchestrate with the floor-flap waves. Our first performance caught a hiss of reproval from the cardboard-crown king: 'Shut up; they can't hear me sending you back.'. Had our 'waves' backed, our bottoms would have hit the walls!

But by the time we were at our four different secondary schools creativity lost its innocence. 'I've sent them all to different schools so they won't quarrel' was my mother's naïve logic. It didn't work out that way. We had caustic and hysterical arguments, trying to prove which school had the strictest, the oldest, the craziest, the *worst* staff of the four! But we all had the bonding experience of creative dance and unlimited drama. Twice a week we rushed from our various schools to our dancing class. A small cup of milk and one biscuit had to suffice until we arrived home at 7pm to start our homework.

We all thrived on the discipline of dance and the rigorous rehearsals. No-one would have dared to have been late or absent for dance or drama. But then no-one wanted to.

Railway Children

We were railway children. Not in the heroic sense of E Nesbit's characters; but a firm and friendly liaison with the LNER gave us an Olympic arena for our energy.

The field adjoining the Avenue — to which we all had access through our back gardens — was, in the main, a lush and level meadow allowed to grow to a June height of tall grass. Buttercups, cowslips, harebells, sorrel, scabious, ragwort and rose-bay-willow-herb all kept pace with the grass and grew unhindered until the hay was cut. There were no restrictions about picking so we usually returned home with bunches of unprotesting flowers to press or give as peace-offerings. We grew up long before the catch-cropping of grass to make smelly silage.

At the far end of the field a sweeping incline to the railway became our sledge run in the winter and our tea-tray track in the summer. When the hay had been gathered in and the sun had burnished the grass stubble and clay soil to an earthenware glaze we slid on our tin trays at alarming speed to be halted by the fence of the railway embankment. The more daring chose the track that led to the gap in the fence where the tray and its rider shot through onto the embankment precariously lodged within a yard or two of the oncoming train.

Mrs Allgood — like Stephen Spender's mother — kept her daughter, Mollie, away from children who were rough, so it was unprecedented that Mollie should have joined the gang on that dry summer day. 'Get your bum on the tray!' Ken tried

The LNER steam trains were our constant companions and the stage for memorable meetings.

to bulldoze Mollie into action. 'That word is rude,' said Mollie, fingering the elastic under her chin which kept her panama hat rigid on her forehead. 'Well, *bottom* then!,' Ken conceded to decorum. 'That's rude, too' Mollie pouted.

Ken then tried his final shocker: *Arse* in an accent which bore no relation to his mother's tongue.

'My mother says' — and it could have been Mrs Allgood speaking — 'my mother says that nice people never talk about anything ... round there.' She gave a furtive glance to and from Ken's trousers. 'All those words are **rude!'**

Pulling the two corkscrew curls that dangled on Mollie's well-fed cheeks, Ken spat out: 'Well, then, how did your father and mother make you and your Archie?'

Ken's facts of life had been advanced by having two elder brothers while Mollie's were still at gooseberry bush level. She reddened, not having the least idea what Ken meant, then, turning away, eyes magnified with tears, she rushed towards home. Ken threw a withering glance at the blue baby ribbons dancing frenetically from Mollie's lace-edged knickers. Nancy, the peacemaker, though scared of Ken, came to Mollie's defence. 'I think you're very cruel to Mollie, Ken; **you've** got a nice mother. What would **you** do if you'd a mother like Mollie's?'

Ken screwed his eyes, clenched and bared his teeth and crunched out a low-toned reply: 'I'd kill 'er!'

Then kicking his tin tray and dismissing all feminine frailty, he shot out: 'Oh, I've had enough of this. I'm going train-spotting at the station. Coming, Alec?' He excluded the girls. We followed; it was a habit we never seemed able to break. Of course with Ken the walk was on the narrow embankment — the short cut to the station — and very soon an oncoming train hissed, puffed, groaned, clattered, thundered and stampeded, hurling us to the railings where we clung while the coaches battered a hurricane against our bodies. Fear was something one neither showed nor mentioned. 'Great, wasn't it?' said Ken. If he said so, it was; one did not risk dissension with bullies.

We trudged along the uneven ground to the station footbridge. 'Guess you can't climb on to the bridge!' Ken called out swinging like a monkey from the iron girders. We, the diffident ones, walked up the bank, which became the platform, and into Crossgates station. There standing magnificently alone was a huge dappled grey rocking-horse — an arrogant aristocrat. We gathered round full of wonder and curiosity. Who were the lucky children who were going to receive it? We examined his long grey mane, his stylish tail and his shining steel stirrups before we thought to look at the luggage label. It read: 'To the Hyde family from the Danbys.' Carved on his solid base was the date: 1888. If he had been a Unicorn brought by Hercules, or Pegasus ridden by Mercury we could not have been more entranced.

We waited and watched him put on to a delivery cart where he kept a steady eye on the real horse which was pulling him. 'You'd better get on too!' the driver called and we packed ourselves round the stand and steadied the bars and rode home triumphant. For hours we galvanised that horse into constant action.

The next day there was a loud and persistent knock on the front door and on the doorstep was our own burly policeman as frightening as he was familiar and friendly. He held a long envelope in his hand. Taking complete control of the situation he gathered us together with the abrupt command: 'Fetch Ken Turnbull!' I have forgotten the exact words which he read out in a heavy legal-laden Yorkshire accent but the gist of it was that we were being summoned for trespassing on the railway line. Gloom stilled us. The fading light put 'Danby' in deep shadow. We had no words for defence.

Daddy arrived and somehow did not seem shocked to find the policeman. They shook hands as if he were a welcome guest. My mother had already shown that she quite understood that constabulary duty had to be done and that it was done better with a cup of tea.

After an uncomfortable week of frigidity and no verdict, it leaked out through a neighbour that the 'summons' had been typed out in my father's office and our favourite Bobby had been invited to co-operate in the ploy to scare the living daylights out of us. We never trespassed on the line again.

How sensible and salutary this rough justice proved to be. No court, no waste of public money, no red tape, no time-taking probation, no child psychologist and no interfering social workers to take us into 'care'. We gained immeasurably from the protective responsibility — not to say ingenuity — of parents and police.

Postscript

'Danby', the rocking horse — now well over one hundred — is a survivor. Three generations of the Danby family treated him with affection even though these children

were surrounded by real working horses and carriage ponies on their farms in Snainton. The shelling of Scarborough in December 1914 was just a rumble in Danby's ears, for Snainton was a safe twelve miles away. I suspect that from 1917, when the Hyde family inherited him, he did not resent the rougher treatment; sometimes five of us challenged his strength and patience, mounting the bars, saddle, neck and rump. After discovering that the tail could be removed to reveal a gaping rectum, we filled the wooden bowel track with marbles which were evacuated with a plop and clatter, delighting our vulgar little minds.

To complete Danby's survival story, I must go beyond my childhood to the Thirties when he, childless but reposed, settled into our young married life style in Styal, Cheshire — long before jet planes zoomed into Ringway airport. He was a silent witness when we sat stunned on 10 December 1936 listening to Edward VIII's abdication speech. Danby burgeoned again when we carried him across the road for a long loan with the Yates' family at Bollin Hey. There he picked up the vibrations of Hal Yates' pellucid water-colour paintings and approved of the Friesian cows munching Cheshire-green grass outside the nursery window. His next move was only a mile or two away, in the Second World War, to Wilmslow where he became the most permanent object in the disturbed life of my evacuees from Manchester and my nieces evacuated from London. He remained unmoved and unprotected while we spent nights in the cellar ignoring the bombs, in a cavern charged with story-telling and poetry. When Hitler's dominance seemed doomed and my evacuees returned home, Danby started still another new life as a permanent member of the family with my war-baby daughter, and her war-widow Nannie with her two-year-old son. He had a restful but lonely few years in Southport, put 'out to grass' in the attic, then responded, as he always did, to a new generation of grandchildren in their Oxford home. Danby was used to 'open house' and friends of all ages riding him hard, and when the house near Folly Bridge was blackened by fire only his tail was singed.

Now, the red leather saddle is worn out, the mane thinner, the tail truncated through all the boisterous love he has enjoyed and eudured from my grandchildren and their friends. He is aged 107 and the focal point in my daughter's welcoming drawing-room but Danby will outlive us all for there is not a mean bone in his body nor a particle of plastic.

Ariadne, the face that launched two grubby paint-boxes.

The train battered a hurricane against our bodies.

CHAPTER THIRTEEN
HOLIDAYS AFTER THE FIRST WORLD WAR

Littondale — The Stone in the River.

Without any sense of accepting charity, we children did profit from our parents' friends. In the quiet little riverside village of Hawkswick where the slow and shallow River Skirfare bubbles down to join the Wharfe, Professor Moorman and his wife had a country cottage called Garris House.

'We shan't be going to Hawkswick until late on in August,' Dr Moorman said to my mother, 'so why don't you have the cottage for the first weeks of the summer holiday?'

So towards the end of July 1919, the Hyde family set off: Sonny aged three, Coidy ten, Betsy twelve, Nancy fourteen and Kathleen eighteen — Daddy was to join us later. Somehow my mother transported us, but the toil and tedium of that journey has dissolved away from my memory. It must have been: cab to Crossgates station, train to Leeds, change trains to Skipton, 'bus or wagonette from Skipton on to Grassington, past Kilnsey Crag into Littondale. Of course we carried not only our clothes but a store of food to see us through at least a few days. Hawkswick is remote even today but far more remote over 70 years ago.

All I can remember is the frisson of 'arriving' after the disjointed little journey, the sheer thrill of seeing, hearing and smelling a river passing the front door; the thick stone mullioned doorway and windows; the cottage garden, a tidy muddle of marigolds, nasturtiums, daisies and roses, and the welcoming smell of wood fires, oil lamps and clean linen. The Moorman family had left its warm welcome by conspiring with a neighbour that newly-baked loaves, a jug of fresh milk and a bowl of that morning's eggs should be on the kitchen table. Their personal signatures showed in the miscellany of books and magazines: *Gems, Magnets* and *Boys' Own Papers* were pushed in between the *Jungle Book, The Water Babies,* Arnold Bennett's *Old Wives' Tale* and W. Riley's *Windyridge*. Later we found Dr Moorman's own *Songs of the Ridings; Plays of the Ridings; Place Names of the West Riding.*

But the most charming discovery was to find the heights of the two Moorman children, Theo and John, marked out on the frame of the living-room door. We never thought then that the feet and inches of John would grow to be a future Bishop of Ripon.

Before we left, the Hydes' measurements were put on the other jamb of the door but after 1919 neither the Moorman nor the Hyde children were ever recorded again.

I cannot remember any cars passing along that little road from Hawkswick to Arncliffe — there must have been a few by 1919 — but we walked everywhere. We heard from Mother that the great grey crag towering above the villages of Hawkswick and Arncliffe was where Tom, in the *Water Babies,* went down to the cottage by the river. Leaning over the bridge, Charles Kingsley had looked down and seen, coming out onto the lawn, the nicest old woman that ever was, in her red petticoat and short dimity bed-gown and clean white cap with a black silk handkerchief over it tied under the chin, and he made her into the kindly Mrs Do-as-you-would-be-done-by in Tom's watery dream-world.

We had all read at home the story of the Water Babies but the Moorman edition was packed with Wordsworth's lines, classical quotations and words which needed a lexicon to sort out — all well above our heads. But we recognised our Littondale: 'A quiet, silent rich, happy place; a narrow crack cut deep into the earth.'

We could look up at the cold grey crag 'three hundred feet of limestone terraces, one below the other, as straight as if they had been ruled with a ruler and then cut with a chisel' down which Tom came to the cottage.

We, too, scrambled, crunched and slithered over the heaps of fallen limestone; we, too, pushed our tired feet through great humps of bracken and wood sedges but we walked no further than the foothills, well within reach of the sheltering cottage and the clear and cool river.

My own eldorado was the wooden splayed-out paling bridge which crossed the river just beyond the cottage. Solitude is not easy to find in a family of five children but only in solitude can the imagination be intense yet free. Each day, before the others were up and about, I crept out of the cottage to the magic bridge and stood in the middle of it leaning over the wooden railing. The secret was to gaze on one small spot of the big grey boulder which reared out of the shallow swiftly moving water. Then the bridge, with its limestone keel of stone, started to move and I sailed on against the current of the water — on and on towards ...? There was never a 'towards' anything, for space and time were infinite and I was at the helm of the ship. Omnipotent. And then, after untimed time, I relaxed my gaze and flicked it on to the diamonds on the water. The ship stopped and I was back on the bridge immobile and only a hundred yards from the cottage. I had planned that after a few days I would let the others into my secret but I never did, thinking that they might not know how to fix their eyes on the stone and I feared they would mock me for my belief and say, 'Silly, you imagined it!'

And so the carefree days passed. We walked to Kilnsey Crag, Kettlewell, Starbotton and Buckden Pike. We hoarded our pennies to spend at Yarkers' corner shop in Grassington. We watched the village boys tickling trout and the 'gentlemen anglers' flinging their rods and lines teasing the trout with irridescent flies. Even on cloudy rainy days it all seemed 'apparelled in celestial light.'

There were neither coachload day-trippers nor motoring tourists. Folk who made the effort to stay in Hawkswick settled into the warp and weft of everyday life and accepted that church-going and serious shopping could only come at the end of a long walk to another village. There was every good reason not to have any truck with the outside world except to chat to the butcher from Kettlewell in his blue and white striped apron and straw hat; the baker in his floury white overall who gave thirteen-to-the dozen rock buns, and the fishmonger who chopped up the cod and hake in the back of his cart and fed all the village cats. The rears of the horse-drawn vans and carts were meeting grounds for the women shoppers and the cats and dogs. Children gathered at the front to give sugar lumps to the horses. There's something about shopping in the fresh air, whether in an open market or in the road, which sharpens your judgment and fortifies your purse against impulsive buying.

You could set your clock by the shepherds and farm-hands in the village — but you never did; time in rural Yorkshire is too good-natured to be put — as it is now — into a digital watch. Time needs hands and hands need Time. Perhaps Dr Wager, who spent his long university vacation at Hawkswick, was nudged by his chiming grandfather clock each morning to pick out a single blue-ringed egg-cup from his kitchen cupboard and set off to the farm for his breakfast egg. This he carried slowly and smoothly in his left hand, leaving his right hand free to raise his deer-stalker hat to anyone passing by, even to the nine-year-old little girl heading for the magic bridge.

Sadly, towards the end of August, we had to leave the cottage and the river and the crisply laundered air of Littondale and return to the Avenue. The Moormans returned to their cottage, Theo and John an inch or so taller than they were before, to put new heights on the jamb of the door.

Hardly had our thank-you letters all been written and sent off to Hawkswick when a telegram arrived with the appalling news that Dr Moorman had been drowned in the river in front of the cottage.

He was 47, at the peak of his career as Professor of English and recognised as the authority on West Riding Yorkshire dialect. His wisdom, wit and kindliness shone through his every action as a husband, father, friend, tutor and writer. We could not believe that the friendly little River Skirfare could be so cruel. Our whole world crumbled. We grieved for Frances, his wife, and his children Theo and John.

It was ironic that one of his finest poems, written in the dialect of the *East* Riding, expressed the wish of an old Yorkshire fisherman that he should be drowned at sea. The poem ends:

> 'T'grave is whisht and foulsome,
> But clear is s'aut sea-bed;
> Thoo can hark ti t'billows dancin'
> Ti t'tune o t'tide owerhead.
> Yon wreaths o'flooers i t'kirkyard
> Seean wither an' fade away,
> But t'sea-tang wreaths roond a drooned man's head
> Will bide while Judgment Day.'

I had to let half a century go by before I had the heart to visit the Hawkswick cottage again. It is still a lovely and loving village with genuine Hawkswick-proud folk running Garris House as a guest house and cafe.

The bridge is now heightened and strengthened with metal bars and metal chain netting. The chest-high wooden palings have gone. The boulder is unchanged, looking as it always did like a cumbersome petrified armchair tilted in the never-stopping stream.

But gaze as I did on the same spot of the same stone, the bridge and the stone and I never moved.

The magic had gone. 'Where is it now, the glory and the dream?'

Holidays on the Hyde Farms

Auburn House Farm

Auburn must be the smallest village in the country for now there is only one dwelling: Auburn House where my Uncle Dawson farmed for over 30 years. Auburn has not always been so small for before the Norman Conquest it must have been a flourishing village until the sea gradually eroded it away.

The bell from Auburn Church now hangs in the courtyard of Boynton Hall but where it lay for centuries before is a mystery. This picture confounds the often repeated tale that the bell can be heard in the sea!

SEREN.mo PRINCIPI
IACOBO
EBORACENSIUM
DVCI, etc.
1648
GERMANICUS.
Bridlington Bay
Auburn village lost in the sea
Hyde village lost in the sea
Sandyford
Whitby
Robinhoods Baye
Scarbrough
Filey
DICKERING
Bridlington
Flamborough head
Bridlingto key
Killham
THE WAPON
Hornesey Burton
Lockinton
Leken feld
Chery Burton

My uncle had the Domesday records in which it said that the chief landlord in 1086 was Eleburne Carle (the original spelling of the name) who also owned Fraisthorpe and much of Bridlington. At one time there were two other landlords in Auburn: the Prior of Bridlington, Gerard Salvayn and John de Heslerton, Lord of Lowthorpe. The Priory property remained inviolate until the dissolution of the monasteries by Henry VIII in the 16th Century.

But all through the centuries the sea was merciless, so much so that in the 15th Century it was necessary to move the village chapel of St Nicholas (aptly named as he was the patron saint of sailors) brick by brick away from its site by the sea to the extreme end of the village just inland from Auburn House. All that remains of it now is a grassy mound in a field not far from the house (a discovery I did not make until 1995 when visiting the present proud and lively owners).

A report written in 1731 is full of gloom: *Auburn having been so washed away by the sea that there are now only one messuage and two cottages left therein containing fifteen personsfi six of whom are Quakers.*

The messuage was, of course, Auburn House.

My Uncle Dawson, a riveting raconteur with adults, never told his tales to children but I once overheard him, in *Ancient Mariner* style, mesmerising his listeners down by the sea with his familiarity with the 'Auburn Dolly' which growled from the ocean bed even when the sea above was calm. The 'Auburn Dolly' rumblings, he told them, were the pounding of heavy breakers slinging shale and rubble against the crumbling walls of Auburn village long since locked in the sea-bed. Grumblings of defiance for all that was lost.

After five years frayed away by the war we returned in 1920 to Auburn farm on the east coast. The North Sea was, as we had left it, fierce or friendly, lashing or lapping, roaring or whispering but always powerful and permanent. Old East Riding folk still sometimes called it the German Sea and on maps before their time it is: German *Ocean*.

My uncle's foreman's cottage was still there, standing precariously on the edge of the low cliff — all that was left of the lost village of Auburn. One crumbling wall gave stark proof that the sea's appetite was not yet satisfied. My uncle's farm, Auburn House — standing where the old Bridlington to Beverley road must have been — was safely inland fortified against wind and weather with house-hugging walls all round and a sturdy coppice of trees on the north side bent by vicious North-easters.

Now alien concrete pill-boxes punctuated the coast, some silted up sinking into the sand; others lurched at strange angles as if to emphasise their impotence now the war was over.

This part of the coast has been described as monotonous but there was nothing tame about the great white thrusting headland of Flamborough with its sea-sweeping lighthouse beam and the contrasting curve of the sand-margined Bridlington Bay. Flamborough Head completed our cyclorama, protected our bay and defined our territorial waters. Beyond that headland, as far as we children were concerned, was

Auburn Farm

There was nothing tame about the great white thrusting headland of Flamborough with its sea-sweeping lighthouse beam and the contrasting curve of the sand-margined Bridlington Bay.

'Come unto these yellow sands!'

another world: Filey with its nannies and babies playing in the rock-pools and Scarborough with its incomparable coastline, its elegant Spa and Marine Drive. Scarborough was special. Scarborough was for days out and meeting our North Riding relations.

During our five-year absence the sea had sucked away at the low cliff and the paths which we had trodden as children, or driven on with the pony and trap, were now in part crumbled away. We scalloped round each break in the cliff to make new paths as folk must have done in the past and would do in the future. As before there were no trees, no bushes, just prickly sea grass and tough smelly ragwort, which we remembered as 'Stinking Willy'. Inland the wheat still lent its ears to the sun and the ripe oats and barley rustled and brushed against the sea-breeze.

Uncle Dawson had not changed. The old order was built into the stubborn rhythm of his everyday life. He looked exactly as he was five years before, a brown and bristly figure in prickly Harris tweeds, the same tawny colour and texture as his moustache and beard as if they had all been woven on the same loom. With his knee-breeches, thick leather gaiters and boots he was permanently weather-proofed against August sun or January snow. He preferred that children were neither seen nor heard so we were never invited into his book-lined shaggy-tobacco den.

To say that he was a 'confirmed bachelor' seems to imply that earlier in his life he had sown a few wild oats, but there was not one wild oat in his life nor in his fields. He assumed that God had put women into the world for some level of domestic service which he could hire, and so, with his large double-bed inviolate, he was able to become a model of husbandry.

He had little conversation for children. His macabre and distant greeting on the sands after not having seen us for five years was: 'You'd better not be picking shells — some of them have not gone off!' We had been instructed to call at the House and pay our respects to Miss Thompson, the housekeeper, a woman who ruled everything and everybody except her master. Discipline started outside the back door: 'Scrape your shoes, wipe your feet, wash your hands at the pump and come in quietly. Nancy, you are the eldest here today so say grace.' We stood around the kitchen table, hands clasped and then sat down in silence. Not one word was spoken through the predictable boiled eggs and bread and butter, teacake and custard pie, except for Miss Thompson's frigid remark: 'So Kathleen's not come with you — well, I can understand that. She seems to have come under some refining influence since she left home.' A final grace, thrust on the 'youngest' unnerved me and I stopped myself in the middle of: 'For what we *are about* to receive and changed to a stumbled: 'Thank you God for the tea' with the childish hope that God would forgive.

The kitchen, unlike the friendly one at Fraisthorpe, was dark and overshadowed by the closed-in farmyard buildings. In the darkest corner of the kitchen a slatted door barred the dingy stone steps which led to a smugglers' underground tunnel to the sea. Miss Thompson used it as a threat: 'That's where naughty children end up — in the smugglers' cave.' Fortunately my uncle had the steps filled up and the door bolted and barred but I can still remember the horror of peering into that black cold abyss and the dank old bones smell which still crept up into the warmth of the kitchen.

The relief and joy of turning our eyes to the western sun and heading inland to Fraisthorpe cannot be described. We hopped, skipped, danced and ran along the cart road which linked the two farms, winding our way for a mile — between the fields of corn. No question of opening gates: we bounded over them and basked in the laughter which came from Uncle Harry and Auntie Florrie as we spilled out our version of the Auburn visit. Miss Gratrix, their loving and gentle housekeeper, was not displeased with the adverse comments we made on Miss Thompson, but she was far too polite to encourage us. Whereas the lines on Uncle Dawson's face showed the wear and tear of 'gaffering', Uncle Harry's face was furrowed with fun. Every wrinkle turned upwards and seemed to make him look younger. Dawson's farm men were under orders; Uncle Harry's men worked *with* him.

Not many farmers are gardeners, at least not in the decorative sense of the word, for they prefer to grow things 'to feed the house'. But there was no garden of any kind at Auburn House. The fold yard, fenced within a few yards of the front door, always seemed ripe for 'muck-spreading'. Uncle Harry had an easy-going, sweet-smelling walled front garden where one plant could trespass on another without being hoed into obedience. Little low box hedges kept the beds from being unruly and the smell of the box mingling with sweet peas, roses, sea-pinks and mignonette made gossip and laughter burgeon.

There was no nonsense and no charm in the earn-your-keep architecture of the Auburn buildings whereas Fraisthorpe was like a child's drawing of a dream cottage but wrapped in the green-gold-red sequence of Virginia creeper. Three little gabled dormer windows watching the central porch added a coquettish look to its four-square frame.

Both uncles teased unmercifully: Dawson with a frown, Harry with a twinkle. Yet to the numerous adults who came almost on pilgrimages to Auburn, Dawson Hyde was a character; a raconteur of Yorkshire legends and local tales which he delivered in North or East Riding dialect varied according to the characters in his stories and the listener's familiarity with Yorkshire haunts and dialects.

He had no truck with the artificial idea of 'summer time' and its meddling with clocks. Asked the time he would take out his large gold hunter and say: 'Do you want Bollington time, Auburn time or time o'day?' 'Time of day' was registered on the face of his watch and the sun; Auburn kitchen clock was always half an hour ahead and Bollington time — Bridlington — was fixed by the government and used by my uncle only for market days and cattle sales.

Local historians, writers, artists, clergymen and a wide assortment of friends, preferably male, revelled in his dry wit and wry humour and shared, and added to, — his collection of antique books, maps and pictures of Yorkshire. He was known for miles around for his gruff kindliness and there must have been at least a score of needy families who regularly received 'anonymous' food hampers with extra treats for Christmas dinners.

On his death in 1930 hundreds of people followed his coffin and filled Carnaby Church and the grave-yard. The columns in the local papers spoke of his 'unfailing fidelity to his friends', the 'genial host', a library 'furnished with fine books and paintings', 'canny wit', 'bounteous heart'. He just was incapable of suffering little children!

The Minister conducting the service used the same words which had been said 20 years before in the same church at my Grandfather's funeral:

No supplicant was ever turned away from a Hyde farm. Each was given food and drink and very often a shelter for the night.

From 1922 onwards we could be independent of both houses and free to invite friends to join us in camping holidays in one of Dawson's fields near the sea. That summer we three sisters had bought ourselves a cumbersome soggy bell tent, designed, one could have thought, to absorb rain rather than dispel it. We had no worries as we had been trained in our Guide camps to put a finger on any dripping point, follow its path down the canvas and thus make a track for the next drops. There seemed to be more faith than fact in this hopeful exercise so we accepted, in any case, that 'camp' and 'damp' were synonymous!

To transport the tent, our three friends and ourselves and all the camping paraphernalia, we hired a flat truck with never a thought that the tyres might be flat too. A few miles outside York the lorry came to a squealing halt. 'Tyre's bust!' the driver snorted in a tone as flat as the tyre: 'Yer'll 'ave ter git yersens there uz best yer can!' It was the first Saturday in August — a Bank Holiday.

The bell tent with its load of clumsy wooden pegs was too daunting to move but we heaved our kit bags and a muddled miscellany of hardware — enamel buckets and bowls, primus stove and tin openers — to the nearest bus stop. Eventually a bus came, and, looking like bleached gypsies, we tried to ignore the stares of amusement and disdain shown by the other passengers. We clutched bowls and buckets, and all the other unsightly gear, on our knees. Suddenly there was such a cacophony that the driver drew to a halt, the conductor leapt along the bus and the passengers clung to one another. It seemed as if the whole bus was falling apart — the large tin alarm clock at the bottom of the tin bucket was not just ringing but was doing a St Vitus dance of death from side to side. My hand was beaten up trying to stop it. Silence was at last restored and the bus went on when I'd stifled the clock and the bucket with my new navy gaberdine mackintosh.

The journey from York to Bridlington is now obliterated from my memory but I do remember our night in the granary at Fraisthorpe and trying to ignore the odd rat, the frequent mice and the bats suspended in sleep from the beams.

We were wakened by the wind and the rain on the granary roof. It was one of those east coast summer days when the wind rides roughshod over the fields and the North Sea growls through its angry grey foam. The lorry arrived, and apart from waiting to be paid, the driver had no intention of lengthening his stay to help us to unload. The bell tent in its sack must have been in the rain all day and all night for it took three of us to drag it to the spot where, the day before, we had optimistically bored a hole for the pole. All the damp six of us were needed to wrench the drenched tent out of its soggy sack and a whole hour went by before we finally heaved the pole upright and persuaded wet guy ropes on to wet wooden pegs. We were past caring that the whole canvassy pyramid looked like Chesterfield church spire. At least it was up.

Just as we were settling on our damp ground sheet to eat 'Dry ship's biscuits' — mercifully living up to their name — we heard the swish of heavy boots through the wet grass and there under the dome of a huge, black umbrella was Uncle Dawson booming out in his deliberately toughest Yorkshire: 'Tak that tent doon!'

It was, of course, Sunday, the day after our arranged arrival, and Uncle Dawson's God — apparently a fearsome Methodist sabbatarian — was being blasphemed. By the time we six girls had walked back to Fraisthorpe, dried ourselves by the kitchen fire and had been stoked up with delicious food by Miss Gratrix ('Have another piece of cheese-cake, honey') we could entertain Aunt Florrie and Uncle Harry with grotesque impersonations of Uncle Dawson and his unforgiving God.

We warmed ourselves through and through with the best medicine in the world: deep, long, gulping draughts of laughter.

Caring for our souls and the Sabbath was not Uncle Dawson's only concern, for part of his creed was that children, like horses, should be well-shod. At the end of each holiday we were summoned, not to the blacksmiths, but to Auburn kitchen. There on the pegged hearth-rug were set out about thirty pairs of shoes blinking their toecaps in the firelight. The shoe-maker from Bridlington, in front of his pyramid of white boxes, exuded pride and hope.

'You can't try shoes on with bare feet.' Miss Thompson, as usual, took on the role of her master's voice. 'Go back and get your stockings on.'

Socks which had been abandoned four weeks before had now become a muddled miscellany of brown, black and white loners clinging damply together at the bottom of our kit-bags. After the frenzy of snatching and squabbling: 'That's mine — No it isn't — This is yours!' The socks acquired roguish partners. I finished up with one white — too small and one brown — too big which made a problem for the shoe-man in deciding my shoe size.

There was no hint of the 'flippant Twenties' in this down-to-earth collection; every pair of shoes, black or brown, were thick-soled, toe-capped, brogue-seamed, flat-heeled and tied with tough laces. Even when the shoes were so big they dropped off our feet, Miss Thompson insisted: 'Use the shoe-horn, child, and undo the laces before you take them off!'

After about forty minutes of pushing, pulling and toe-wiggling, we were landlocked into shoes ill-suited to the Ariel beings who danced bare-footed on the sands.

'Wear them now and break them in:' Miss Thompson said, pushing us through the back door, no doubt much relieved that the session was over.

It was now late afternoon and a north-east chill rippled our skimpy gingham frocks and tightened the skin of our sun-tanned limbs. We clomped our way back to camp, heaving and hoisting shoes which, we remarked, could more fittingly have anchored the Mauretania.

CHAPTER FOURTEEN
LOVE FIFTEEN

For most of 1924 I was 14, the awkward age when dreams of what one might be are light years away from what one is. Like many adolescents of that and this period, I was awkward and shy with those who were unfamiliar but impudent and pert with those I knew well. But not with parents and their friends; it was a heinous sin 'to answer back'. Elders were always assumed — often inaccurately — to be our betters whom we had, without reasoning, to respect.

My mother had brought us up to be clean and plain. Not in so many words but she made it quite clear that beauty was elsewhere. She had no feminine penchant for dressing up, making up or making up to men although she looked engagingly feminine herself. Beauty, as far as my mother was concerned, was quite distant from her daughters and I cannot remember any of us having one feature or talent praised. Beauty, in my mother's book, was something caught on the brush by a Burne-Jones, a Watts or a Rossetti and their limpid ladies were definitely not for man-handling.

Unlike the Pre-Raphaelite ladies with their loose girdles and their close-fitting morals, our English rose skins were too often blemished with a blackhead or a spot, a condition which evoked no sympathy from my mother who loftily assumed that it was lack of washing. It was a lonely and nerve-wracking business, nose against mirror, going into battle against any guilty pore and then trying to disguise it with an unhygienic dab from a secret powder compact.

So we grew up through those threshold years with a Kiplingesque idea that a schoolgirl's role and goal was to be a *man*, my son! How romance ever insinuated its way into our lives was to be marvelled at. But in a naïve way it did. My mother, as I have already told, had a genius for attracting into our home people who shared high-minded thoughts, words and music. Regular visitors were George Wilkinson, a magnetic lecturer in English at the Training College in Leeds, and our oldest cousin Austin, a superb raconteur of North and East Riding dialect and, at that time, Second Master at Woodhouse Grove School.

Throughout our childhood, our home vibrated with do-it-yourself entertainment, and we children — a captive audience — needed no persuading to change roles and become the entertainers. Mr Wilkinson's repertoire of spoken verse excluded the obscure and the analytical for words flowed from him with joyous compulsive rhythm as different from the elocution-of-the-day as a brook is from piped water. He had no academic snobbery but revelled in simple but shapely verse full of imagery, rhyme and rhythm. So, without reference to print, we absorbed and knew by heart the poems he constantly repeated at our request. Of these I still remember: Alfred Noyes' *Whither away is the Spring today?*, his 'Go *down to Kew in Lilac Time;* George Meredith's *Love in a Valley,* and Swinburne's *When the Hounds of Spring are on Winter's traces,* and how we rollicked through de la Mare's *Three Jolly Farmers* and Lear's *Jumblies.* I am grateful that we had this free ride before being caught in the grip of the modern intellectual poets whose stark prosaic lines took much of the joy and the music out of verse-speaking.

So we grew up thinking that making love was making music or making up poetry or writing heart-to-mind letters where we were more fluent than face-to-face. We measured our boy-friends on their wit and wisdom in 'putting it into words'. Bed had nothing to do with it. Bed was unromantic — a place for settled-down marrieds. To us a double bed symbolised all that was stuffy, middle-aged and bourgeois. We were remarkably ignorant of what could happen between sheets!

We girls sparkled and responded to George Wilkinson — a charmer — but as he was married and middle-aged, he was reserved for relaxed hero-worshipping. The next best thing, as far as I was concerned, was his son, Peter, who though not as verbally romantic as his father, was accessible and approved of by my mother and cousin Austin. Fortuitously for me he was also at Woodhouse Grove, a sixth form boarder, so it was easy to arrange a family visit of the Hydes and Mr Wilkinson to Woodhouse Grove with Austin as our host. My heart soared with the idea of Sunday tea and evening service at a boys' boarding school — *his* school.

The visit began rather badly by my heading for the swing on the huge chestnut tree in one of the Grove's lovely gardens. 'Not on a Sunday, my dear, not on a Sunday'; Austin's Primitive Methodism died hard. I should have remembered that this was a Methodist school. I tried to make up for it by screwing my eyes and my hands longer and tighter during 'grace' before tea. As we stood outside the school ready to be led into the evening service by the Headmaster, Dr Towlson, the boys filed past, each one deferentially raising his straw boater. Elation ran high until I noticed my beloved lifting his hard hat to our side of his face evidently to hide his blushes and to avoid eye-contact.

Before the day was out, however, invitations were given and accepted for father and son Wilkinson to join the Hyde camping colony at Auburn. I was as chuffed as the steam train which carried us back from Apperley Bridge to Leeds. Now — what bliss — such good reasons for keeping a correspondence going. That there was nothing in the letters more passionate than cricket or lacrosse did not daunt me. I hung on every word and read and re-read each one until the folds cracked. There was little comic relief in either our letters or holiday conversations apart from hearing how the school-leavers had, on the last day, all thrown their boaters into the River Aire and how the juniors had caught them neatly as they floated down-stream.

Meanwhile, at home and at school, life went on. Like our mother we were 'joiners' — though not at her esoteric level. We were obsessed with Girl Guiding. As with all our ploys, what we lacked in genius we made up in enthusiasm. The sleeves of our Guide uniform were as rigid as armour with badge after badge sewn on in

Woodhouse Grove School, Apperley Bridge, featured frequently in our family life. Before the First World War my cousins Henry and Alan Danby were boarders and my cousin Austin was on the staff. Austin returned after his service in the RAF to be deputy head and held this position when my first boy friend was a boarder and I was a visitor.

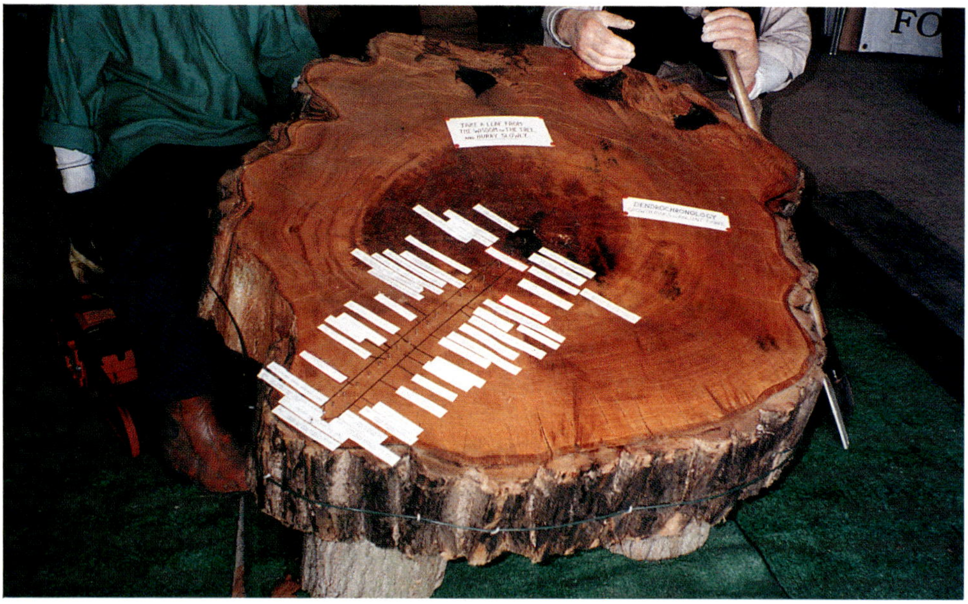

From this ancient chestnut tree was suspended the swing which I was forbidden to use on a Sunday! Now in 1995 the tree has had to be cut down and the imaginative forester and staff have saved a slice for posterity with every ring's history recorded.

pairs from shoulder to cuff. According to our Guiders' testimony we could, between us, cook, nurse, carve wood, paint, signal in morse and semaphore (to whom and for what was never made quite clear), run, jump and make baskets. We could turn a conglomerate of string and rope into sheet-bends, sheep-shanks and clove-hitches (presumably handy for dealing with a drunken sailor). We could sing, recite, play the piano, throw a javelin, read maps, follow nature-trails, make book-ends out of tent-pegs and, of course, dig latrines.

This last navvy job was our major opus shown proudly to visitors who came to see us on the open-day in camp.

'And who', Aunt Maggie asked, trying to breathe out instead of in, 'will deal with the detritus?' That phrase became a family joke for all unpleasant chores. Our cousin, Fred Hyde, a journalist and an amateur naturalist and geologist could not understand why we giggled when he used the word in its proper context when telling us about the birds' nests in Bempton Cliffs.

One of our Guiding ambitions was to polish our Tenderfoot badges so hard that the contours on the trefoil, the GG and the Be Prepared were completely flattened out. But we *were* prepared for anything and everything except how to cope with our disturbing emotions. We were totally unprepared for any sexual adventures within or without marriage.

Everything was sublimated into song! We sang round mock camp-fires indoors and real camp-fires under the stars; we sang as we stirred porridge in monstrous smoke-smudged billy-cans; we sang as we felled branches, chopped wood or carried buckets of water from the well. It was a huge gamut of activity, with green bottles falling off walls, London burning, woad daubed on ancient Britons, mowing meadows and yip-pie-addying our way through every community song in Britain with the occasional relief of less raucous songs from France. I write with a flippant pen but Guiding made good use of our adolescent energy and helped to make us sturdily independent of parents and false materialism. Adolescents always want to be with their peers. Clubs were our answer as they may be still. I joined the Crusaders — a Church of England youth movement — pressurised by my what-a-friend-we-have-in-Jesus form-mate Hilda; kind and sweet as she was, her fervour was exhausting and I never became wholly committed.

After the war, my father and his next-door crony bought a part of the field adjoining our garden to make a lawn tennis court as a private club for a few Avenue neighbours. Not to be outdone, Betsy and I invited 'best friends' to join a junior club called, for no apparent reason, The Crescent Tennis Club for which we made elaborate quarter-moon-shaped badges. In our solemn rules, membership was fixed at *fifteen* neither more nor less. That we never cajoled more than ten to pay the subscription did not deter us from sticking to our coy motto: 'Love Fifteen'. Boys who joined us never stayed long enough to pay their subscriptions, bored, one might hazard a guess, with serving balls which invariably were not returned. The Suzanne Lenglen headbands and eyeshades we affected gave us, we liked to think, 'style'. Unfortunately that is where mimicry stopped; there was little drive or style in our strokes. Lobs and volleys tended to hover enticingly in the air, giving more aggressive opponents all the time in the world to smash them to the ground.

Camping holidays at Auburn had now become a more communal affair. The only obligatory passport was that one should be persona grata with Uncle Dawson. The Wilkinson father and son were not only granted permission to camp but were invited by Miss Thompson to Auburn House to 'eat with the Master' before going for an outing in his car: a Bean. This open hooded tourer, tough, male, bulky and resolute, could have been designed for my uncle. It had a bonnet like an iron helmet and a stubborn look on its face warning the heathen that it would be behind closed stable doors all day Sunday.

Saturdays were reserved for outings when the favoured few were shown rare spots in Yorkshire and given a commentary on the history and the folklore of every farm and hamlet. To our surprise the Wilkinsons charmed Uncle Dawson to include Betsy and me in a motor-drive to Kilburn. 'I'm taking you to see a carver friend of mine working on some stuff for Ampleforth College.' We drove from the brown crumbly soil of Auburn to the white chalk of the Hambleton Hills, both of us in our striped Macclesfield silk dresses, Peter between us, his hair Brylcreamed, white shirt, school tie and cream flannels. Nobody would dare to be less than well covered with my uncle who more than filled the driving seat in his heavy Harris tweeds.

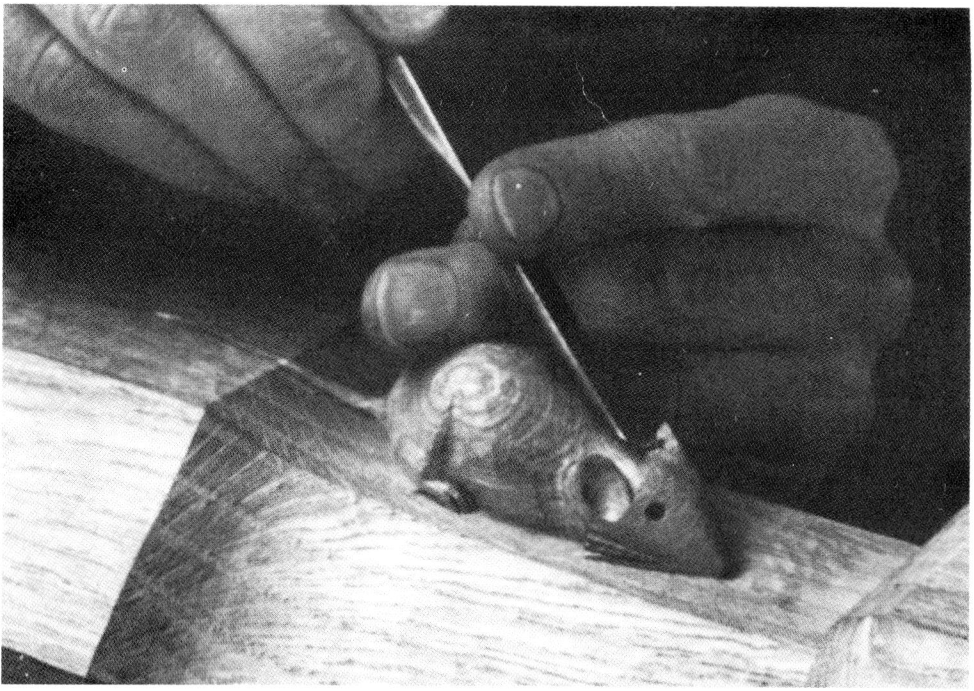

Thompson's original mouse with four paws.

'There's the white horse, look, twenty miles away. It's a hundred yards long, forty times the length of one of my Clevelands. Twelve people can picnic on just one eye...' But as my uncle would never picnic on or off a white horse, we were never able to put it to the test.

We came down to Kilburn on an air-rippling day and saw the trunk-length slices of oak catching the silver northern light and turning it to gold. To watch Robert Thompson in his village workshop was to see centuries of craftsmanship and centuries of oak captured in the strength and gentleness of one man's hands.

We followed his gnarled but sensitive fingers pointing out his insignia: the mouse, its four paws embedded in the foot of a small oak table. We watched him show a boy apprentice how to wield an adze and make small ripples in a slab of wood on the workshop floor. As Thompson held part of a church screen for us to examine and touch, I — thinking that praise called for words, not Yorkshire appreciative silence — volunteered: 'How marvellous to be able to do that!'. To which he replied quietly and with typical Yorkshire understatement: 'It's simple really; it's just knowing what to cut away'. We had no idea then that this village carver, Robert Thompson, was to become famous, the world over, as 'The Mouseman'.

It was a golden day. Sledmere, through which we returned, shone a sunset gold; corn was standing tall with gold-pricked ears; virginia creeper, not yet autumn-red, flickered gold and green, sunburnt hands touched giltily and guiltily while in the cottage gardens' brazen tiger-lilies were blatantly seducing the bees. Barley glistened and shimmered silver-gold in that special East Yorkshire light as if signalling that soon it would be September. Yes, soon it would be September and my fifteenth birthday, and I felt, deep in my heart, that I could now hold my own with my older sisters. Perhaps I had just begun to realise that being loved makes one more lovable and, yes, more important.

That night back in camp Peter and I escaped on our own into the snuggest of our tents. My mother was not wrong in assuming that her friends' boys had as little passion to spend as they had pocket-money, so she trusted us to be away for six weeks, she coming now and again to stay at Fraisthorpe. The only nearby adult was Peter's papa.

'Time was away' so I do not recall the hours we had spent in whispered talk and occasional bird-like pecks but just as Peter's hands moved uncertainly towards the curve of my silk-covered breast, a voice at the tent door shattered our intimate world. 'Peter, do you know what time it is?' It was not a social question but a firm rebuke. Deflated and confused, our heaven became hell. Dear George Wilkinson, so human, so witty, so responsive to women, did not seem to understand how tentatively we moved within that fragile opalescent bubble of dawning love.

The next night, with exaggerated bonhomie, he arranged a sing-song and a supper, and quietly checked that we were all in *his* tent. Though we sang warmly of lads and lasses kissing as they came through the rye, we had to put our own modest desires into cold storage and assume an air of detachment which hurt.

Adolescence was — and probably still is for many of our young — painfully precarious.

'Shall I have it bobbed or shingled?
Shall I have it shingled or bobbed?

CHAPTER FIFTEEN
LEAVE TOMORROW BEHIND

'Shall I have it bobbed or shingled? Shall I have it shingled or bobbed?' So rang the silly words of the silly tune which took us into the early Twenties. Skirts, hems, sleeves and hair had all become shorter; hats had become closer; cigarette holders longer; eyebrows thinner and everybody *danced.*

We tended to invite to camp-holidays friends who, like us, were crazy about

'When cares pursue yer, HALLELUJER
Helps yer through the darkest day!'

Greek and creative dance and who, in the wispiest of tunics, could range from Greek friezes to Bacchic orgies or Pyrrhic war dances in a sandy world of our own. So entirely were the Auburn sands our personal possession that we took our portable gramophone down to the beach and there to Elgar's *Salut d'amour,* Chopin's *Preludes* and Brahms' *Waltzes,* we went through our Greek repertoire. It was merciless treatment for the '78' records, for the North Sea behaved very differently from the Aegean and

In a sandy world of our own.

often we were blinking through sandy eye-lashes to wipe sandy records with cold sandy hands. Changing needles — which we did far too infrequently — was little help to the composers and the orchestras who became grittier with every performance. But we were not always in this aesthetic world. In 1923 the 'cat's whisker' wireless set had transformed our lives, for by twiddling a minute wire, as thin as a hair, on to a small crystal we could, through headphones, be transported to the Savoy Hotel in London and hear the Savoy Havana and later the Savoy Orpheans bands playing the jazz and the blues on which we thrived.

Through the newly-discovered magic waves we felt cosily close to America and twanged out: *Home in Pasadena* and *California, here I come* as if we should be in USA the next week. We added to our ballroom repertoire of the waltz, the foxtrot, and the two step, the quick-quick-slow of the slow foxtrot, the more sophisticated and sinewy tango, maxina and missouri walk. We kicked our way through every variation of the Charleston, the quick and the frenzied *Sing Hallelujah!* and the flatfooted My *Cutie's due at two-to-two.* Freed from our Liberty bodices, we coiled and writhed to the *Black Bottom* — a new experience for our formerly decorous pelvises.

In the Maxina, unlike other ballroom dances, the two partners both faced the same way, arms outstretched with clasped hands at shoulder-level. The rhythm dèr de dèr de dèr de DER moved the couple forward. On the fourth beat the right leg swung high and across the body, turning the couple to an angle of 45°, then after the next four steps the left leg swung across the body reversing the 45° angle to the right. The 'man' (usually a girl in our limited circles) had to keep a decorous space between his body and hers otherwise she would be swiped across her bottom with his shoe.

This intended-to-be-elegant dance was in our repertoire but on the following occasion it turned out to be my swan-song for the evening.

My mother's college friend, the village school-mistress of Cloughton near Scarborough, had lent us her school-house for a holiday. We loved the clocked gable, the classrooms with desks for play not work and to have the run of the playground to ourselves.

Across the road, nearer the sea, was a splendid country house owned by the Swarthmore Quakers to use as a holiday home, Cober Hill. Through another friend of my mother's we had an open invitation for the social evenings of song and dance, (It had never occurred to us before that Quakers *did* dance!)

Every night, except Sunday, we went through the traditional dances of waltz, veleta, the Lancers, cotillion, and the Paul Jones. As the week went on and we girls gained confidence, having been praised for our dancing, Betsy and I boldly introduced the Charleston, Black Bottom and the Maxina.

On these occasions we put aside all our sisterly differences and donned a 'Heavenly Twins' act, becoming the only couple on the floor - giving, in fact, exhibition dances. For this Maxina Betsy held my hands tight, not out of affection, but to steer me in the right direction. Putting on her performance-smile she was also doing a ventriloquist mutter: 1, 2, 3, 4. 'Lift higher, can't you!' Goaded into action every fourth kick I twisted my waist tighter, flung my leg higher until, in one massive effort, my clumsy well-worn sandal hurtled through the air then shot along the polished floor like a curling stone on an ice-rink. There was no Quaker silence, just roars of laughter.

My sister jilted me. I sat shamefaced trying to buckle the strap of my retrieved sandal through tears. The Warden took pity on me and coaxed me onto the floor again for a Paul Jones - the final dance. More shame here as no one said 'Excuse me!' to claim me as a new partner.

Two sympathetic elderly ladies finally drew me into the hand-linked circle to join in singing the 'Goodnight' song (words to the tune of 'Begone, dull care'). I choked over it:

> The day is done; we've danced and sung,
> Our eyes have seen delight.
> The day is past, we part at last.
> To each and all: 'Goodnight'.

But what gentle, innocent, wise and kindly folk they were. No drums, no microphone, no flashing lights and, of course, no bar. And all this simplicity in the 'Roaring Twenties'.

Every seaside town had its plethora of hotel ballrooms, palais-de-danse halls, pier pavilions and dance music shops. These, like the Penny Bazaars, were open-fronted to the street and pianists and singers kept up a non-stop encouragement to come in and buy. So from sixpence to nothing more than two shillings, one could buy a well-presented, skilfully scored song-sheet often demanding expert piano playing. I suppose these shops, the radio and the picture-houses with their tireless pianists providing 'atmosphere' and filling in the intervals with songs-of-the-day were the reason for our knowing verse after verse of popular songs off by heart. With very little money to spend, we made the song-sheets, records and our memories the phonograph albums of those musical times.

We tried, starry-eyed with the performances of Fred and Adele Astaire, Jack Buchanan and Gertrude Lawrence, to make our bodies and voices have semblance of their brilliance while singing away to *Lady be good* and *Who stole my Heart away.* We thrilled to Jack Smith's *Whispering just while you gather near me* and the quiet purr of his *Afraid of You.* Artists so suave, so elegant and so beautifully articulate took us into another world. English country dancing had a revival in the Twenties and all over the country, in school, village and church halls people of all weights and ages were doing the up-a-double, back-a-double of *Gathering Peascods, Black Nag, Sellingers' Round* and *Rutty Tufty.* It was all part of the back-to-nature cult — the folksy revival of raffia and cane work; lino cuts; hand-loom weaving and bottled fruit. 'Ambridge' rather than Mayfair. Of course it all fitted in with one or another of my mother's 'isms' (Steiner perhaps?) and we upped and doubled with the rest while privately considering it rather gauche and undemanding. Right across the country there were demonstrations of and classes for Dalcroze Eurythmics, structured series of restrained hand and leg movements rigidly beating out the bar lines. We girls dismissed it as 'dancing to numbers' for it had neither the technique nor the spatial artistry of our Greek or natural movement dancing. Predictably Mother joined the Cecil Sharpe folk song and country dance revival and helped Frank Kidson in his research and restoration of old Yorkshire songs and poems. We were in on all that.

A year had gone: a dullish year of geometry, algebra, Latin and team-games; a brightish year of school-holiday hand-holding visits to the 'pictures' ('cinema' as I was schooled into saying by Peter); a bubbling year of flannel-dances, rugby 'hops', the Arts Ball and rare visits to the theatre. An experimental year of run-up Magyar dresses, fringed and shingled hair and surreptitious reads of the *Wells of Loneliness* and *The Sheikh* with brown paper covers hiding the titles. A year when the 'cat's whisker' had given way to the four-valve wireless set and a new world opened out to us with the muscle-moving rhythms of Jack Hylton, Debroy Somers, Jack Payne, and we said goodnight lovingly to Henry Hall's *Here's to the Next Time.*

Of course we returned to Auburn for the perennial camping holiday. Our Liberty bodices had now been exchanged for cotton camisoles which neither uplifted nor flattered us. It was fashionable to have a boyish figure, and for once fashion was on my side.

On the last Sunday of our holiday it seemed as if the larks became satellites of sun and song, proclaiming that tomorrow the reapers and the binders would be out for the first cutting. 'Ister starting cutting ti'morn?' Foreman had asked. But today — today we were driving in Uncle Harry's Humber to Rudston and Sledmere.

Motoring for most people in 1925 was a luxury for which one prepared with veils over hats, rugs over knees and leather straps over the petrol cans. Today, the huge hood was pleated optimstically into rest behind the back seat. We climbed on to the running board, sank on to the buttoned leather seats and yet sat high and upright as if for a royal progress.

Uncle Dawson's big black Bean remained piously in the stable while the three grown-up male cousins, Austin and Horace Hyde and Alan Danby — who now qualified for Dawson's hospitality — did a God-granted inspection of the Auburn fields — on foot.

Our first stop was Burton Agnes, a historic home, too warm-hearted and lived-in to be called 'stately.' The era of open-to-the-public, huge car-parks, cordoned-off rooms and tea and coca-cola in the stables, had yet to come. Even if it had been open, farmers are neither gawpers nor trippers — preferring to stop and have a chat with those whose living depends on the land and to whom weather is important. 'Flamborough looked near this morning; it'll rain before the day's out ...' was the kind of homely forecast which outstripped the Met Office. So we were soon on our way to Rudston calling at the church to see the graves of the Macdonalds of the Isles, an incongruous row of Celtic crosses linking a sacred patch of the Yorkshire wolds with the Western Isles of Scotland. We crossed the church-yard to stand baffled

A medley of 1920's motor cars

The Jowett, a modest little motor car both in price and power, was my father's first car. (In this photograph are some members of the Jowett company)

Uncle Dawson drove a Bean, a tough 14 tourer, but never on Sunday!

Sunday was the day when we all squashed into Uncle Harry's Humber to visit friends and relations.

Aunt Alice Wainwright and her three children (Alfred pretending to drive) in their baby Austin.

Once a year we were driven in the Allgood's Austin 16 Saloon to their Masonic party in Leeds.

Lagonda

The Golightly bride went off on her honeymoon in a sporty Lagonda Coupé. In the double dickey seat behind was her lavish trousseau.

Miss Scotson-Clark, escorted by Colonel Bousfield to Sports Day in his chauffeur-driven Daimler Saloon de Luxe.

by the uncarved ancient monolith twenty-five feet high and, more than that — so local legend has it — deep down in the ground. Time moved backwards into infinity and then was nudged forward: 'Sir William Strickland and his men did a daft dig two hundred years ago, but they never got to the bottom of it, and I don't know what good it would have done them if they had,' was our farming uncle's down-to-earth comment, which showed little concern for the earth-probing of the archaeologists and their continuing interest in the tallest stone in Britain.

Starting the car was no press-button affair so my uncle was always ahead of us swinging the starting handle and quickly stepping on to the running board and into the driver's seat to keep the engine going. A squeeze of the black rubber ball blared a signal through the polished Klaxon horn that it was time to be off. We left Holderness for the Wolds and took the white ribbon road on which chariots of the Early Iron Age must have thundered for there were chariot burial mounds nearby. On to the farms of Cottam and Cowlam where they and the two rather forlorn little churches were all that remained of the two villages: 'Wiped out with the Black Death' so my uncle told us.

Sledmere was our main goal, for there Uncle Harry had a tale to tell of living history — of folk he had known. The village and the great house at Sledmere have more than a picture-postcard prettiness. They are handsome, solidly built and cared for by generations of the industrious and imaginative Sykes family not least Sir Tatton Sykes. It is in the nature of Yorkshire farming folk to identify with and be proud to till the lands of the great patrician Yorkshire families: the Boyntons, the Stricklands, the Halifaxes, the Middletons and the Sykes ... There is no question of servility for these independent tenant farmers are strong and highly respected characters in their own right, faithful custodians of their several hundred acres, which they have inherited from their forebears, and will, in time, hand on to their sons. Well, that's how it was when we were young — and I hope may still be so.

When we arrived in Sledmere my uncle ignored the feminine grace of the Gothic-type cross but gathered us round the more masculine block erected by Sir Mark Sykes just six years before as a memorial for the First World War. There, carved in stone, was the story of how Captain Sykes rallied 1000 farm wagoners from the Wolds to go to France to fight against the Germans. Every character was faithfully immortalised: the mothers, wives and children bidding their men goodbye; the young farm hands with their loaded wagons and well-loved horses; the same men stiffened into their uniforms; the boats taking the recruits across the Channel — all recorded lovingly in panels of frieze profiles. More hostile chisels had been at work on the Germans grotesquely caricatured with leering mouths and bayonets at the ready. Uncle Harry's chuckles at the stone cartoons died down as he moved to the memorial to read out from the list of dead the names of those known to him: 'Young men', he said, 'whose guns had never killed more than a rabbit on the harvest field and who probably before the war had never ventured further than York or Scarborough'. To travel by train almost the length of England and then by boat to France where they could not understand one word of the language was enough to

First World War memorial depicting the East Riding Wagoners recruited by Sir Mark Sykes and immortalised in this monument in Sledmere.

make even tough young Yorkshiremen squeamish.

> 'An I tell yer, I felt that neet
> Squeamish an'wamble and flayed
> Getting nearer and nearer to t'war
> Where aboard t'boat I were laid ...'

In this poem by W J Turner, the young wagoner Paul tells in his own East Riding dialect how he felt the first night ('neet') on the boat. Later I was to hear my cousin Austin Hyde's voice over the air bringing this poem to life in his preserved East Riding. More recently George Nellist, verger and cleaner, said the whole 23 verses to me in the quiet of Sledmere Church vestry.

We left Sledmere after a quick look through the iron gate of the Park and church and started homeward. We called at two or three farms, but never quite responded to the genial: 'Come thi' ways in', since news of cattle and crops is more fittingly exchanged outside in the farmyard.

And so back to the usual lavish Fraisthorpe Sunday tea where 12 of us sat round the dining table with the crisp white damask cloth falling below our knees. Miss Gratrix, the housekeeper, in her usual place at the head of the table, was always quick to notice an empty cup or plate which she would fill. Uncle Harry and Auntie Florrie relaxed into banter and gossip encouraging the seven girls — the Hydes and the Danbys — to make good stories out of their exploits. If any one of us tried to put a brake on the ravenous appetites of the eight-year-old boys — Sonny, our brother, and Henry, his cousin — Miss Gratrix gently came down on their side: 'Have another bun, honey; there are plenty more in the larder.' Yorkshire teas, especially Sunday ones, are not designed for time- or weight-watchers and only the clanging of the single bell for the evening service prompted us to leave the table and put on our kept-in-storage-in-the-attic panama hats. The beamish vicar and a few supportive neighbours were already in the garden. So exactly did the ladies' multicoloured chiffon and voile frocks duplicate the shades of the sweet peas, they could have been enlargements of the flowers fluttering behind them. Holding audience from a sea-bleached basket chair, old Henry Jackson — Florrie's father — wore his frock coat, starched white shirt and cravat, with easy elegance looking like the Lord of the Manor, which he was not. A closer view of the stiff white cuffs framing well-kept hands would have shown that the gold cufflinks bore a royal crest. But you have already heard that story.

We followed the faithful few into the church, past Wag-lad sweating at the end of the bell-pull and Cissie Hall trying not to as she kept the harmonium going non stop with *Jesu, Joy of Man's Desiring* until the vicar took over. There was nothing musically ambitious about the service; the hymns fitted the happy few as confidently as old slippers and we murmured the prayers and responses from well-worn memories. The 20 or so unequal voices soared into approximate harmony through easy familiarity with one another and sheer good will. I think my aunt must have chosen the hymns for when we pleaded: *Dear Lord and Father of Mankind forgive our foolish ways,* we caught her indulgent smile and roguish wink from Uncle Harry. And we knew that, as long as they were there, Fraisthorpe would always be our shelter from the stormy blast however perverse and foolish we might be.

After our hats had been collected like so many soup plates, we walked back to our field camp site in Auburn in a fine drizzle and joined our girl-friends who were peering critically into half-crown-sized mirrors in their powder-compact boxes in the hope of disguising their peeling noses. This sudden and rather futile attempt to prettify ourselves was in response to an invitation from the four attractive young men camping near the beach to join them for a ukelele evening of song. We oozed over *What'll I do*?, sank into bathos of *All alone* and brightened up on *Yes, sir, that's my baby* ... We sublimated sex into song in, as I look at it now, a symphony of romantic innocence.

We arranged to walk into Bridlington the next day to treat ourselves to knickerbocker glories and the latest records and buy crabs down at the old harbour to bring back for our supper. It was a damp, cool Monday morning when sea, sky and sand were grey. 'Aren't you coming with us to Bridlington?' Peter asked, rather as if the reply was of little consequence. 'Sorry, I've got a blister on my heel and can't walk.' It was not a remark to further romance but a truth which I had thought could be used as a ruse to keep him by my side alone for a whole afternoon. Cool closed-mouth goodnight kisses were as far as we had gone in this disturbing calf-love. But we had read Donne's love sonnets together, become Rupert Brooke's heirs of grief and mirth and tried out our sketchy philosophy after a fluttering through Bertrand Russell's: *Analysis of the Mind.* This last was Peter's way of scoring intellectual dominance, an easy role for him as I, an unworldly 15-year-old was flattered by the attention of an 18year-old Cambridge law student. I sat humped on cold damp sand and watched the little group walk away, becoming smaller and smaller and closer and closer, and felt excluded from their laughter. The strains of: *I want to be happy* strummed on the ukeleles gradually faded into the distance. I was alone with a secret feeling of jealousy, loneliness and a fickle sun.

It was nearing the end of the holiday. Next week I should be 16 and back at school wearing my green felt school hat and gloves. It was not the North Sea which sent a chill fretting from head to heart but the thought of *'Lord, behold us with thy blessing once again assembled here'* and that my limbs now bare and brown would be banished from the sun and Peter would be returning to Cambridge.

And I pondered — as young and old have pondered through the centuries — Who was I? What was I? What did it all mean? If there were a God, whose God was it? Uncle Dawson's God, the stubborn Sabbatarian? or Miss Scotson-Clark's God of decorum and duty, bound between the covers of the Book of Common Prayer and Hymns Ancient and Modern? Or was it my mother's God, ubiquitous and infinite, spreading protective wings over Christians, Moslems, Buddhists and Jews?

I sat gazing at the sea and wondered ... Thoughts zig-zagged. A strange one emerged. If my mother had met Dr Marie Stopes in 1908 instead of 1920, would I be here? No-one would have missed this unborn fourth girl. But what marvels of joy and friendship I would have missed.

Gradually the wondering changed to *wonder* ... I was here, alive ... and as I gazed out to sea — where the village of Auburn lay locked in the ocean bed — a small boat thrust its mast heavenward and put all its trust into one white exultant sail.

Postscript

There are now no more farming Hydes. The Lodge at Fraisthorpe is no longer a farm-house but the home of international hauliers. In the stack-yard where hay, straw and wagons formerly stood there are giant juggernauts which can take 10,000 lbs of turkeys to Greece and bring back 10,000 lbs of peaches. The house has been transformed: the old flagged kitchen is now studded with power points and stream-lined with the latest units. Dairies and larders — replaced by freezers — now house a sauna and a jaccuzi. Stables, no longer smelling of horses and hay, have been smartened into cost-effective offices. The granary — once our rustic theatre — is now a disco den for more sophisticated teenagers.

What a difference central heating and a bathroom with piped hot water would have made to my Aunt Florrie's life. She was too finely wrought to cope with the cold and hard physical work of a northern farm-house. She died of pneumonia (no antibiotics in 1934) aged 52.

Auburn House always seemed to us a grumpy old farm, bluntly masculine both outside and in. Set in the shadow of the protective coppice, it seemed reluctant to open itself out to the sea. Its fold yard and its muck almost reached the never-used front door.

When I revisited it in researching for the first edition of this book it was utterly deserted and looked as if it would never attract a buyer. I did not know that very soon after my visit a great sea-change was happening, Robin and Mary Jackson (both of farming families in Fraisthorpe and Auburn) had rescued it and lovingly created a transformation.

The old fold-yard, now sunlit with white-painted walls, had surrendered its hundred years of muck to make luscious beds for the newly-planted bushes, grass and flowers. Naturally they burgeoned.

Inside the house scaring things have gone: no sign of the bone-rotting smugglers' cave nor my Uncle Dawson's dark smoky den. A window has been cut out of the den's thick wall to make a room with a view of the new garden and the sea. The front door welcomes visitors over a new-mown lawn. The back staircase which led to the men's dormitory has been removed and this room has been transformed into a master bedroom with its en suite bathroom. Of course the big black kitchen range has given way to an 'Aga' and every kitchen wall has its fitted units.

But its owners *are* farmers and not 'furriners'. Indeed they would like to be one-hundred-per-cent farmers but the Government and the EC command them to 'set aside' several fields of barley, oats and wheat, and let the weeds take over.

Hundreds of cars — duly paying their parking fees - now pack the beach and the sand-dunes, and disgorge bikinied bodies.

A mixed blessing for the owners, for, although bins are provided for litter, the appalling detritus of plastic containers, cans and paper has to be cleaned up every Monday, a sordid job for bred-in-the-bone farming folk.

And whatever would Uncle Dawson say to all this for it was he who started the parking fee 'to keep the cars away'? And what full-blooded Yorkshire tirade would be levelled at the nudists splayed out on their official strip of the Auburn sands?

"Auburn", by the Rev. Richard Wilton

Here Auburn stood
By pleasant field surrounded,
Where now for centuries the ocean flood
With melancholy murmur has resounded.

Here Auburn stood
Where now the seabird hovers —
Here stretched the shady land and sheltering wood,
The twilight haunt of long-forgotten lovers.

The village spire
Here raised its silent finger,
Sweet bells were heard and voice of rustic choir
Where now the pensive chimes of ocean linger.